Byzantium Triumphant
The Military History of the Byzantines 959-1025

By Julian Romane

Pen & Sword
MILITARY

First published in Great Britain in 2015 by
Pen & Sword Military
an imprint of
Pen & Sword Books Ltd
47 Church Street
Barnsley
South Yorkshire
S70 2AS

ISBN 978 1 47385 570 1

Typeset in Ehrhardt by
Replika Press Pvt Ltd, India
Printed and bound in England
by CPI Group (UK) Ltd, Croydon, CRO 4YY

Pen & Sword Books Ltd incorporates the Imprints of Pen & Sword Aviation,
Pen & Sword Family History, Pen & Sword Maritime, Pen & Sword Military,
Pen & Sword Discovery, Pen & Sword Politics, Pen & Sword Atlas,
Pen & Sword Archaeology, Wharncliffe Local History, Wharncliffe
True Crime, Wharncliffe Transport, Pen & Sword Select, Pen & Sword
Military Classics, Leo Cooper, The Praetorian Press, Claymore Press,
Remember When, Seaforth Publishing and Frontline Publishing.

For a complete list of Pen & Sword titles please contact
PEN & SWORD BOOKS LIMITED
47 Church Street, Barnsley, South Yorkshire, S70 2AS, England
E-mail: enquiries@pen-and-sword.co.uk
Website: www.pen-and-sword.co.uk

Contents

Foreword

This book is a narrative of political-military events in the Byzantine Empire from 959 to 1025. Sources for this narrative are the works of Byzantine historians, Leo the Deacon, John Skylitzes, and Michael Psellus, interpreted through Byzantine military manuals. This is war, as seen by the Byzantines. The Byzantine historians are the lineal descendents of the first Greek historians, Herodotus, Thucydides, and Xenophon. We will do well to understand that ancient and medieval authors did not write in the ways of modern writers. Before printing, lectors read books to audiences and explained or expanded on the texts. The written word was expensive; authors were laconic. If they said much, it was because very much more could be said. The lector supplied explanations. And so, like the lector, I have interjected the passion and the blood that the source narrative might hide in dry prose. This is not fiction. This is a presentation of a Byzantine historical narrative as the Byzantines understood it.

So, dear reader, why should you read this book? Because there are no narratives of tenth century Byzantine military history except this. The importance of this book is to reveal the actual nuts and bolts of Byzantine political-military operations. During this time, the Byzantine emperors launched a series of offensives in the east and west. My narrative clarifies the reasons for these advances and why they succeeded. Many commentators have made powerful statements about the nature of these campaigns without looking at them. Famously, Arnold Toynbee in his *Study of History* claims that Basil II's Bulgar campaigns and especially the Battle of Kleidion caused the 'breakdown' of Byzantine civilization. Byzantium may have 'broken down' (whatever that may mean) at this time but the Bulgar war didn't do it. Certain other commentators make the point that John Skylitzes made much of the Bulgarian campaigns to influence policy under Alexius I. A good look at Basil II's problems in the Balkans and Alexius I's problems (delineated in his daughter's history) demonstrate that here there are two different sets of problems and that the story of one is not the related to the other. Moreover, some commentators blame the collapse of the east after Manzikert on Basil II's eastern policies but again, the problems Basil faced were very different from the Seljuk war.

A major problem in the understanding of the Byzantine Empire is that many of her modern historians have little understanding of real affairs. They do not see the Byzantines as the proud violent people that they were. Arguments over honour, land, money, theology, all were good reasons for a hard fight. And then they faced a lot of real enemies who were intent on their destruction. They fell on their knees and begged the Theotokos for forgiveness but only after the sword had fallen. We need to remember the battlefield. It stank. It stank of sweat, and of blood, and of excrement, and it stank of fear. Often, in modern accounts we see the Byzantines as effete intellectuals spinning overly subtle plots to gain power. Rather, they were hard and harsh men and women who had the determination to grab what they desired, without regard to methods.

Of course, there never were a people who called themselves the Byzantines. Those people called themselves the Romans. Their state was the legitimate and only valid state in the world, the Roman Empire. The first major use of the word Byzantine to identify the people and empire of medieval East Rome was by Hieronymus Wolf in 1557, in his published collection of historical sources, *Corpus Historiae Byzantinae*. The term was used in seventeenth century French scholarship and, famously, Edward Gibbon used the term often in his *History of the Decline and Fall of the Roman Empire*. So, Byzantine, it is. Modern pedagogical curriculum, in history classes in high school and undergraduate levels, never quite gets to the Byzantines, yet rarely do the Byzantines get away without a mention. And so the Byzantines are relegated to an academic limbo where, if you look for it, there is lots of material but if you mention the Byzantines to people who have a basic knowledge of their school history classes, they just might say, Who? But for those of us for whom Byzantium is a passion, it is enough to know that some people are interested.

Introduction: Byzantium Background

The Great City spread across low hills on a peninsula between sparkling blue seas. To the south lay the Bosporus and to the north, beyond the further point of land, unfolded the Golden Horn, home to a gathering of ships more numerous than any other in the world. Buildings of two and three stories crowded mile after mile of cityscape out of which, here and there, rose stone piles of massive geometric forms, topped by graceful low domes, sparkling gold in the sunlight. Encircling the city, high walls punctuated by huge towers provided protection for the myriads of people within. Great cisterns supplied water; organized and regulated markets provided many different foods. Connected together by boulevards, wide forums graced many neighbourhoods. Here imposing public buildings and private mansions pointed the way to the imperial palaces. At the apex of the peninsula stood a labyrinth of grand structures, a huge hippodrome, large throne halls, well tended gardens, and hovering over all, great domed churches, including the greatest of all, the imperial church of Holy Wisdom. This was the capital of the last ancient society of the Mediterranean world. It is the Year of the World, 6467 (AD 959).

Our story covers the sixty-six years from 959 to 1025. This is the lifetime of Basil II Porphyrogenitus, who was born in 958, and became emperor in 960. He along with his brother, Constantine VIII, assumed direct power over the empire in 976. Basil died in 1025. In the decades before these years, the balance among eastern Mediterranean powers shifted in Byzantium's favour. The compact and centralized empire of Constantinople proved resistant to the waves of political change that swept across the Near East. The enemies of Byzantium fragmented while the empire renewed its strength. The Byzantines capitalized on these conditions during the life of Basil II. For the first time in centuries, the empire of Constantinople fought successful wars of expansion, using the results of study and practice to develop a unique method of warfare. These wars are the subject of this book. Using the literary sources and recently uncovered information about Byzantine weapons and tactics, this book describes in as much detail as possible the wars during the life of Basil II Porphyrogenitus. The experiences of centuries contributed to the methods of

Byzantine military operations. Therefore, we will start with a brief account of the origins and development of Byzantium.

Origin of Byzantine Society

The Emperor Constantine founded the city some six hundred years before. He ruled the lands from the island of Britain to beyond the banks of the Euphrates. Strong armies were at his command, throngs of administrators waited on his word, the true church, as he saw it, willingly followed his lead. The Ever Victorious Emperor desired to merge the Classical traditions of Greece and Rome with the Good News of Salvation through Christ. The society that emerged from Constantine's city embraced both traditions through the centuries. The Classics, influenced by the Bible, and the Bible, interpreted through the Classics, formed the basis of Byzantine civilization, the empire of Constantinople.

Two centuries later, warlords had seized the western provinces of the Roman Empire but Augustus at Constantinople still ruled the east. In legal theory and with Church recognition, this sole emperor was still the ultimate if distant universal authority. Within another fifty years, the Byzantine Caesar launched offensives that reunited many of the western provinces to the imperial dominion. Then the darkness began falling. Strange tribes invaded Italy and the Balkans. The imperial armies mutinied and revolution broke out in the Great City. The Sassanid Empire resurgent, invaded the east taking Syria, the Holy Land, Egypt, and most of Anatolia. Soon all that remained of the Roman Empire was the Great City and the North African provinces. However, sailing from Carthage, Emperor Heraclius rebuilt the armies, reorganized the administration, and defended the Great City, besieged by the Avars in the west and the Sassanids in the east. A brilliant series of campaigns broke the Sassanid Empire. Heraclius had restored much of the empire and recovered the True Cross. Then, out of the sands of Arabia, another enemy suddenly appeared. The soldiers of the Prophet burst into the Roman provinces in the east, sweeping across Syria, the Holy Land, into Egypt and then across northern Africa. As the Arab armies smashed deep into the empire, the Byzantine eastern armies retreated into Anatolia, dividing the lands into areas assigned to each major army. The descendents of Heraclius proved powerless to stop the disintegration of the empire.

In 717, Leo III seized the throne. He defended the Great City through another severe siege, fending off the Bulgars in the east and the Muslims in the West. His counter attack was nowhere as complete as that of Heraclius but he stabilized the frontiers and settled armies in Anatolia, protected the Aegean, and pushed the Bulgars back. Leo and his son, Constantine V, fought difficult battles, managed finances, and increased military strength in a time of great trouble. The darkness swirled around and surrounded the empire; the earth itself heaved and exploded, as the volcano island of Thera erupted. The only possible way for the empire to survive, the emperors believed, was through divine intervention in human affairs. Already deeply devout, a sense of the Mystical Presence of the Holy Trinity, the Mother of God, and the Blessed Saints pervaded the Byzantine consciousness. Only the most correct exercise of proper devotion could maintain the Mystical Presence. The question revolved around the proper uses of images in sacred places. Leo was sceptical of them; his son was hostile to their use and so for over a century strong controversy rang through the halls of church and state.

The Reformation of the Byzantine Empire

Slowly, through the reigns of Leo III's descendents, the empire gained strength: the Caliphate disintegrated, the economy improved, perhaps the weather too. A woman emperor compelled, so they thought, the Italians to proclaim a Frankish king as emperor, but still the Byzantines grew stronger. In 829, Theophilus ascended the throne. He was the sixteen-year-old son of Michael II, a former commander of the guard and favourite of the clique who had murdered the previous emperor. The new emperor had to find a wife so an heir would ensure imperial continuity. The imperial bride-show became the accepted solution of choosing a wife for the heir apparent or young emperor. The Sacred Palace issued an invitation for any attractive young woman of accomplishment to come for an inspection by the court. After the court chose those young women considered acceptable, they lined up in a great hall and the imperial suitor walked along the line, chatting and looking at the candidates. He chose the one that best suited him; she married him and became empress. Theophilus chose Theodora as his wife and empress. The argument about the use of sacred images, the icons, continued. Theophilus was strongly against their use but Theodora believed their power was beneficial. The split between emperor and empress reflected a profound divide in Byzantine society: many men, particularly ascetic monks, despised the icons while many women held on to them and secretly used them in personal devotions. After Theophilus died, Theodora became regent for her young son and oversaw the reinstatement of the icons as part of the way of the orthodox. This finally settled the questions of the icons. Theodora became the Blessed and her feast of celebration, the Restoration of Orthodoxy, remains an important feast day of the Orthodox Church.

Theodora, when her son, Michael III, was sixteen, held a bride-show. The lovely and chaste Eudocia became empress. However, the Emperor already had a mistress, Eudocia Ingerina; moreover, he only enjoyed horses, racing, athletics, high jinks, and drinking. Later historians awarded him the label 'the Drunkard'. As he grew older, he became less amenable to his mother's influence and finally he had her prime minister killed and eventually sent her to a convent. He dropped one favourite for another, choosing the equestrian, Basil, as his boon companion. Michael III had his longtime mistress, Eudocia Ingerina, married to Basil in order to legitimize the child she carried while he allowed Basil's dalliance with his sister, an ex-nun. He made Basil co-emperor, to do the work he did not like. However, Michael was unstable; fearing that the senior emperor would turn on him, Basil killed Michael and became sole emperor. Eudocia Ingerina delivered a boy, Leo. While Basil was the child's legal father, most people believed he was the natural son of Michael III, hence of the original imperial line. Basil had his own son designated as heir but that son died and Leo became Emperor Leo VI, known as the Wise (886–919).

The Imperial Dynasty

The reign of Leo VI was, with vicissitudes, quite successful. Leo wrote or oversaw the writing of a fine book on military affairs. The economy continued to improve, the great controversy regarding icons faded. Nevertheless, a new church-state controversy erupted, centring on Leo himself. As a young man, almost sixteen years old during the reign of Basil I, Leo married Theophano after a bride-show. They had a daughter but Theophano did not accept Leo's dalliance with another woman. She died at about the age thirty, and subsequently was elevated to sainthood. The other woman, Zoe Zaoutzaine, daughter of Stylianus Zaoutzes, commander of the imperial guards, remained Leo's favourite. When Theophano died, Leo married Zoe and crowned her empress. The scandal at the time was intense because popular opinion accused Zoe of the murder of her husband who had died suddenly just after the death of Theophano. Alas, Zoe died of a dread disease within eighteen months of the marriage (896). Unfortunately, for Leo, the Orthodox Church was sceptical of second marriages. A third marriage was 'moderate fornication' outlawed at one time, but now just strongly discouraged. Leo soon married a young woman named Eudocia (899) but after about a year, she died in childbirth along with her infant boy. Leo found solace in the arms of a lovely young girl, Dark-Eyed Zoe (Carbonupsina). The laws of Church and state forbade a fourth marriage. Leo knew a fourth marriage was nothing but trouble and did not press the issue until the dark-eyed beauty delivered a son, Constantine (905). The fact that the delivery took place in the Imperial Porphyra, the purple birth chamber in the Sacred Palace, demonstrated that if the child were male, he would be imperial heir. Three days after the child received baptism, Zoe returned to the palace escorted by an honour guard. Within months, Leo VI married Zoe and crowned her empress. Church leaders led uproars of protest that Leo met with political pressures and swift select punishment. The controversy continued even beyond Leo VI's death (912).

Two factions emerged around the issue of the fourth marriage; one supported the independence of the Church and questioned the young Constantine's legitimacy; the other supported the imperial family and called the young man Porphyrogenitus (Born in the Purple), indicating his absolute legitimacy. Behind these factions, older issues simmered: many of those who opposed the fourth marriage disliked images in church while many supported the young man because he was the great-grandson of the Blessed Theodora, restorer of Orthodoxy. Leo's half brother, Alexander, who had never amounted to much, immediately succeeded to the throne. This brother was enthroned with the young Constantine VII Porphyrogenitus, aged six. Alexander expelled the Empress Zoe from the palace and seemed about to get rid of the young Constantine VII; however, his death followed Leo's in thirteen months and left Constantine sole legitimate ruler at the age of seven. Alexander left instructions for the regency following his death but the arrangements fell through. With the breakdown of a settled process, a power vacuum opened, an invitation to competing forces, including the Empress Zoe, some powerful noble families members, and a number of commanding military officers.

The commander of the imperial fleet, Romanus Lecapenus, more ruthless than the rest, became sole regent (919). Zoe returned to her convent; Romanus' daughter, Helena, married Constantine VII; his supporters defeated the army commander, Leo Phocas, and had him mutilated. He became Emperor Romanus I, enthroning his wife and sons. Unscrupulous, untrustworthy, yet cunning and a superb administrator, Romanus' reign was successful. While Romanus ruled, Constantine VII reigned. Studious, enjoying reading and writing, Porphyrogenitus produced massive compilations of data about the empire and its history. As a living connection with the past, he received the loyalty and love of many of his subjects. While Constantine had to work as an artist and earn money, Romanus never managed to gain popularity with the city or the Church. He even failed to win the respect of his sons. They seized Romanus and imprisoned him in a monastery. However, just as the brothers were going to do the same to Constantine, the tables turned on them and they went off to a monastic life.

Sole Rule of Constantine VII

The Porphyrogenitus preferred a quiet life; he let those around him manage the imperial administration. He trusted above all his wife, Helena Lecapena, mother of his six children, one son, Romanus, and five daughters. She, and a favourite, Basil 'the Bird', oversaw the administration of the city: their critics accused them of unscrupulous corruption. The frontier wars continued with raids by one side following raids from the other. The military leaders of both sides greatly profited, the only losers being the peasants and towns people caught between. While the administration provided stability if not honesty, a beautiful young woman captivated the young Romanus in his sixteenth year.

Her name was Anastaso, changed to the more acceptable Theophano when she married the imperial heir (956). Beautiful, witty, vivacious, intelligent and skilled at man-management, this woman is the most controversial person in the Middle Byzantine Period. Her romantic exploits were a matter of wonder to the Byzantine chroniclers and she has caught the imagination of Byzantine scholars, particularly in France. Melchior de Vogue, a French savant of the nineteenth century, commented that Theophano 'disturbed the world as much as Helen, and even more'. Hugues le Roux, nineteenth century French novelist described Theophano as '...this young woman of supernatural loveliness, containing in the delicate perfection of her harmony the power that troubles the world'. Charles Diehl's sketch of her life melds romance with fact. In the late twentieth century, Peter Schreiner said she had bewitched Romanus and '...took the name of Theophano when she climbed out of bed and into the throne'. A woman's point of view comes from Lynda Garland's sketch of Theophano's life, in which the Empress's concern is for her children amidst a hostile world, but the story remains remarkable.

Among the servants of the imperial establishment, none was more important than the House of Phocas. The house first appears in the person of a regimental commander in the east about 872. His son Nicephorus Phocas the Elder was a successful military officer in campaigns against the Muslims in both Asia Minor and Sicily. By the time of his prominence, the family was doing well in their Cappadocia home base, as landowners and military governors. The Elder's son Leo was a general who fought against the Bulgars. Defeated in battle, he nevertheless attempted to gain power during the Porphyrogenitus' childhood but Romanus Lecapenus outmanoeuvred him. He was condemned and blinded. His brother, Bardas, however, retained favour and military command, advancing his two sons, Nicephorus and Leo, to high and deserved positions in the army. Along with the Phocas brothers, a younger nephew on the distaff side, John Tzimiskes, also gained high rank.

Chapter 1

Romanus II: The Conquest of Crete and War in the East

E mperor Constantine VII Porphyrogenitus, son of Emperor Leo VI the Wise, died in November, during the third induction, in the year of the world, 6467 (fall AD 959). His son, twenty years old, succeeded him as Emperor Romanus II. The new Emperor continued his father's policies, depending on one of his father's ministers, the eunuch Joseph Bringas. Promoted to *parakoimomenos* (sleeps at the emperor's side) by Romanus, Bringas controlled the civil administration that continued to run smoothly. Public opinion, there certainly was such in the Great City, viewed the young Emperor as a good person, handsome and well able to fulfil the ceremonial roles expected of the Emperor, yet prone to the distractions and vices of the young. With age, he would mature. A military success would certainly strengthen an already good beginning. Romanus' advisors directed his eyes to the island of Crete.

Battle for Crete

In the never-ending struggle with the Islamic powers, Crete had fallen to the Muslims over a century before (around 824). As a base for pirates, Crete was a thorn in the imperial side. Marauders from the island raided for plunder and slaves, disrupted trade and depopulated the islands and seacoasts of the Aegean. Constantine VII's forces had attempted to capture Crete in 949 but failed. At that time, the old palace eunuch, patrician Constantine Gongylios, led an expedition costing some 120,000 numismata. The Patrician sailed in a fleet of transports guarded by *dromon* fire-bearing battleships with a force consisting of some 9,000 soldiers and about 20,000 mariners. When the army landed on Crete, Gongylios assumed its size and strength would intimidate the Muslims. He did not enforce strict discipline nor did he order the construction of an entrenched base camp. The Muslim commanders soon saw the lack of sound military practice, and they secretly gathered their forces and attacked the Byzantine army. Very unprepared, Gongylios' army disintegrated under the Muslim assault. The Muslims killed or captured most of his soldiers and Gongylios only escaped because his personal attendance hustled him onto a boat.

The reduction of Crete would improve trade and shine lustre upon the new reign but a defeat could weaken Romanus' imperial standing, perhaps fatally. The imperial bureaucrats pushed their wheels and gears in motion to ensure victory or at least avoid embarrassing defeat. Of utmost importance was the question of commander-in-chief. Able military aristocrats won battles but then, in the recent past, had proven difficult to control, often striving for their own assumption of imperial power. Eunuch bureaucrats were not eligible for imperial status but had proven to be poor commanders. The Emperor and his main advisor, Bringas, decided that a member of the aristocratic Phocas family from Cappadocia would prove both able and loyal. Romanus II appointed the *domestikos ton scholon* (Commander of Imperial Guards) Nicephorus Phocas as *strategos autokrator* (Commander-in-Chief). The new imperial general organized an expeditionary force of elite units and oversaw the readying of unique transport ships that had ramps on their bows allowing foot and horse to embark fully armed and able to manoeuvre into formation immediately. Together with a strong fleet of *dromon* fire-bearing battleships, the loaded transports sailed to Crete in summer 960.

The fleet anchored off the Cretan coast near Almyros, to the west of the great Muslim fortress of Chandax (from the Arabic, 'The Moat', and now Heraklion). A Muslim force deployed on highlands overlooking the coastline, waiting for an opening to disrupt the Byzantine landing. The transports manoeuvred into lines and rowed toward the beach. As the boats grounded, ramps allowed the foot and horse to disembark fully armed and mounted. The Muslim force, not seeing any chance of disrupting the Byzantine deployment, dressed ranks and assumed battle position. Nicephorus' troops formed a battle-line shield-wall, bristling with spears, organized in a centre and two wings. The commander ordered trumpets to sound the advance as he directed the imperial war standard forward. The army marched directly against the Muslim force above the beach. As the Byzantine archers shot an arrow storm against the Muslim rear, the armoured front crashed into the Muslim line. The defending line waivered and then broke. As the Muslim soldiers fled the field, the Byzantines pursued, killing many of their enemies. The routed soldiers ran back to the gates of Chandax. The Byzantines followed but the fortress's defences were ready so an immediate escalade was not possible. Nicephorus ordered his soldiers to build a secure camp as a fortified base for his army and its supplies. The fleet found a safe anchorage in which the admirals secured the transports while the *dromon* battleships patrolled to burn any Muslim ships bringing supplies or attempting to attack the Byzantines.

Once the commander secured his army and fleet, he began organizing an attack against Chandax. His first need was a reconnaissance of the hinterland in order to see if there were significant forces in the neighbourhood besides those in Chandax. He assigned a company of elite horse to *Strategos* Nicephorus Pastilas, a renowned soldier who had fought against the Muslims for many years, had suffered captivity numerous times and always managed an escape. This commander of the *Thrakesian* theme had battle scars on his face and chest that made unusual patterns distinguishing his appearance. Nicephorus Phocas instructed Pastilas to sweep across the land, plunder the manors and villages, and return swiftly to the base camp. The land was rich in produce, fruits, cattle and sheep. The raid should relieve much of the need for sea delivered supplies. Nevertheless, Pastilas' company found a rich land, seemingly devoid of enemies. Indulging in the fine food and wine, they failed to notice that the local forces concentrated in the nearby hilly forests. Suddenly, as out of nowhere, a strong force of Muslim soldiers appeared, drawn up for the attack. They charged the Byzantines, who just had time to mount and deploy. Still, they faced superior numbers and the weight of the attackers began to tell. At their head fought Pastilas, smashing the enemies with his swift sword. While Muslim archers stood and shot arrows at him, infantry carrying stout spears closed in and rushed him, killing his horse by ramming their spears into its front. Pastilas leaped off from his falling mount and swinging his sword, continued to cut down his enemies. Finally, a group of archers caught him in their fire and put an end to him. When he collapsed into a bloody pile, his company of horse broke and fled, only a few of them making it back to the base camp.

The commander, disappointed with the outcome of the raid, nevertheless now saw the strategic situation. Facing strong enemy forces in Chandax, he also faced a Muslim relief effort from the hinterland. If he concentrated his effort against one enemy force, he had to fear an attack in the rear from the other. The situation called for caution and careful manoeuvring. His supplies secure from the sea, he strengthened the fortifications of his base camp and began to consider the best means of attack. Nicephorus Phocas, with his engineers, led a company of horse around the fortifications of Chandax, looking for vulnerabilities. The walls were strong, built of beaten earth, both high and wide, facing a double deep moat. (See above, Chandax means moat.) The commander ordered his men to build a stockade, cutting the town off from the landside, so the only egress was from the sea. Then, assembling his men in camp, Nicephorus told them that he insisted on strict discipline and order.

The example of the disaster that befell Pastilas clearly showed, he argued, what happens in the face of the malicious and cunning Muslim enemy. By exactly following his orders, victory would be theirs. The soldiers, led by their officers, drew their swords and pledged to follow their commander.

While his men completed strengthening their camp, Nicephorus chose able and experienced young soldiers, forming a separate battalion. He had heard from his local informants that the Muslims had organized an army, collecting the local militia. This army was some 40,000 men strong and their plan was to bring the Byzantines to battle, overwhelm them with numbers, and with the support of the soldiers in Chandax, push them into the sea. On the next night of the full moon, Nicephorus led his battalion out of his camp quietly, unnoticed by the enemy. Directed by native scouts, he hurried while darkness remained to where the enemy force was encamped on an easily defended hill. Some of the soldiers silently blocked the exits from the hill and others found places to assault the force on top, thus turning their enemies' strengths against themselves. Nicephorus gave the signal to sound trumpets and drums. At this, his soldiers surged up the hill and attacked the sleeping Muslims. Awakened by the tumult of trumpets, drums, and screams, the sleeping militiamen found swift death at the hands of the Byzantine elite troopers. Panic seized many of the militia who rushed pell-mell down the hill only to find more of Nicephorus' troopers waiting for them. The slaughter continued and the Byzantines killed many. The commander, in order to have proof of this victory, ordered his men to decapitate the dead bodies and put the severed heads in leather bags. To each trooper who had a bag with a head, he promised a *miliaresia* (a silver coin worth 1/12 of a gold solidus). The Armenian troopers responded with special gusto. The force returned to the base camp while darkness remained.

As the morning brightened, Nicephorus directed some of the heads impaled on a line of stakes set up in front of the stockade his men had built, which separated Chandax from the hinterland. His men shot the other heads against the city walls, where they exploded with a bloody splat. Some women appeared on the city wall and wailed at the loss of loved ones. Whether the town was seriously demoralized remained unknown. Immediately the Byzantine army deployed to attack. At the sound of the command trumpet, the escalade surged toward the wall, ladders at the ready, archers shooting arrow storms against the wall top, throwing machines bombarding the wall, the men exhorted by their officers to achieve bold accomplishments. However, the walls held. The defenders returned fire; they crushed ladders under large stones dropped on top of them, and repulsed all efforts of the Byzantines to gain a foothold on the wall's top. Nicephorus saw that the defenders were too strong to fall to this attempt; he ordered the trumpeters to sound the recall before too many of his soldiers were seriously injured. Withdrawing from the attack, the Byzantines set about turning their camp into a permanent settlement, rather than simply a daily make shift and prepared to sit out the coming winter. The engineers designed and began constructing large siege machines; the officers exercised and trained the men and stockpiled sufficient supplies to maintain the army for months. Nicephorus had decided to let the people of Chandax have a taste of famine before he tried another assault.

Siege of Chandax

His army spent the winter practising with their weapons, training to improve assault skills and building a variety of siege machines, throwing machines, and many ladders. As spring came, in March 961, Nicephorus marshalled his forces, ordered them into a massive column and with trumpets sounding and drums beating, marched against the walls of Chandax. The commander directed the leading companies of soldiers to position their ladders for attack while the column shook itself out into assault formation, with heavy infantry prepared to mount the ladders as archers and javelin throwers moved into support position. Suddenly, on the battlements, a woman appeared, making gestures and signs that the Byzantines assumed were magic incantations. Pulling off her skirts, she exposed her nude body and made explicit signs of contempt for the soldiers below. As she danced along the battlements, a practised archer took aim and transfixed her nude body with an arrow. She stumbled and fell from the wall right in front of the assault troopers. They rushed her as she struggled to rise, and crushed her to death. The enraged soldiers scrambled up the ladders as the defenders, waiting for them, struck hard at the men trying to reach the wall's top. The Byzantine effort, disrupted by the soldiers' anger at the woman, failed to achieve a foothold on the wall. The Muslims had repelled them, killing and wounding many.

Nicephorus ordered the stone-throwing engines forward. They cleared the walls of defenders with powerful bombardments. However, clearly, the defenders were just out of range of the stone shower and an assault on the walls was not possible. The commander ordered a massive battering ram forward. As the ram stuck the wall, the throwing machines kept the wall above the ram clear of defenders so they could not interfere with the machine. However, the defending commanders were quite sure that the ram would achieve little against the pounded dirt wall. Nicephorus also knew this but the actions of the ram was a cover for another operation: while the ram drew the Muslims' attention, a crew of miners dug in the moat, cutting into the alluvium upon which the wall sat. While the ram slowly clawed a path through the wall, the miners excavated out a large gallery under the wall, propping up their ceiling up with wooden piers. When the ram finally made a narrow breach in the wall, the Byzantine engineers decided all was ready in the underground gallery. The miners placed pitch, flammables, and the materials of Greek fire in the gallery and set them alight. Slowly, smoke made its way through the ground, venting in the area of the wall. Soon, a cloud of smoke engulfed the wall section. At once, two massive towers and the connecting wall section jolted and broke off sections of masonry, slid down into the moat, and collapsed. The rising dust, billowing smoke, and the unexpected sight of what appeared solid and firm slide into rubble shocked the city defenders dumbstruck.

Nicephorus, however, was ready. His infantry formed an assault column with their shields and sturdy pikes lining a formidable front, backed up by a deep formation of heavy infantry ready to push their comrades through any enemy. Within the powerful column, archers and javelin throwers advanced to support the leading infantry. The Muslim army quickly recovered from their shock and formed a cordon across the breach in the wall. Facing these men of Chandax, in the form of the Byzantine assault column, were plunders, rapists, and enslavement. The defending army locked shields with a will to protect their families, their homes and their own lives. They fought hard. Nevertheless, the assault column inched ahead as the deep formation pushed their comrades forward. When one man fell in front, another replaced him and the struggle continued amidst yells, screams, trumpets, and curses. Eventually, the Muslim cordon unravelled as man after man fell to the Byzantine blades and the remaining defenders turned and fled. The Byzantine soldiers pursued the fleeing defenders, cutting them down as they tried to hide in the city's narrow streets. Breaking into the houses, the soldiers raped and murdered with abandon. After three days, Nicephorus managed to suppress the soldiers' passions and ordered his soldiers to accept the surrender of those without weapons. Since the surrendered men counted as booty along with the women and children, accepting surrender only increased the total amount of plunder.

Once the soldiers stamped out the remains of resistance in the city, Nicephorus collected the imperial fifth of the loot for the Emperor and divided out the prisoners who were of the leading families for his anticipated triumph (7 March 961). Then he allowed the soldiers to plunder whatever they could find. Since Chandax was the base for pirate operations for many decades and had held off all enemies, the treasures of the city were rich pickings, indeed. Once the Byzantines had well picked over the city, Nicephorus directed the slighting of the walls. Organizing a mounted force, he then rode out into the countryside, plundering as he went, eliminating opposition when it appeared. Units spread throughout the island of Crete, restoring the land to the Byzantine Empire. On a hilltop overlooking the devastated Chandax, the Byzantines build a fortress they called Temenos. Nicephorus settled older soldiers and those who wanted to stay as garrisons guarding the island. Before he returned to Constantinople, the commander assigned some of the fire-bearing *dromon* ships to guard the sea-lanes leading to Crete.

Leo Phocas Campaigns in the East

During the late summer of 960, others were looking for plundering opportunities. Since Nicephorus had collected units from the eastern sections of the empire, he significantly reduced the size of many garrisons. Beyond the imperial frontiers, in northern Syria, predatory eyes focused on the Byzantine east. The militant Muslim dynasty, the Hamdanids, controlled the military frontier facing the Byzantine border. Based at Aleppo, forces of Ali ibn Hamdan, Sayf ad-Dawla (Sword of the Dynasty) prepared for another of the almost yearly forays into the empire. Inhabitants of the Muslim frontier lived in areas dedicated to military settlers, in some ways similar to the Byzantine themes. The Syrians called such an area a *thughur*. Here dwelt soldiers, generally light horsemen, armed with bows and javelins. One of their occupations was raiding across the border and fighting with Byzantine soldiers who also occupied their time with raiding. During the years when the Caliphate was strong, districts sent money to the frontiers to pay for mercenaries. These often took the form of slave-soldiers, called *ghulam,* either heavy infantry or horse soldiers. The Bedouins, always looking for action and plunder, eagerly joined these expeditions. In addition, individual young men, keen for adventure and plunder, came in the summer to fight for Islam; these were the *ghazis* (fighters for the faith). The Emir at Aleppo, the Sword of the Dynasty, called for holy war against the Byzantine Empire, promising plunder or paradise to those who came to fight.

Erupting out of Cilicia, the forward base of the Hamdanid Emirs, a massive force swept across the Byzantine frontier, burning and looting, capturing women and livestock, killing those who opposed them. News of the invasion reached Constantinople and Emperor Romanus acted quickly. Nicephorus Phocas' brother, Leo, also a famous soldier, never suffered defeat. In command of a small force, Leo Phocas had defended the Danube frontier: he had repulsed a Magyar invasion using unexpected ambushes and night raids to confuse and disorganize the enemy. Because Nicephorus had taken many soldiers from the eastern provinces to Crete, the Emperor appointed Leo commander of the western provinces (*domestikos* of the West). This is probably when the office of domestikos split into a commander for the east and west. Leo transported the elite mobile units of the western Byzantine army to Asia, being careful not to so weaken the western frontiers as to invite attack. As it was, he had only a small force, compared with the invading Muslims, but Leo did not intend to hit the invaders head on. Rather, as his force passed through the burnt and plundered landscape, he avoided direct confrontation with the Muslims. He marched to the mountains bordering Cilicia, which overhung the roads leading to the lands around Tarsus. In the narrow passes and overhanging heights, he prepared ambushes to catch the Muslim forces as they returned with plunder.

The Muslim armies had collected and were marching home under the eye of the Sword of the Dynasty, Ali ibn Hamdan. Mounted on a very large mare, he rode about, inspecting his soldiers and glorying in the richness of plunder and numbers of slaves. He often flung his spear up in the air and, as it twirled and fell, he caught it only to repeat the stunt. With his entourage, his massive horse, and twirling spear, the Sword of the Dynasty was clearly visible as his army marched toward the mountains. Leo Phocas' army spread out into a series of bases, waiting to ambush the Muslim army all along the road they were taking. The Sword of the Dynasty's army slowly threaded themselves into the narrow mountain road, breaking their formations, and spread out all along the road. When the army and its plunder were at the most vulnerable, Leo Phocas gave the order to attack. As the Byzantine trumpets rang out, all the soldiers drew their swords, and charged the drawn out Muslim army. The different bands that made up the Muslim army had no cohesion. The army quickly disintegrated. Everyman tried to escape by himself: some made an escape, some hid, most perished. Leo was particularly interested in capturing Ali ibn Hamdan. The Muslim commander escaped the first assault, gathered his bodyguard around himself, and fled. Byzantine horse pursued but by scattering gold and silver coins in heaps, the Sword of the Dynasty and his guard got away.

The ambushes continued until what was left of the Muslim force had retreated beyond the frontier. Leo ordered all the booty gathered together. Here were heaps of goods, both Byzantine and Muslim. These, after taking the Emperor's allocation, Leo distributed to the troops. To the captives that the Muslims had taken, Leo gave supplies, and sent them home. The Byzantines bound their many prisoners taken from the defeated army, preparing them for the march toward the slave markets. Leo and the Byzantine army celebrated their victory with song and prayer, after which they began the march to Constantinople and their triumph. Leo Phocas and his army marched into the Great City by the Golden Gate and proceeded down the Mese, a main boulevard leading through the imperial forums to the great palace. Here Emperor Romanus, his empress, and family received the conquering general. Then, leading picked troops, some carrying heaps of treasure along with crowds of fine captives, Leo marched around the great Hippodrome to the cheers and admiring chants of the citizens of Byzantium.

Nicephorus Phocas gave the people of Constantinople an even greater spectacle when he returned from his victory in Crete. Awarded a triumph similar to his brother's, his army was more imposing and the spoils paraded through the city were more impressive. Heaps of gold and silver, masses of coins, gorgeous garments, carpets, full sets of armour, helmets, shields, and weapons, all gilded, then a multitude of former elite individuals, now slaves, passed in front of the cheering crowds in the Hippodrome. Soon after the triumph, Emperor Romanus II received the victorious general, presenting him with munificent gifts and reappointing him *domestikos* of the east. Nicephorus crossed the Bosporus and assembling his army of veteran warriors, pushed quickly to the frontier. The forces of the Sword of the Dynasty, already weakened by Leo Phocas' ambushes, continued to waste away because, at this time of year, the volunteers and subsidized troops had all gone home. The local troops occupied their strongholds and avoided combat with the crack Byzantine troops. Nicephorus, while maintaining strict discipline, led his forces in an extensive plundering expedition. They sacked farms, villages, and small towns, capturing livestock and prisoners for the slave market. What his men could not transport away, they destroyed. Isolated in their fortresses, the local soldiers could only watch. Nicephorus then attacked the strongholds, battering them into ruin. He took some sixty rich fortresses including the Sword of the Dynasty's seat, Aleppo. The Hamdan Emirs had built a palace, al-Hallaba, in Aleppo's suburbs, a large beautiful structure filled with treasure. Since it stood outside of the city walls, the Byzantines easily captured it. The soldiers plundered everything they could find and burned the palace. They also gained entrance to Aleppo, sacking the city and killing the inhabitants. Loaded with plunder and important prisoners, Nicephorus was on the march to Constantinople when he received the news: Emperor Romanus was dead.

References

Death of Constantine VII: Leo the Deacon, I, 2–3; John Skylitzes, 248–9. Skylitzes references refer to the page numbers of *Ioannis Scylitzae Synopsis historion*, edition princeps, ed. I. Thurn (CFHB, 5, Berlin and New York, 1973).

For the reign of Leo VI the Wise: see Shaun Tougher, *The Reign of Leo VI (886–912)*, New York, 1997. This is a nice detailed and chatty book.

For the reign of Constantine VII, see Steven Runciman, *The Emperor Romanus Lecapenus & his Reign*, Cambridge, 1929, still in print. Sir Steven's first book, but like the rest, always cogent.

For background, see Arnold Toynbee, *Constantine Porphyrogenitus and his World*: Oxford, 1973. This is a true masterpiece by a master.

Nicephorus' Campaign on Crete: Leo the Deacon, I, 4–9; John Skylitzes, 245, 249–50.

For background about Byzantine battles for Crete, see John Wortley, translation of John Skylitzes, p. 237, note 30.

For details on the naval operations, see John Pryor and Elizabeth Jeffreys, *The Age of the ΔΡΟΜΩΝ*: Leiden 2006, pp. 262–6.

Byzantine Military Thought and the Battle on Crete

Byzantine military handbooks had a long history. (See Appendix II.) Of particular import for the fighting on Crete are the *Taktika* of Leo VI and the later *Praecepta militaria* of Nicephorus Phocas, the Byzantine commander in these battles. While I leave details of any analysis of these books to the relevant appendix, Leo's information is consistent with Nicephorus' actions on Crete. Various sections of the *Taktik* illuminate the possibilities open to Nicephorus and so from the context of the battle we can see why he made the choices he did. First, section 2, 'Concerning the Qualities Needed in the Commander': Nicephorus certainly just about sums up the qualities Leo recommends as pictured in 2, 18.

Second, in section 3, 'Concerning the Importance of Strategic Plans': As the battles on Crete unfold, it is clear that Nicephorus has a handle on the operations, concentrating and manoeuvring his forces to achieve his ultimate objective. See especially 3, 1–2. Third, section 11, 'Concerning Camps': Nicephorus builds a strong camp as soon as possible and uses that camp as a base from which to manage his operations. See especially 11, 1–2, 19, 26 Text available as George Dennis editor and translator, *The Taktika of Leo VI*: Washington DC, 2010.

Nicephorus' own *Praecepta militaria* was written sometime after the battles on Crete but show Nicephorus' regard for clear discussion of battle tactics and decisive operations. Holding his heavy infantry as a shield, he throws his heavy cavalry at weak points in the enemy's lines, trying to grind them up. Text available in Eric McGeer, *Sowing the Dragon's Teeth*: Washington DC, 2008, text, translation, and commentary *Praecepta militaria* pp. 12–59.

Siege of Chandax: Leo 2, 6–8.

For Nicephorus' discussion on the form and use of camps, see *Praecepta militaria*, V, 1–66.

The narrative makes the siege seem a well organized smoothly running operation, as it probably was; however, without a great deal of forethought and accomplished technical advisors, no commander can hope to accomplish much in a siege. Just what went into a successful siege is illustrated by the two manuals ascribed to Heron of Byzantium. The *Parangelmata Poliorcetica* describes the construction, complete with plans, of various siege engines, Heron talks of everything from ladders, rams, shield covers, and towers. Nicephorus needed men who understood construction and crews of skilled artisans at their command. These men had to select and ship a mass of prefabricated materials to build ladders, throwing machines, and the ram. Clearly these constructors understood the plans and measurements used in Heron's text. And, equally clearly, so did Nicephorus as commander in chief.

Even more important than the machinery, the *Geodesia* describes the most critical information of siege work. These are the mathematical and arithmetic formulae that generate accurate measurements for the height of the walls, their thickness, the range for throwing machines, and all the dimensions needed to insure weapons and units of men reached the points on the battlescape necessary for success.

The *Geodesia* also provides the type of information that Nicephorus and his construction staff needed to successfully mine the wall. Unseen distances and depths, maintaining direction and concealment, and many other factored were correctly ascertained. Without the mathematical expertise and highly skilled artisans Nicephorus' siege would have failed. Text available in Dennis Sullivan, *Siegecraft, Two Tenth-Century Instruction Manuals by 'Heron of Byzantium'*: Washington DC, 2000, *Parangelmata Poliorcetica* and *Geodesia*, text, translation and commentary.

Leo Phocas Campaigns in the East: Leo 2, 2–5; 9–10; Skylitzes 252–3.

The Byzantines had studied Muslim warfare for centuries. The *Taktika* (18, 103–49) gives an extended discussion of the Muslim armies of the Near East.

Leo Phocas used an indirect strategy to savage the Muslim armies on the Arab-Byzantine frontier. When he was emperor, Nicephorus composed a manual describing the principles and practice of 'little war', Περι παραδρομής, translated by George Dennis as *Skirmishing*. Text available in George Dennis, *Three Byzantine Military Treatises*: Washington DC, 1985 (pp. 144–239).

The Byzantine triumph, based somewhat on the old Roman Triumph, and developed into the later western European Royal Advent, is well analysed. See Michael McCormick, *Eternal Victory, Triumphal Rulership in Late Antiquity Byzantium and the Early Medieval West*: Cambridge, 1986. See pp. 176–8.

Chapter 2

Nicephorus Phocas Seizes Power

The City

Emperor Romanus II died in early spring 963. News of unexpected death has always been disturbing; news of an emperor's sudden death was frightful to both the high and low. Romanus was a vigorous young man: he should have ruled for decades; if he were not the best of emperors, certainly he would not be among the worst. As the mainmast, the moderator of Byzantine society, his person held the riggings of power in place. With the Emperor's sudden death, each person could see vistas of great heights or of the abyss. Nicephorus Phocas, as one of the most powerful in the empire, was a candidate for great elevation or a target for mutilation and disgrace. His rivals for power were few: the empress, the patriarch, and the Lord Chamberlain. Each represented a major institution in Byzantium. The Empress Theophano was mother of two boys, Basil aged five and Constantine aged two, both heirs apparent. Reportedly, the most beautiful woman of the age, her reputation, supported by the fact that she had convinced Romanus to marry her, was of a ruthless unscrupulous manipulator. Rumour spread that she had poisoned her father-in-law, the Porphyrogenitus, and indeed that she poisoned her husband. However, Romanus' death left her vulnerable, along with everyone else, and she clearly did not have a plan immediately after Romanus' demise.

The Patriarch Polyeuctus had been on the ecclesiastical throne since 956; he was a difficult and headstrong administrator but he was an excellent manager of the many interests of the Church. Made a eunuch in young age, he was a stern moralist and respected for his integrity. He suggested that Romanus died because his companions were corrupting him and he ignored the Lenten fast, going hunting for deer instead. His companions did bring him back alive from the hills in which they were chasing deer. He seems to have suffered internal injuries, perhaps from a fall. His end was soon in coming. The Imperial Senate and all high civil officials assembled, and Polyeuctus recognized Romanus' two sons as emperors under the direction of their mother, Theophano. While this brought some stability to a chaotic situation, the administration fell deeper into the hands of the palace eunuchs, under the Lord Chamberlain, Joseph Bringas.

As a member of the senate, Bringas saw to the installation of Theophano as regent, thus ensuring his own power and keeping his hand in the corruption game.

Constantinople was a very complex urban structure. Many competing interests struggled with each other in a sophisticated moneyed economy. The later Roman-Byzantine tradition of government ensured a convoluted state – private series of enterprises that dominated most economic activity in the city. Given the large number of competing people and the high stakes of the game, what many saw as corruption was the grease that smoothed the wheels of action. The state organized business, bakers, food markets, silk, and weapon manufacturing among others, but private ventures surrounded the state enterprises that had far less state regulation or involvement. Here were building trades, carting-teamsters, and specialty foods, many distributers of alcohol and the like products, inns, taverns, artists, and the education industry. All sorts of organizations dealt in these businesses: younger sons and daughters of great families, clients of powerful people, sharp thrifty individuals, families of business people, and another major player, the Church in many forms, from property owner to hospitals and charity institutions. In addition, of course, there was another layer of enterprises: gambling and prostitution, protection and security, thieves, purse-snatchers, and toughs. These organized themselves in the usual structures of artificial clans, called in English, gangs or the mobs. Threads of all these businesses ran into the palace.

In the sophisticated society of Byzantium, most of the ruling elite came from the rich and well-born families because education was a necessary attribute for important positions and that required a childhood spent in school rather than on a job. However, there were exceptions. A poor family could have one of their young boys castrated so he became a eunuch. A dealer in such commodities would then buy and train him. That way, the eunuch might find a position where he might gain influence. Should he succeed, he would, of course, repay his patron with influence and look out for his family's interests. While there were numerous places where he might find employment, the Church, great houses, foreign courts, the ultimate positions were in the palace. Here, eunuchs managed the institutions of the private parts of the palace and this allowed them to exercise personal influence on the workings of government. They could influence a positive or negative decision; they could expedite or retard implementations; and they certainly could build up a collection of favours given in return for other favours. All governmental actions came from the issuing of laws, meetings of the main officials, and the judicial courts. However, if someone wanted to circumvent or short circuit the 'system' then the time had come to get to an important eunuch. This, of course, was no problem – for a price.

This was all very clear to the eunuch Lord Chamberlain, Joseph Bringas. The death of Romanus threatened his position and his webs of influence radiating from the palace. Polyeuctus, he could handle, the patriarch was honest but liked power. The Empress' family was still in the city; she understood how things stood. The one factor the Lord Chamberlain could not control was the military. Triumphant generals who were also great landowners were not amenable to either the favours or blackmail of palace eunuchs. Not that the brothers Phocas would reform Constantinople – that's not happened to this day, rather, they would bring in their own team to take over the influence business. Commander Nicephorus Phocas was a serious threat to Joseph Bringas.

The General Nicephorus' Dilemma

All these things weighed on the mind of the commander as he absorbed the news of Romanus' death. He understood that Joseph Bringas was no friend. He despised the eunuch whom he saw as venal and untrustworthy. As wife and empress of his lord the emperor, Nicephorus respected Theophano; as mother of acclaimed emperors, he honoured her. Except as living symbols of the Christ-beloved state that he served, the imperial family had little meaning in his own personal life. Nicephorus was a widower and his son had died while sparring with a cousin with lances on horseback. The general had turned to the consolation of Holy Church. He had personally helped his friend, Saint Athanasius, with gifts. Together, they helped found the Great Laura monastery, the first monastery founded on the Holy Mountain of Athos. As one deeply involved in Holy Church, although a layman, Nicephorus knew and admired the Patriarch Polyeuctus. Here was a man he could trust.

Considering his options at the start of the interregnum, Nicephorus could call together his army, accept acclamation as emperor and march on Constantinople: that would mean war, and better than most, the general understood that war was always a gamble. He could do nothing: however, that way his enemies might gain power and then, they would surely destroy him and his family. Better than either path, he could go to the Great City with his personal entourage and contact those people who would support his effort to achieve an outcome that would be neither threatening nor violent. Welcomed by an admiring public, Nicephorus celebrated another triumph and contributed great treasure to the imperial coffers. With the celebration and thanksgiving completed, the general retired to his house in the city.

Suddenly, Nicephorus received a summons to go to the palace. He understood that this could only come from Lord Chamberlain Bringas and suspected that once he entered the palace, he would disappear. He set off, but he went to the Great Church, Hagia Sophia, instead. Probably, the general had anticipated this course of action and as he entered the Great Church, the Patriarch Polyeuctus met him. The general, in his splendid attire, addressed the patriarch, in his official robes, in a corner of the church, talking loud enough so those nearby might hear them but not so loud as to interfere with others in the sanctuary. That way there would be no suspicion of sinister collusion. Nicephorus announced his concern: that he had done great service to the Roman State. He defeated her enemies, enriched her treasury, and smote her enemies. Now he faced destruction from a noble member of the Imperial Senate who seemed to believe that working in secret could escape the Eye of God. This was beyond reason, Nicephorus argued.

The patriarch nodded agreement, and signalling to his attendant bishops and acolytes, Polyeuctus led a procession, accompanied by Nicephorus and his entourage, from the Great Church to the Sacred Palace, where he ordered the Imperial Senate to assemble. Once the important officials, spiritual and temporal including the lord chamberlain, convened, Patriarch Polyeuctus charged them to consider that the general Nicephorus, at great personal effort and danger, had greatly promoted the interests of the Roman State. He should receive honours. The Imperial Senate and the People of Rome had proclaimed the two young sons of the imperial family as emperors, as was proper. The senate should confer the office of Supreme General and Commander in the East on Nicephorus, with the proviso that he made binding promises that he would do nothing to undermine the state constitution. For, the patriarch continued, Emperor Romanus held Nicephorus in high regard and awarded him those positions.

The Imperial Senate, by unanimous vote, agreed with the patriarch's proposal. Even Lord Chamberlain Bringas voted yes, according to some unwillingly but pressured by his peers. The general swore that he would honour and respect the two child emperors for as long as they lived and the senate agreed to appoint or remove no one in high position without Nicephorus' consent. Then the senate appointed Nicephorus Supreme General and Commander in the East. With these acts accomplished, the senate adjourned and each departed for their homes.

The Throne Beckons

In the later spring of 963, Nicephorus travelled to the main army base in Cappadocia. Here he received new recruits for training while waiting for the arrival of veteran soldiers, both local troops and the regiments from the capital. The training included using different weapons and drilling to orders given by trumpets, drums and cymbals. His stated intent was to concentrate a major force and attack the emir of Aleppo, to end the threat from that power. Nevertheless, other events intervened. The nature of those events comes to us through a fog of propaganda justifying the outcome. The result was, of course, that General Nicephorus Phocas became emperor. Since he had sworn to allow the imperial children peaceful occupancy of the throne, he needed an overwhelming reason to take the throne for himself. He blamed the greed and treachery of Lord Chamberlain, Joseph Bringas. Moreover, the chamberlain eunuch did not have a reputation that would refute such charges. They might be true. The story, told after the event was as follows: disappointed that the general had safely escaped his trap that winter in Constantinople, Bringas was hunting for a way to destroy him. The chamberlain summoned the Patrician Marianus Argyros to the palace.

Marianus, an older individual, had commanded the army of the west and fought in Italy and the Balkans. Bringas secretly met with Marianus in a private corner of the palace. He told Marianus that he would make him General of the East and then Marianus could get rid of Nicephorus. After the destruction of Nicephorus, Bringas would proclaim Marianus as emperor. Marianus had survived conspiracies in the time of Romanus I Lecapenus (920–944) and Romanus II favoured him. He knew the price of imperial involvements. His response, as recorded by Leo, was 'Hush! Stop whipping a small monkey to get him to fight a fierce giant. My opinion: look to John, known as "Little Soldier" (Tzimiskes), he is ambitious and hard-hitting. Make him General of the East. If anyone can rid you of Nicephorus, it is he.' Of course, since someone killed Marianus in the disturbances connected with Nicephorus' accession, he would never deny this story.

Bringas followed Marianus' advice and wrote to John Tzimiskes, offering to make him General of the East and then emperor, if he would agree to arrest Nicephorus and send him to Constantinople in chains. At the same time, Bringas removed many of Nicephorus' relatives and friends from their offices and forced them to leave the city. However, the attempt to turn the Patrician, John Tzimiskes General of the Anatolic Theme, failed. He was a nephew of Nicephorus Phocas, a son of Nicephorus' sister who married into the House of Curcuas. When he received the letter, he took it straight to Nicephorus' camp. Leo tells us that upon entering his uncles' tent, the Little Soldier sat down and woke up the sleeping commander and told him that he had been sleeping long and deeply, indeed! While Nicephorus was sleeping the good Lord Chamberlain had plotted his murder. How could they, John Tzimiskes continued, allow an effeminate creature like this Joseph Bringas try to split them apart? This artificial woman, this creature of doubtful sex knew nothing but the woman's sneakiness. He then handed Bringas' letter to Nicephorus, who read it with amazement. Leo continues: Nicephorus asks John what he suggests. John is adamant. They must collect the army and remove Joseph Bringas.

Whether the Lord Chamberlain opened himself to the charge of soliciting murder through direct contact with two important people, neither of whom he was sure would agree with him, or Leo's account simply reflected the official explanation for Nicephorus' usurpation remains a question. However, Joseph Bringas' reputation for subtle and smooth manoeuvres is not evident here. By the same reasoning, however, Bringas certainly intended to eliminate Nicephorus because if he did not, Nicephorus would get rid of him. Now, the commander had reached the point of final decision: he and John mobilized the recruits and marched toward the main military base in Cappadocia, Caesarea. This was the concentration centre for both the veteran thematic troops and the imperial regiments from the capital. Once the officers organized and arranged the camp, Little Soldier John, ranking commander as General of the Anatolic Theme, called all the officers together, disclosed the evidence of the Lord Chamberlain's treachery, and recommended that the army proclaim Nicephorus as emperor. At dawn in July 963, the officers, with Little Soldier at their head, surrounded the commander's tent, drew their swords, and acclaimed the new emperor. Nicephorus, acting surprised, as was the custom in such events, immediately refused, citing the deaths of his beloved wife and son. He suggested that John receive the honour instead. The officers, with John at their head, steadfastly refused and Nicephorus finally relented, accepting the imperial office. He retired to his tent, where he put on the scarlet buskins, strapped a short sword to his side, and grasping a great spear, strode to the speaking stand. Below him the army gathered, soldiers of all the formations, veterans and new recruits. He spoke of the justice of their cause, of the worthlessness of Bringas' administration, of how much he depended upon them, his soldiers, and that hard fighting was ahead. With great enthusiasm, the soldiers pledged their loyalty and support.

After a thanksgiving service in the Caesarea cathedral, Emperor Nicephorus rewarded John with the rank of Magistrate and made him General of the East. Then he appointed new or confirmed existing generals of the themes, sending them back to their home bases to ensure support for the new regime. He was particularly concerned about the commands that controlled the strategic seaways on the Black Sea coasts and especially the coasts of the Sea of Marmara through the Bosporus in order to secure provisions for his forces. Always the careful general, questions of supplies for his armies were more important than just numbers of soldiers to Nicephorus. Having settled the command structure, he mobilized his field army for the march to Constantinople. He organized his force into a massive rectangle. With light cavalry outriders scouting ahead, keeping an eye on the flanks and rear, the heavy infantry battalions marched in close order, abreast of ranks along the front and rear and in line of files along the sides. Inside the large area this enclosed, light infantry, heavy cavalry, and the supply trains moved, protected from immediate assault by the lines of heavy infantry, but able to sally forth against an enemy, should any appear. This was the formation used to march through enemy territory, and Emperor Nicephorus was taking no chances on a possible pre-emptive attack from Bringas or his supporters.

As he marched on the capital, Nicephorus sent a letter, delivered by Bishop Philotheus, addressed to the Patriarch Polyeuctus, head of the Church, to Joseph Bringas, head of the administration, and to the Imperial Senate. The letter stated that Nicephorus was legitimate emperor: he would protect, honour, and educate the two child emperors; he would expand the territory of the empire; any who refused to recognize him as emperor were rebels and he would deal with them as such. Lord Chamberlain Bringas had anticipated for this eventually. Bishop Philotheus, he arrested and threw into prison. He ordered the Macedonian Guards Regiment consolidated, appointing General Marianus to command the forces in the capital, assisted by nobles loyal to him. Soldiers guarded the walls and gates of the city. Nicephorus' brother, Leo, and father, Bardas, were living in the Phocas' townhouse in the city. When word of Nicephorus' arrival across the Bosporus came, Leo dressed as a common labourer and left the city through a sewer pipe that ran through the sea wall. He had arranged a skiff to meet him, and he took the skiff across to Nicephorus' camp. The Magistrate Bardas, old and infirm, went to the Great Church seeking asylum. The women, children, and servants remained in the townhouse, protected by loyal retainers from haphazard incidents and by Byzantine custom from official harassment.

Crowds began to collect in the streets, chanting slogans against the Lord Chamberlain. To restore order, General Marianus led a battalion of Macedonian Guards through the main streets, catching and punishing the demonstrators. What was a raucous affair became a riot. Townspeople turned on the troops and fought them in close order, something the soldiers did not expect and they lacked training for this type of fighting. While men and boys surrounded the troops, pushing them back and forth, women began throwing things from the upper stories of the buildings lining the street. A clay tile or flowerpot stuck General Marianus on the forehead and split open his skull. The soldiers called it quits and the townspeople allowed them to withdraw to their barracks, taking their wounded commander with them. General Marianus died the next day. The riot spread through many parts of the city. Districts erupted when gangs of one section plundered other sections. Old scores, debts, arguments, all found an outlet as neighbours plundered neighbours. Upheaval and violence spread, threatening ongoing businesses. The bakers, particularly worried about looters, closed their shops. The story spread that the Lord Chamberlain Bringas pressured the Bakers' Guild to stop selling bread to punish the populace for supporting Nicephorus but even if he wished to close the bakeries, he had no way to enforce such a ban across the city. However, fear of looting would accomplish just such an action.

In the centre of Nicephorus' supporters in Constantinople, sat Basil the Bastard. This man was an illegitimate son of Emperor Romanus I by a Slav bondswoman in the imperial household. The young man was very precocious; Romanus had him made a eunuch and saw to his education. Basil loved books and study. He became Grand Tutor to the young Purple-Born Constantine VII and together the two developed a close relationship based on scholarship. After Romanus' legitimate sons managed to dethrone their father, Basil helped Constantine bundle the sons off to a monastery. Constantine made Basil patrician and lord chamberlain. His administration was efficient and relatively honest as such things went in Byzantium. After Constantine died and his son, Romanus II, became emperor, Basil was out of favour at court. Romanus II replaced him with one of his own subordinates, Joseph Bringas. Basil escaped prosecution for malfeasance of office and remained rich and influential. However, he had no love for Joseph Bringas. Calling together his personal retainers and those for whom he had found favours, in all about three thousand men, he armed them with swords, shields and helmets and led them to Joseph's house. They broke in, plundered the premises, and proceeded on to the houses of Joseph's supporters. While some continued to spread the riot, Basil and some of his close followers went to the naval dockyards. He found the officers and men ready to support Nicephorus as emperor. They fitted out some of the fire-bearing dromones and sailed across the Bosporus to support Nicephorus, with the approval, Basil said, of the people and senate.

Nicephorus embarked on the admiral's ship and escorted by the Byzantine fleet landed at a monastery near the great Golden Gate. Setting up his headquarters in the monastery, he dispatched some guard battalions to seize the Great Palace. As they approached, Joseph Bringas saw his personal guards defect and soon he was alone. He ran into the Great Church to find sanctuary. As he entered the church, the old blind Bardas Phocas was able to leave and return to his home. While his soldiers secured the Sacred Palace, Nicephorus' servants removed his military trappings and dressed him in imperial robes and insignia. The new emperor mounted a fine white horse, draped in purple with imperial ornaments. With his guards leading and following, Nicephorus rode into Constantinople through the Great Golden Gate and down the main thoroughfare, the Mese, through the Forum of Arcadius, the Forum of Theodosius, and the Forum of Constantine to the Great Church. All the way, crowds welcomed him and cheered as he passed. Dismounting at the entrance to Hagia Sophia, the churchmen, in their high vestments, welcomed him. Proceeding to the interior, at the high alter Patriarch Polyeuctus anointed and crowned the new emperor. The date was August 16, AM 6470 (AD 963), the anniversary of the deliverance of Constantinople by the Holy Mother of God from the Muslim invasion of AD 718 and, nineteen years before this date, of the advent of the Mandylion, taken from Edessa, through the Golden Gate to Hagia Sophia. Both feasts feature in the *Synaxarium Constantinopolitanum*.

References

Death of Romanus II: Leo, 2, 10; Skylitzes, 254–5.

Structure of Byzantine society in the tenth century: for details on the Byzantine economy see Angeliki Laiou and Cecile Morrisson, *The Byzantine Economy*: Cambridge, 2007, especially Section III; also, the most important collection of writings on Byzantine social history, see Angeliki Laiou, *The Economic History of Byzantium*, vols I–III: Washington DC, 2002, without a doubt the best source of information on the Byzantine economy in all of its aspects.

Physical structure of the Great City: see John Freely and Ahmet Çakmak, *Byzantine Monuments of Istanbul*: Cambridge, 2004, especially pp. 154–199.

The Empress Theophano and women in Byzantine elite society: see Charles Diehl, *Byzantine Empresses*: New York, 1963, especially 'Theophano', 114–35; Lynda Garland, *Byzantine Empresses*: New York, 1999, especially chapter 7, 'Theophano' 126–35; while not specific about Theophano, for a good discussion about women in elite Byzantium, see Judith Herrin, *Women in Purple*: London, 2001.

The General Nicephorus' Dilemma: Leo, 2, 10–12; Skylitzes, 254–60, 13, 1–7.

Nicephorus and St. Athanasius: Albert Vogt, 'The Macedonian Dynasty from 867 to 976 AD', in Tanner, editor, *Cambridge Medieval History, vol. IV, the Eastern Roman Empire*: New York, 1923, p. 70.

The Throne Beckons: Leo 3, 1–8; Skylitzes, 260–1.

Basil the bastard: 'Basil the nothos (bastard)', in Alexander Kazhdan editor, *The Oxford Dictionary of Byzantium*, vol. I: New York, 1991, p. 270.

Joseph Bringas: *Ibid.*, 325–6.

Chapter 3

Nicephorus II Phocas: the Conquest of Cilicia

The New Reign

A grand procession of high officials, military officers, ecclesiasts, and important people led the new Emperor out of the Great Church into the Sacred Palace. Entering the Hall of the Imperial Throne, the crowd took their respective stations as Nicephorus mounted and sat upon the throne of the Roman Empire, receiving the acclamations and pledges of support from his court. Within a few days, he took the machinery of administration firmly in hand. There was no question of who was in charge. His father, Bardas, he elevated to Caesar; his brother, Leo, he appointed *kouroplates* and *magistros*; Basil the Bastard, he elevated to the rank *proedros*; and his fellow general, John Tzimiskes, he appointed *magistros* and Domestic of the East.

Nicephorus II Phocas was fifty-one when he ascended the Imperial Throne of the Byzantine Caesars. The Emperor enjoyed a robust late middle age. He was stocky with broad shoulders and a deep powerful chest. A strong hooked nose offset his black piercing eyes, staring out from pronounced bushy brows. Thick black hair on top, cut to a disciplined military fashion, framed his face. A moderate but neat black beard, streaked with white on his cheeks, gave balance to his appearance. Words of command came easily to him but tempered by the common touch of the popular military officer. Initially, Nicephorus was clear that he did not intend to change his abstinent life style, unmarried and vegetarian, like the holy monks he so admired. However, his monastic spiritual advisors, whom he respected deeply, convinced him to accept a conventional married life, because as they explained, a position of great power can lead to temptations for the abstinent of a perverted nature. Nicephorus agreed that he must marry so now came the question, whom would he marry?

After the fact, speculations and never-ending rumour have swirled around the Empress Theophano from her time to this time. Certainly, Nicephorus had known her as a member of the imperial family since she had married the young Romanus in the time of the Porphyrogenitus. He had met, and pledged his loyalty to her two young children, Basil and Constantine, when he pledged loyalty to their father, Romanus II. Whether she had actually suggested to the general that he should assume power after the death of Romanus and facilitated his road to the throne, is an intriguing story for which there is no evidence. The circumstances are possible but the fact that Nicephorus originally decided not to marry tell against it, unless, of course, that was merely subterfuge. However, here, we can easily get lost in wheels within wheels and simply say she was probably not directly involved in Nicephorus' effort to seize the throne. However, once the new Emperor had ascended the throne, a very different set of circumstances emerged. If Nicephorus did not marry, the Empress would find herself in a convent, just like Romanus I's daughters, but if she married him, then she would remain empress. Here all sorts of motivations on many sides come into play: the care of the child Emperors, Basil II and Constantine VIII; the management of the Sacred Palace and its female staff; official contact with important women and their concerns, both of a legal and ritual nature. The imperial government needed an empress. Therefore, Nicephorus needed to marry. Who better but the widow of the father of the child Emperors?

For both bride and groom this was a marriage of convenience. The Emperor acquired an empress and stifled an area of possible opposition. The Empress maintained her status and the management of the female side of the Sacred Palace while raising her children. As the preparations for the wedding proceeded, a rumour arose, that Nicephorus had stood as baptismal sponsor of the young Emperors. Interested but unidentified parties informed Patriarch Polyeuctus of the rumour and he immediately rebuked Nicephorus for attempting an improper union, for Church Law forbade godfathers marrying within six degrees of godchildren. Nicephorus, taken aback by this charge, informed the Patriarch that, indeed, he was present at the baptisms of the children, but it was his father, the head of the House of Phocas, who stood as godfather. This explanation satisfied Polyeuctus but emphasized the fact that there were some who opposed the marriage with Theophano. Nevertheless, once he had decided on the union, the new Emperor sweetened the marriage bed with gifts. He gave to the bride impressive jewellery and imperial robes and the revenue of many rich estates, which produced fruit and fine grains.

During the winter following his accession, Nicephorus provided rich rewards for his supporters and, for the populace, exciting shows and many horse races in the Hippodrome. While the entertainment went on, he spent his time training his regiments of professional soldiers in the practices of war. Every day, his men drilled in archery, lance, spear, and swordplay. In these drills, he emphasized horsemanship and synchronized unit actions with the intention of using these men as cadres to train large numbers of troops. Just after the equinox of spring, 964, the Emperor announced a campaign against the Muslims.

Conquest of Cilicia

In late winter, John Tzimiskes, Domestic of the East, had marched through Asia Minor toward the Cilicia. He commanded an elite body of cavalry, both archers and lancers. Advancing into the mountains that separate Cappadocia from Cilicia, Tzimiskes' force ran into the yearly expeditionary forces of Emir Sayf ad-Doula, intent on raiding and plundering the Byzantine lands. Immediately attacking the Muslim cavalry force, the Byzantines cut many down; the rest dismounted and fled into the mountains surrounding both armies. Collecting on a height, the Muslims held off the Byzantine force. Tzimiskes had his soldiers dismount, and surround the height. Slowly the Byzantine solders advanced up the hillside all around the height, killing or pushing back their enemies. Coming to the top, the Byzantine soldiers killed all of the Muslim soldiers, about 5,000 men. Blood ran down the hillsides, so later people called the place 'the Mountain of Blood'. Having broken the main striking force of the Muslims, John sent word back to the Emperor; the time to advance had come.

For centuries, the Byzantine army had maintained a fortified base at Caesarea, the main Byzantine town of Cappadocia. The forces from the themes of Asia Minor joined here in order to await the imperial *tagmata* marching from Constantinople under the direction of the Emperor. Nicephorus planned a major effort to expand the empire. He had already conquered Crete. Now he intended to take the lands of Tarsus. Beyond the Cappadocian, highlands, through the mountain passes, spread the rich Cilician plains. Great walls surrounded the main city of Tarsus that sat among a series of castles and fortified settlements. For centuries, the people of the Tarsus plain had raided and plundered Byzantine lands. Muslim warriors took Christian women and goods. The Byzantines fought the Muslim and did the same to their homes, when they could. Nicephorus decided that this border war would end with his conquest of Tarsus and the Cilician plain.

First, Byzantine light troops, mounted and foot, spread into Cilicia, to harass and disrupt the local soldiers. Then, the imperial army, theme troopers and imperial *tagmata*, advanced through the passes and made for Tarsus. As his light troops spread fire and destruction, the Emperor oversaw the construction of a large armed camp near the city. The walls of Tarsus were strong: a double wall of cut white stone, complete with battlements surrounded the city while the river ran through the city's middle, supplying fresh water. Floodgates controlled the river's flow so, when necessary, the city defenders could divert the water into a moat that enclosed the whole circuit of the walls. The supplies in the city were plentiful and the populace intensely disliked the

Byzantines. Nicephorus knew that he would not easily take the city. He settled a good part of his army in his camp, and blockaded Tarsus' gates. As he set out his siege lines, soldiers from Tarsus attacked the Byzantines to disrupt and dishearten them. Insults to the Emperor and the Byzantines flew from the walls of Tarsus. Nicephorus let them have their fun as he organized a large elite strike force.

While the Byzantine blockade continued, the Emperor led a special force through the countryside, capturing, plundering and destroying castles and fortified towns. His army using escalade tactics took Adana and Anazarbus, the largest cities after Tarsus, and some twenty other fortified bases. The strongest Cilician fortification after Tarsus was Mopsuestia, a small city. Nicephorus led his force to the city, but saw that only a regular siege would carry the place. He blockaded Mopsuestia and surrounded it with heavy throwing machines, bombarding the walls with stones and fire. The Mopsuestians responded with a bombardment of their own, hurtling rocks and flaming arrows at the Byzantine machines. Nicephorus saw that he was not going to overthrow Mopsuestia and he withdrew his forces from the city. When autumn turned to winter, the Emperor collected supplies, having thoroughly looted Cilicia and cleared off the land. The army marched back to Caesarea. Nicephorus chose the best slaves and goods of the plunder and sent them to the imperial treasury in Constantinople. The rest he handed out to his soldiers along with their regular pay. He dismissed the troops from the themes, sending them home with their bounty, requiring them to return in the spring with repaired armour, sharpened swords and healthy horses. The Emperor stayed the winter in Caesarea with his *tagmata*.

While waiting for the spring, the Emperor brought his excavating engineers to Caesarea and planned how to break into Mopsuestia and Tarsus. He drilled his *tagmata*, both horse and foot, practising fortification assault tactics. When the spring of 965 came, the theme forces again collected at Caesarea. Nicephorus commanded the might of the eastern section of the empire, a little less than 40,000 men. The trained army of *tagmata* and *themata* soldiers were about 25,000 including heavy infantry, light infantry, archers, horsemen and *kataphracktoi*. Of this total, the *kataphracktoi* were some 600. The rest were volunteer light troops, carriers, and camp helpers. Marching from Caesarea toward the Cilician plain, the army was moving through a narrow defile. The Emperor saw a soldier discard his shield. Nicephorus ordered the shield recovered by one of his staff and carried in his train. That evening, officers found the man who threw away his shield. He and his captain faced the Emperor, who was adamant that he would punish such behaviour. He ordered the captain to flog the guilty man, cut off his nose, and exhibit the man through the camp. The next day, the Emperor saw the man marching along without suffering punishment. The Emperor immediately stopped the unit and called its captain to his presence. Because the captain failed to carry out the imperial order, the Emperor had the captain severely flogged and his nose cut off. Thus, he dismissed the disgraced officer from the army.

Arriving at Tarsus, the Byzantines rebuilt their camp, surrounding it with a palisade. Then Nicephorus sent his light troops out to not only plunder as they did in the last year, but also to destroy all the fields and orchards. Uprooting the crops, cutting all the trees, and demolishing all the buildings in the area, the Byzantines beheld Tarsus now sitting in the middle of a wasteland. The inhabitants of Tarsus, as they saw the Byzantines destroy their wealth, assembled their infantry, and marched out of the city, ready to do battle to repel the Byzantines. Nicephorus was waiting for them to come to battle. The Emperor led out the imperial army. In front, rode the *kataphracktoi*, the ironclad horsemen, 'horses without legs', men and beast enclosed by iron except for their eyes, in a blunt wedge-shaped formation some 500 strong. Behind the ironclad horsemen, there were foot archers and slingers, ready to send flights of missiles over the horsemen, to rain on the enemy. To the right of the foot, the Emperor in person commanded a cavalry force of mixed heavy and light warriors. To the left of the foot, Duke John Tzimiskes led another mixed cavalry force. All together, the Byzantines fielded about 10,000 men. The infantry of Tarsus stood with their banners waiving, challenging the Byzantines to attack. The Emperor Nicephorus gave the signal. The trumpets and drums sounded. As one, the Byzantine force moved forward. Gathering speed, the ironclad horsemen drove toward the enemy as arrows and stone fell from the sky. At the first contact, the men of Tarsus broke and ran, only to be overrun by the cavalry centre and wings. Very few made it back to the city. After that engagement, the only defending soldiers to be seen at Tarsus kept to the walls of the city.

Having secured the area around Tarsus, Nicephorus rode out of camp with a select group of elite soldiers, his special mining engineers, along with many labourers and marched toward Mopsuestia. The Byzantines rebuilt their siege lines, set up the throwing machines, and bombarded the town. The defenders replied in kind. As this continued, Nicephorus and his mining engineers found that part of the wall that looked most vulnerable to underground attack. Having chosen a spot masked by barricades holding throwing machines complete with river access beyond the town's line of sight, the miners began digging, hiding the dug soil in the river. In time, the engineers had excavated and propped up two towers with their connecting wall. At dawn of the day for the attack, the Emperor marshalled a strong force with scaling ladders facing the undermined section of wall. He was at the fore. The Muslim warriors, all in their white robes, thronged the wall parapet, threatening the Byzantines with arrows and stones if they came closer. Nicephorus had given the order to fire the mine. Eventually, with a great crash, two towers and the wall between suddenly collapsed, burying many defenders and leaving the town open to assault. The Emperor gave the signal. Trumpets and drums sounded and the Byzantine army surged into Mopsuestia. The town was soon theirs. The Byzantines rounded up and enslaved all the men, women, and children; then they looted the city.

Nicephorus and his force returned to the besieged city of Tarsus with many of their prisoners and loot. The leaders of Tarsus believed that a fleet from Egypt would come with reinforcements and provisions. However, the Byzantines guarded the coasts and their fleet drove the Egyptian ships away. Once the people of Tarsus understood that there was no possible relief, they intended to avoid the fate of Mopsuestia, and so sought terms. Nicephorus agreed that any person not wanting to stay under Byzantine rule could leave with safe passage to Syria. They could take only the clothes on their backs. The terms agreed upon, those who so desired left the city and the Byzantines took over. Nicephorus shared all the public loot with his soldiers, taking for himself and the state only the great standards that the armies of Tarsus had captured from the Byzantines over the years. The land of Cilicia became the Lesser Theme of Cilicia garrisoned and governed from Tarsus. Deserving soldiers received 'soldier's properties' and so became local landowners.

In October 965, the Emperor Nicephorus entered Constantinople with his victorious army, marching down the Mese road, through the imperial forums to Hagia Sophia. There, he placed the recovered standards as a sign of victory. The Emperor had brought back the city gates of both Mopsuestia and Tarsus. Plating them in gold, he set the gates of Mopsuestia on the city wall near the Golden Gate, and that of Tarsus on the palace walls. He also entertained the populace with chariot races as the city rejoiced in this first major recovery of land in Asia in hundreds of years.

The New Reign Turns Sour

In early 966, the excitement and enthusiasm of the new reign began to fade. Many people saw that the Emperor's administration was not concerned about their welfare. Early in the reign, people in Constantinople suffered from 'requisitions' and theft as the imperial soldiers helped themselves to what they wanted. This did not abate when the Emperor went on expedition but only got worse when Nicephorus returned with his victorious army. When the civilians complained, the Emperor belittled the actions of his soldiers by saying that with the great number of men under arms, he would be surprised if there were not some difficult people. When the soldiers continued to plunder shops and houses and then roughed up the civilians trying to defend their property, Nicephorus was actually amused and refused to discipline his soldiers. However, the incidental misbehaviour of the soldiers was not as unsettling as Nicephorus' need for revenue. He debased the coinage by introducing a new coin, the *tetarteron*. This was a lighter *solidus*: the standard *numisma* weighed about 4.40 g while the *tetarteron* weighed about 4.02 g, making it 1/12 less in weight. This provided two coinage weights but the Emperor decreed that both coins be accepted at the same value yet he demanded taxes be paid with the larger coin while expenses were paid in the smaller. At 72 standard *numisma* to the lb of gold, the *tetarteron* gave Nicephorus 5¼ extra coins to the lb of gold, an automatic profit of more than 8 per cent.

While he manipulated the currency, he also sought to increase tax revenue. His fiscal agents looked for any unpaid back taxes and demanded immediate payment. The Emperor imposed many new taxes and ignored the traditional exemptions for senators. Moreover, he stopped payments normally granted to charitable and religious institutions. He even managed to coerce the Church into agreeing that he would have final say over who would become bishop. Nicephorus used this power to strip revenue from the Church in excess of their actual expense. As he increased his revenue, his actions began to disrupt the economy of the city. Nicephorus' brother, Leo the *kouropalates* (superintendant of the imperial household and palace), bought large amounts of provisions, especially grain, and stored then in warehouses. The amount of the purchases was enough to cause shortages in the city markets but crop failures exacerbated the difficulties, especially when Leo released the supplies at high prices.

Nicephorus needed to increase his revenue because he had ratcheted up the Byzantine war machine. Not only did the wars in the east continue but also the Emperor deliberately started a war with the Bulgarians to the north and invested deeply in an Italian war. In the east, he maintained more than 40,000 men and all their supporters. In the Balkans, he had some 20,000 men and in Italy, he supported at least 10,000 men. All together, with imperial guards, strategic garrisons and his fleet, Nicephorus was paying almost 100,000 soldiers. This was an extreme effort for the Middle Ages and put the economic structures of the empire under heavy pressure. The people of Constantinople became very unhappy.

Popular frustration boiled over on Easter day. Some Armenians and naval personnel began fighting. The fighting escalated and the city guard was unable to quiet the disturbance. After the rioters nearly killed the city *eparch*, Magister

Sisinnios, the guard crushed the rioters. In the end, there were many dead. The rumour spread: the Emperor was very angry and would punish the populace during the horse races in the Hippodrome. Some days later, at the next horse-racing day at the Great Hippodrome, the Emperor presided over the shows from the imperial box. Armed soldiers appeared on the track, formed up into battle units and drew their swords. The audience, having heard of the massacre in the Hippodrome during the Nike uprising in Justinian's reign, feared that Nicephorus was about to launch the soldiers against the populace, as rumour said he would. Panic seized them. The audience bolted toward the exits, which were narrow steep stairs. Crushing and trampling each other, the terror killed many people. The Emperor simply stayed in his seat, the soldiers did not advance against the audience, and soon the panic subsided. Nevertheless, there remained many dead and hurt. Nicephorus let it be known, that he was merely providing a demonstration of armed skirmishing for the audience's entertainment. Popular discontent remained serious.

This became clear to the Emperor on Ascension Day. Forty days after Easter, the Emperor traditionally celebrated the feast at the Church of St Mary of the Spring at the Pege monastery outside the city walls. After the celebration, he returned to the palace in a great procession that marched down the Mese past the great forums. When the procession entered the Bread Makers' Square, a large group of people whose relatives died in the Hippodrome panic received the Emperor with loud jeers. They called the Emperor 'murderer' and 'cursed killer', and described him as 'painted with citizen's blood'. Soon, they began throwing mud and stones at the Emperor and his entourage. His Armenian guards formed up and pressed the crowd back but the crowd attacked them. The guards closed formation and pushed through the thoroughfare to the Forum of Constantine. While the Emperor and his party were moving toward the forum, a thrown stone struck Nicephorus. The next day, investigation pointed to a woman and her daughter who had thrown stones from their roof. The Byzantine courts tried her and her daughter for treason, found them guilty, and had them burned to death.

The civil disturbances did not surprise or upset Nicephorus: he expected this sort of behaviour from the ungrateful drunken sots who made up the population of the imperial city. Rather than worry about the mob, he began building a new fortified wall in the palace district. The old Grand Palace had grown slowly over centuries and was rather open. A main façade faced a plaza that led to the Great Church, the Mese thoroughfare, and the senate house. None of this suited Nicephorus, so he demolished many fine old buildings and constructed a walled enclosure with his palace inside. The citizens called this construction 'the Tyrant's Acropolis'. In subsequent reigns, the name

Boucoleon described Nicephorus' palace, from the sculptures on either side of the main gate, one side picturing a bull, the other, a lion.

References

Beginnings of Nicephorus II's Reign: Leo, 3, 8.

Marriage of the Emperor to Theophano: Leo, 3, 9; Skylitzes, 260–2.

For commentary regarding the marriage of Nicephorus and Theophano, see Diehl, *op. cit.* , 114–35; Garland, *op. cit.*, 126–35.

Detail about relationship of godparent to family of child, Leo p. 100, note 79, ODB, vol. II, p. 858. 'Godparent'; *ibid.*, p. 1306, 'Marriage Impediments'.

Conquest of Cilicia, Leo, 3, 10–11; 4, 1–6; Skylitzes, 268–70.

In his book Περίπαραδρομῆς, translated by George Dennis as *Skirmishing*, Emperor Nicephorus is very clear that the most important factor that raises moral and ensures enthusiasm in the soldiers is that both officers and men own their own homesteads that support them (19.30–50).

In addition, Nicephorus affirms that the soldiers are exempt from civil authority and are to be judged by their regimental commander or if the question is very serious, by the general commanding the theme (51–66).

While these men must receive their pay and share of plunder, they must suffer hardship and privation; they must labour and follow orders without question. With excellent equipment and fine mounts, the soldiers will fight for the Holy Empire and the Christian Religion (23–30).

With such an army, Nicephorus continued, victory is never far away if the forces follow a careful and aggressive pattern of manoeuvre with sharp, brutal fighting and ruthless destruction. He outlines specific action important to both security and attack in detailed description that could easily be adapted as orders. (See table of contents to *Skirmishing* and section to which they refer.)

For army organization, see the appendices.

The Reign turns Sour: Leo, 4, 6; Skylitzes, 274–6.

For coins see Sears, *Byzantine Coins*, pp. 296–7 with pictures.

For Great Palace and Nicephorus' wall see Appendix IV The Great Palace.

Chapter 4

Nicephorus II Phocas: Wars in the East and the West

The War in Italy

Emperor Justinian had reunited the Italian peninsula under the banners of the Roman Empire in a long and bitter war. In just a few years after his death, a tribe of Germanic warriors swept into northern Italy and the Italian cities opened their gates to them, preferring the loose rule of the Lombard warlords to the stringent dictates of Byzantine bureaucracy. Being Italy, just because some groups preferred the Lombards, so there were other groups who held fast to the empire. This divide rippled all the way down the peninsula. The cities on the Po River and those of Tuscany along with the lands around Spoleto and Benevento supported the Lombards. The Byzantines continued to hold many coastal towns, including the young Venice, Ravenna, Rome, Naples and the far south of Italy. The situation simplified in 774 when the Carolingians conquered the Lombard kingdom and annexed northern Italy. South of Rome Lombard dukes coexisted with Byzantine holdings of different types. Some, like Naples, were Duchies recognizing a tenuous Byzantine suzerainty; in others, imperial officials commanded direct power.

The Theme of Sicily had long been the main bastion of Byzantine power in the Western Mediterranean. In the reign of Basil I (867–886), Sicily had fallen to the Muslims of North Africa, whom the Byzantines called the Carthaginians. These Muslim Carthaginians then continued to raid Southern Italy, the Peloponnese, and the Adriatic coasts. The Emperor Basil appointed the grandfather of the Emperor Nicephorus, also named Nicephorus Phocas, to command in Italy. Taking a rag-tag army, this Nicephorus defeated the Muslim raiders and obtained peace in Italy. He extended imperial control over much of what the Benevento Lombards claimed, including Benevento itself. He also ensured that the local population did not unnecessarily suffer at the hands of his army. Having set Italy at peace, he returned to Constantinople to become Domestic of the *Scholae*. Basil's successor, Leo VI the Wise (r. 886–912) established these lands as the Theme of Langobardia. The local Italian warlords fought back. Guy of Spoleto, son of the ephemeral western emperor, Guy of Spoleto (r. 891–5), took Benevento in 895. However, the Byzantine simply moved the theme's capital to Bari. We, at our distance from these events, must not see the manoeuvring and struggles between the Italian Byzantines, the Benevento-Spoleto Lombards, the cities of Naples and the others included in this mosaic of Southern Italy as indicative of great cultural and social differences. The dominant families had long been interrelated and a man could change from a Lombard to a Byzantine by simply changing clothes. Often, when it suited them, the Lombards and the autonomous cities recognized Byzantine suzerainty. Together, they all fought against the Muslim raiders from Sicily and Africa.

Southern Italy remained stable through the reminder of Leo VI's reign but after his young son, Constantine VII, ascended to the throne the Carthaginian Muslims launched major raids and overran much of the land. Constantine's mother and her regency, faced with a major Bulgarian attack, decided that they could not afford to send strong forces to Italy. Having established the new Theme of Calabria, the regency appointed Eustathios, an imperial chamberlain, as commander. He dealt with the Muslim powers, agreeing to pay them 22,000 gold pieces a year and they agreed to withdraw their forces and stop raiding the Italian coast. The imperial admiral, Romanus Lecapenus, pushed the queen mother's regency out of power and proclaimed himself co-emperor (r. 920–944) along with the young Constantine VII in 920. The new Emperor appointed the Patrician John Mouzalon commander of the Calabrian theme, with the intention of raising the money for the tribute locally. The local powers rebelled; they killed John Mouzalon and recognized the Lombard prince of Benevento, Dandulf, as their overlord. Emperor Romanus I saw the necessity of recovering the Italian lands and he began to fit out a fleet and mobilize an army to send to Italy. However, before sending such an expensive expedition, the Emperor dispatched the Patrician Cosmos of Thessalonica to discuss the matter with Dandulf, with whom Cosmos was well acquainted. Cosmos convinced Dandulf that avoiding trouble with Constantinople was sound policy and so the Lombard prince rejected the submission of the Italian themes. At Dandulf's instruction, the themes and Cosmos came to an agreement that restored them to the empire.

Emperor Romanus I's main concerned was the threatening Bulgarian empire. The ambitious Bulgarian chieftain, Symeon, intended to overthrow the Byzantine Empire in Europe. Among his preparations for a great war, he sought to make an alliance with the North African Muslim power, to which the Byzantines were paying tribute to protect their Italian lands from raiders. He sent to the ruler of Carthage representatives who told the Muslims that if they would send a great fleet against Constantinople, then the Bulgarians would attack by land and together they would bring down the Byzantine Empire. The North Africans would hold Constantinople and the Aegean Sea while the Bulgarians would take lands in the Balkans. They would share the plunder and slaves equally. The rulers of the North African empire found the scheme appealing and sent high-ranking representatives back with the Bulgarian envoys to Symeon. As the ship carrying these negotiators sailed past Italy, Byzantine ships based in Calabria seized them and took both the Bulgarians and Muslims to Constantinople. After interrogations, Romanus I understood just how close he was to a possible disastrous war. The Bulgarians, he threw into a dungeon. The North African Muslims, however, he honoured with comfortable quarters and many gifts. He apologized for being late with the tribute payment he owed, explaining that the current circumstances were difficult. Then he sent them home with more fine gifts and gifts for their ruler. The ruler of the North African Muslims was so pleased with the fact that Romanus promised to not allow any war in Italy that would disturb the North African's efforts to attack Egypt that he forgave half the yearly tribute, wanting 11,000 gold pieces instead of 22,000. While southern Italy was never quiet, the peace between the North African Muslims and the Byzantines lasted up to the time Nicephorus II became emperor.

A small Christian stronghold, Rametta, high in the mountains near Messina had requested help in its efforts to withstand a Muslim siege. Nicephorus saw this request both as an opportunity to expand the empire in the west and to stop paying tribute to the North Africans. Indeed, if he began to pay tribute in his new debased coin, the Muslim would demand more of them to make up the difference in weight in gold. Instead, Nicephorus decided that an assault on Sicily would turn the tables on the North Africa Muslims. The Byzantines refitted a number of fire-projecting warships and organized a large flotilla of transport merchant ships. They also put together a motley collection of cavalry soldiers and their horses as an assault force. The Emperor appointed the eunuch brother of the imperial gatekeeper, the Patrician Niketas, as fleet master and appointed his nephew, the Patrician Manuel, as commanding general. Clearly, Nicephorus did not think that this attack was particularly important: Niketas was a profound theologian but only a figurehead as admiral; Manuel was a good soldier and fierce fighter but the science of strategy was beyond him.

The Byzantine fleet made landfall near Messina where they unloaded their transports and organized their forces. The Muslim commanders decided not to face this force directly but retired into the hinterland, concentrating their forces. Manuel marched along the east coast. The cities opened their gates at his approach because all the local troops had joined the Muslim forces in the island's interior. Tauromenium, Leontini, Syracuse, and Himera, all surrendered without significant struggle. Because the campaign went so well, Manuel thought that he had won the war. Instead of consolidating their conquests, garrisoning the cities and guarding the horse pastures, Manuel concentrated his forces and marched toward the enemy in order to wipe out those he considered defeated fugitives. However, the Muslim forces were undefeated. They closely followed Manuel's movements. When Manuel's army marched into rough country, Muslim scouts anticipated his route. The Muslim commanders placed a large force in ambush at a rocky defile through which Manuel was going to lead his army. The Byzantine army, not suspecting that the enemy was at hand, broke ranks and marched along the narrow track in almost single file. Suddenly, the drums sounded and with a great shout, the Muslim forces launched a massive attack on the disorganized Byzantines. Manuel and his army died in the defile; only a very few men managed to escape. The Muslims swept back to the east coast, reoccupying their cities and, using a cleaver ruse, captured the Byzantine fleet before Niketas knew of Manuel's defeat. Except for a few men, the Muslim destroyed both the army and the fleet. Niketas spent his time as a prisoner in North Africa copying religious texts.

A few years later, in 969, Emperor Nicephorus sent the Sword of Mohammad, which he had captured during his Syrian campaigns, to the ruler of the North African Muslims. The Emperor demanded that the North Africans release their captives or the most powerful Byzantine emperor would go to war against them. (Of course, the important part of the message was the unspoken converse, that if the North Africans released the Byzantine captives, the Byzantines would maintain the peace.) This ruler, Al-Muizz Lideenillah, was deeply involved with his campaign to conquer Egypt. Since he preferred that the Byzantines not interfere with his ongoing battles, he sent the captives, including the Patrician Niketas, back to Constantinople.

The Bulgarian War I

After Nicephorus returned from his campaign in the east, he received emissaries from the Bulgarian Tsar Peter during winter 965–6. They had come to demand the payment of tribute that Romanus I had paid to support his granddaughter, Maria Lecapena, when she married Tsar Peter. However, she had died and, anyway, Nicephorus had no interest in paying tribute. The Emperor received them at full court in the Golden Hall Throne Room. Nicephorus, in full regalia, sat on the throne with his father, the Caesar Bardas, sitting next to him on a golden chair. When the emissaries presented their demand for payment, Nicephorus turned livid and yelled at them, 'A dreadful fate awaits the Romans

(Byzantines), slayers of enemies, should they act like prisoners and pay ransom to these disgusting and dirty Scythians.' Turning to his father, he asked in a sarcastic manner, 'Did you beget me of a slave and not know it? How can I, Holy Emperor of Romans, pay a bounty to these disgusting and dirty dogs?' The Emperor then ordered the imperial guards to slap the emissaries across their faces. The Emperor yelled, 'Go! Tell your leather-eating ruler who is clad in animal skins that the High and Mighty Emperor of the Romans is coming now to your lands, to pay you all in full. You shall lean, bastard slaves, to hail the Romans as your lords and not to demand ransom of them as if they were your servants.' Nicephorus then dismissed the emissaries.

After the Bulgarians left the city, Nicephorus mobilized the army of Europe along with the elite *tagmata* and marched toward the Bulgarian frontier. The Byzantines attacked and took the Bulgarian border strongholds. The Emperor marched the length of the frontier and returned to the capital. He did not intend to invade the Bulgarian Empire: too often Bulgarian ambushes destroyed Byzantine armies advancing through the Balkan Mountains and valleys. But, the Bulgarians did not know that. Nicephorus calculated that Tsar Peter would station his army near the Byzantine border, expecting a coming attack. While Bulgarians watched the Byzantines, Nicephorus commissioned the son of the ruler of Cherson, Kalokyres, to go to the Rus and convince them to attack the Bulgarians from the north. The Emperor made him a patrician of the empire and promised to give him a total 1500 lb of gold to accomplish this.

The War in the East

Nicephorus remain more concerned about the east than either Italy or the north. After the urban civil disturbances settled down in spring 966, Nicephorus began preparing for another major campaign in the east. His manner of war utilized an indirect strategy by which he avoided large battles or great sieges but rather he raided enemy lands, taking and holding important but ill-defended strategic points. From these points, manoeuvring his forces in large units, he destroyed productive areas and blocked main supply routes. Rather than met enemy forces head-on, he would surround and harass them endlessly. His main tactic was surprise and his main military virtue was patience. If an operation took a long time, he accepted that and persevered. Moreover, he was not concerned about cost. He would simply grind more money out of the empire. Resting his authority on his army, which idealized him, the Emperor proceeded on the assumption that military success would silence all criticism.

Besides capturing Cilicia, Nicephorus had added the island of Cyprus to the empire. In 965, he sent the Patrician Niketas Chalkoutzes as commander with a strong body of troops to seize the island. Previously, Cyprus was a joint condominium between the Byzantine and Muslim powers. Niketas' *coup* met no resistance because the sudden attack was a complete surprise to the Muslim communities. When the Nicephorus marched east, leading his elite *tagmata*, he was marching as a victorious emperor. He joined forces with the thematic armies, ensured that Cilicia was settling down as a new theme, and advanced into Syria, where a Byzantine army had not been for over two hundred years. He led his army to the great city of Antioch and set up a camp. Rather than attempt to capture the city, the Byzantines occupied significant sites near Antioch to hold the city under a light blockade. People and goods could still get in and out, but there was always the threat of a Byzantine raid. Nicephorus paraded his army in front of the main city gates, to ensure that everyone inside the city knew that he and his forces were there. Then the Emperor split up his army into units and sent them off to ravage the countryside.

In the fall of 967, a great earthquake struck Byzantine Asia Minor, destroying many towns and villages, although Constantinople was unaffected. In Syria, Nicephorus captured a marvellous relic of The Saviour, which he sent back to Constantinople, to be enshrined in the Church of the *Theotokos* in the Great Palace. He captured forts in southern Syria, crossed Mt Lebanon and came to Tripoli. Here he hoped to connect with his fleet, which was sailing along the coast, but the winds did not cooperate and the fleet could not make the trip. Therefore, rather than besiege Tripoli, Nicephorus marched north to the fortress town of Arka, which dominated a rich plain. Surrounding the walls with a triple palisade, the Emperor had the fortification undermined. The towers collapsed and the Byzantines gain rich loot along with needed supplies. Many forts and towns fell to the Emperor's forces. The large towns remained under threat. Nicephorus spent a whole year plundering Syria. He was still there on 22 December 968, when he witnessed a spectacular solar eclipse. In spring, 969, Nicephorus decided to return to Constantinople.

Before he left, he instructed his commanders and captains how the campaign should proceed. He pointed out that while they plundered and looted the countryside, the great city of Antioch remained unconquered. That was the way it should be, he said. Clearly, the rulers of Antioch, after constant harassment and incessant raids, would willingly submit to Byzantine domination. That way, the empire would gain a new city with its wealth and structures intact. The Byzantine camp sat at the foot of a hill known as the Black Mountain, situated between Antioch and the Mediterranean. Pointing to that hill he said that there, they would build a fort that would secure their hold on the land and would eventually convince the city of Antioch to surrender. With that, the Emperor picked up a stone and carried it to the hilltop, expecting each person in the army to do the same. In three days, the Byzantines had constructed a well-walled fortress, from which they would continue to strangle the supply lines of Antioch. He left in the Black Mountain fort a force of five hundred crack cavalrymen and a thousand elite infantry. Then the Emperor marched back to the imperial city with his *tágmata* and allowed the *themata* troops to return home.

The Emperor had appointed Michael Bourtzes as commander of the Black Mountain fort after elevating him to patrician status. His orders were to enforce the blockade of Antioch and ensure they did not receive any supplies. The Patrician Bourtzes was under the direction of the Camp Commander (*Stratopedarches*), Patrician Peter, who commanded the Cilician theme. Peter, an imperial household eunuch, held command as a financial official (*logothete* of the *stratiotikon*) since a eunuch could not hold direct military command. Nicephorus ordered him to release the local *themata* and hold Cilicia with just some of the elite *tagmata*. Michael Bourtzes did not want simply to wait out the season until spring when the Emperor would return. He negotiated with the masters of Antioch, attempting to talk them into surrendering but they refused. However, in his negotiations, he became acquainted with a resident of the city, Aulax. Bourtzes gave him valuable gifts and promised more for accurate measurements of the height of the Kalla Gate towers. Bourtzes had ladders made to the proper height and then waited until the Patrician Peter had come on an inspection tour with an elite force. On a moonless rainy night, Bourtzes led three hundred picked men to Antioch and placed their ladders against the Kalla tower. Killing the sleeping defenders, his three hundred men seized both gate towers. With the gate under control, Bourtzes sent to Peter to bring the rest of the army in order to take the city. Peter hesitated because he knew Nicephorus had specifically forbidden the taking of Antioch by armed forces that would plunder and damage the city. Nevertheless, in the morning the people of Antioch found that a main gate was in the hands of the enemy. They organized an attack to retake the gate and towers. Bourtzes' messages became increasingly desperate as day passed day under the missiles and assault attempts of the city people. Rage at the Byzantine attack swept the city. A mob attacked Christopher, the archbishop of Antioch, killing him and plundering his residence and church.

Peter found himself in a difficult position. If he refused to help Bourtzes and the defenders killed the three hundred, then that would be his fault; yet if he helped Bourtzes and took the city, then he would be disobeying a direct order from the Emperor. On the other hand, at least they would capture Antioch. Peter set off toward Antioch with as many soldiers as possible. When the people of Antioch saw the Byzantine army advancing against the city, they lost heart and retreated from the Kalla gate. Bourtzes, seeing his chance, descended from the tower and, with his sword, cut the ropes holding the gate bar and then his men removed the bar and opened the gate. Peter's force advanced through the gate and eliminated all opposition. The Byzantines had captured the City of Antioch. Shock shook the Near East. The Muslim governor of Jerusalem accused the archbishop John of inviting the Byzantines to march to Jerusalem and he incited a mob to attack the Church of the Holy Sepulchre. They killed the archbishop and fired the building, which resulted in the dome collapsing.

The Bulgarian War II

The celebration of Nicephorus' eastern conquests entertained Constantinople for days. The Emperor, however, became very concerned about developments to the north. After he rejected the Bulgarian emissaries in the winter of 965-6, Nicephorus had sent the Patrician Kalokyres to induce the Rus to attack the Bulgarians from the north, as we said above. The patrician had developed contacts with the Rus prince of Kiev, Svyatoslav. These Rus were a mixture of Scandinavian adventurers, Vikings to the western Europeans, with Slavonic tribal society groups. An agrarian warlike people, willing to trade but preferring to plunder, the Rus maintained Viking warrior traditions uniting them with steppe military practices. Svyatoslav, impressed by the wide vistas that the split between the Bulgarians and Byzantines opened, called forth all his men and ships. Sailing out into the Black Sea, a huge fleet of Viking long ships travelled to the lower Danube. The Bulgarians found out about the Rus' attack and as Svyatoslav's ships advanced up the Danube, the Bulgars mobilized an army to meet them. The Rus managed to push the Bulgars away from their landing site and then formed a strong shield wall that covered their swordsmen. The shield wall phalanx pushed the Bulgars back and was invincible to their counter-attacks. The Bulgars broke and fled the field, collecting in their fortress at Dorystolon. Tsar Peter saw that the Rus were going to overwhelm his land and quickly sent envoys to Nicephorus begging for peace and an alliance against the Rus.

The Rus attack was much greater than Nicephorus had anticipated. He was concerned that the Rus would descend on Constantinople, as they had done in the past and set out to strengthen the capital's defences. He mobilized local forces and increased the number of men in the imperial *tagmata*, especially the heavy cavalry *kataphracktoi*. The wall garrison mounted heavy throwing machines on the towers. They mounted a great chain onto the Kantenarion Tower, on the south side of the Golden Horn. They attached the chain, held up by log floats, to the great tower of the Kastellion on the north side. Nicephorus understood that he could no longer trust Kalokyres to do his will but since Tsar Peter and the Bulgarians were now the weaker party, they were susceptible to Byzantine influence. He received the Bulgarian envoys with great honour. The Emperor told them that if Tsar Peter would abdicate in favour of his son Boris, who had been a guest at Constantinople for many years, then the Bulgarians would receive support to hold off the Rus. Tsar Peter did surrender the throne and Nicephorus sent the Patrician Nicephorus Eroticus and Bishop Philotheus to the Bulgarian court. They requested that Tsar Boris send daughters of the royal family to Constantinople as prospective brides for the young sons of Romanus II, Basil II and Constantine VIII. The Bulgarians sent out the young ladies in magnificent covered wagons, for Bulgarian highborn women did not ride horses. The accompanying entourage included envoys that carried requests for the military force necessary to repel the Rus.

References

Course of Italian War: Skylitzes, 261–6; Wortley, English translation of Skylitzes, notes on pp. 252–6; Barbara Kreutz, *Before the Normans, Southern Italy in the Ninth & Tenth centuries*: University of Pennsylvania, 1991, chapter 5 to 8; C. W. Previté-Orton, 'Italy in the Tenth Century', in Cambridge Medieval History, Cambridge UK, 1922, pp. 148–165.

The Bulgarian War I: Leo, 4, 5–6; John Fine Jr, *The Early Medieval Balkans*: Ann Arbor, 1983, pp. 181–2; Paul Stephenson, *Byzantium's Balkan Frontier*: Cambridge, 2000, general overview of Balkans just before Nicephorus' reign, pp. 18–46, Nicephorus starts war, pp. 48–9, Dimitri Obolensky, *The Byzantine Commonwealth*.

Chapter 5

The Murder of Nicephorus II: John Tzimiskes Seizes Power

Nicephorus as Others Saw Him

There is a contemporary record by someone who came to Constantinople and dealt with Nicephorus extensively. He was Liudprand, Bishop of Cremona, representing the interests of the Western Emperor, Otto I. He arrived on 4 June 968 and left on 2 October of that year. He wrote a detailed account of his stay in Constantinople, describing the people and problems he faced. He appears to have completed the account by the end of 969 and so this is about as close as can be had to a medieval primary source. Liudprand wrote the record to explain why he failed to get the agreements he wanted. He blamed his failure on the Byzantines, particularly Nicephorus. But, it is not the case that he disliked the Byzantines in general: when he was younger, in the reign of Constantine VII, he came on a commercial mission and was favourably impressed with the Byzantines. He learned Greek and began reading the ancient literature, both pagan and Christian. His current mission turned sour from the beginning of his mission because of the way the Emperor chose to deal with Liudprand.

When Liudprand arrived, Byzantine officials assigned him and his entourage to a large open house some distance from the palace. Liudprand found the building dingy, uncomfortable, without food and water. He had to buy supplies from the officials at what Liudprand saw as exorbitant prices. He had to deal with one certain official as the conduit for dealing with anything in the city and Liudprand thought only the worst of this man, who he refused to name in his account. So, from the beginning Liudprand was unhappy with the Byzantine administration.

Liudprand met with Leo the *kouropalates*, Nicephorus' brother, on 7 June. The western envoy hoped to clear up some of the problems with his living arrangements but from the start Leo was offensive and provocative. He started out by describing Liudprand's principal, the Western Emperor Otto I, as $\rho\eta\gamma\alpha$ instead of $\beta\alpha\sigma\iota\lambda\epsilon\alpha$ (this is the way Liudprand writes of this issue in his account). The point is that the Byzantine administration accorded

Liudprand the dignity of an envoy of a secondary ruler, a king, rather than that of an imperial equal. Leo was both assertive and insulting and so the meeting accomplished nothing. However, Liudprand soon received a summons to appear at court during the Pentecost celebration. Nicephorus greeted the emissaries sitting in state in the Great Throne Room. Liudprand found the Emperor to be a repulsive monstrous man. He had a dwarfish fat head with small mole-like eyes. His short beard was wide, thick and turning gray; his neck was thin like a finger. His complexion was dark; his belly large; his legs short. His robe was once very beautiful but now it was old, food stained, threadbare and it smelt bad. He wore old slippers on his feet. Behind him and to his left sat the two small Emperors, Romanus II's children, Basil II and Constantine VIII. Nicephorus started by accusing Liudprand's principal, King Otto, as an aggressor and usurper. Liudprand tried to respond but the Emperor interrupted him whenever he tried to speak. Then, Nicephorus announced that the Pentecost celebration must continue, stood up and began a procession. As Nicephorus left the audience hall and marched into the roadway leading toward the Great Church, the street was lined by ranks of townsmen dressed like soldiers but with small thin shields, cheap spears and bare feet. The courtiers who accompanied the Emperor wore oversized tunics, tattered by age; they had been new in the youth of their fathers. Only the Emperor wore any gold or jewels but the ornaments were actually for a larger man.

The Emperor held a great feast that evening and Liudprand attended. He found himself in fifteenth place in order of protocol, below many he considered of lower diplomatic stature than his principal. He concluded that this was an intentional slight of the August Ottos. His table lacked a table cloth and his personal attendants were not allowed in the hall unlike those ranged above him in the order of precedence. He disliked the food. It was full of garlic and leeks. Moreover, the wine was poor and he was also expected to drink 'bath water' (this was boiled water, which remained warm or at least tepid). Since, previously in the reign of Constantine VII, he enjoyed his stay in Constantinople, he found that Nicephorus' table was different from what he had before. It was evidently very spicy and hot, not to a north Italian's taste of that time. The fact that Nicephorus and the Byzantine military liked to drink water was something that passed the wine-drinking westerner right on by. As the feast progressed, the Emperor asked questions of Liudprand about the realm of the Ottos. When Liudprand answered, however, Nicephorus bellowed out, 'You Lie! Your soldiers are nothing!' The Emperor proceeded to berate and insult the western realm. Later, Liudprand found out that Nicephorus was making a deal to support Otto's enemies in southern Italy at the same time as he pretended to deal fairly with Liudprand. Liudprand found such double-dealing upsetting.

In the end, Liudprand accomplished nothing and left Constantinople feeling cheated, insulted, and made to look foolish in front of the whole empire. He summed up his impression of Nicephorus II: a Greek king, with long hair, wearing a long sleeved tunic with a hood, lying, fraudulent, merciless, fox-like, haughty, falsely humble, cheap, greedy, eating garlic, onions and leeks. His impression of the empire was also negative. Famine haunted the land; one gold coin could not buy two measures of wheat in a land where abundance had been usual. Moreover, Nicephorus, rather than attempting to alleviate the situation, made the famine worse by forcing sale of grain at low prices only to resell it at a far higher price. Constantinople, he pointed out, was once the most opulent and flourishing of cities but was now starving, rapacious, greedy, stingy, and dinner loving. Clearly, this educated and sophisticated bishop of the west did not see Nicephorus II Phocas' rule as a golden age but rather as an example of bad government.

The Reign Fails

The notable citizens of Constantinople saw the Emperor's rule in much the same way as Liudprand did. Nicephorus' many military victories were matters of importance and pride, of course, but the expense was high and Nicephorus was uninterested in how this expense disturbed the population. The debased coinage was bad enough, especially since the good coinage were tender for taxes. That had the force of making them more valuable as they became scarcer. But since the weather turned bad in 968 and the harvest failed, food prices rose. Because Nicephorus needed money to pay his large army and used the debased coin, the effect was to lower the value of the coinage. The result was a strong inflation that caused actual want. But, rather than use government stocks of grain to alleviate the shortages, Leo the *logothete* sold the grain at the high market prices, thus making a high profit on the transactions. More, he forced as a tax the sale to the government of private stocks of grain, for which he paid the old price in the debased coin and then turned around selling the grain at the inflated price. The chroniclers of the time told stories that displayed popular displeasure. One story relates how the Emperor Basil I, finding that food was short, opened the government stocks of grain and sold them below even the usual market price. Another relates that when Nicephorus was enrolling new soldiers for the army, an old man applied for a position. Nicephorus asked him why at his age he thought he could be a soldier. The old man answered him, 'I am much stronger in my old age than I was when I was young.' The Emperor wanted to know how that was so. The old man replied, 'When I was young, I needed two donkeys to carry the grain one gold piece bought. Now, I can carry on my shoulders what two gold pieces will buy.' The Emperor saw the joke but it did not bother him.

The Emperor received the absolute loyalty of his army. He did not care if the city people and landowners failed to appreciate his endeavours. His difficulty, however, began when he failed to perceive that people around him, from whom he gained the throne, began to see him as a liability and threat. During his operations in Syria, he found fault with the efforts of the Domestic of the *Scholae*, John Tzimiskes. Nicephorus removed John from command and exiled him to the countryside. When the Patrician Michael Bourtzes captured Antioch, Nicephorus proclaimed a celebration of thanksgiving but he removed Bourtzes from command and recalled him to Constantinople. The Augusta Theophano, married to Nicephorus as part of the arrangement by which Nicephorus gained the throne, began to have doubts about how long he would keep the throne. While sensational rumour in later chronicles credit her with a love affair with John Tzimiskes, her most important interest remained her children, the young Emperors, Basil II, aged eleven, and Constantine VIII, aged nine. She also had a daughter by Romanus II, Princess Anna. If the political situation should explode because of Nicephorus' miss-steps, her children would be at great risk from both enemies and friends. The danger to Nicephorus came from his own family and household.

In late fall of 969, the Caesar Bardas, Nicephorus' father, died at an age over ninety years old. He had been a moderating influence on Nicephorus' tendency of harshness. After his death, the Emperor became more morose and arbitrary. A few days after Bardas' funeral, the Augusta Theophano approached her husband, the Emperor, asking to speak. She spoke to him about the Magister John Tzimiskes. She reminded Nicephorus that John was the son of Nicephorus' sister, that he was a close part of the imperial family. She begged the Emperor to release him from exile in the countryside and find him a new wife now that his previous wife had died. Nicephorus relented and ordered that John come to Constantinople and appear at court. John did come to the city and often went to court as required. While he was in the palace, he was led through secret passages to meet the Augusta in the women's quarters. There he and Theophano plotted the removal of Nicephorus. Each time he went to the women's quarters, John brought a number of guards with him but when he left the quarters he was always one man short. Those men would stay hidden in the interior of the women's quarters while the plot matured.

In the evening of December tenth, a priest passed a note to the Emperor warning him that his life was under threat and that he should order the women's quarters searched. The Emperor ordered the acting chamberlain, Michael, to investigate the women's quarters. Michael came back and said there was nothing amiss. Later that night, Theophano told Nicephorus that she needed to leave the imperial residence suite in order to make sure that the instructions for the care of some young Bulgarian princesses being held as hostages were followed. She told Nicephorus not to lock the door because she would do that on her return and she left the suite. As midnight approached, when Nicephorus had gone to sleep, John's men who had been hiding emerged and went to a balcony that overlooked the sea. They gave the signal and John Tzimiskes, Michael Bourtzes, and others rowed along the shore in a small boat through the strong winds and swirling snow. Landing beneath the high palace walls near the statue of the lion attacking a bull (so *Bucoleon* palace), John whistled the counter signal. The men on the balcony then lowered a basket on a rope and pulled up the conspirators one by one, with John being the last. Once together, guided by one of the Augusta's eunuchs, the group entered the imperial suite. They were amazed and frightened when they found the Emperor's bed unoccupied, thinking that perhaps the plot was revealed, but the eunuch pointed out the Emperor, sleeping on the floor as was his want, resting on an animal skin and covered by a scarlet felt blanket. His head rested toward a triptych deesis icon, Jesus flanked by Mary and John the Baptist.

The conspirators surrounded the sleeping form and all at once began kicking him awake. Nicephorus woke and looked up, when Leo Balantes smote him across the forehead with a sword. Blood gushed out of the wound and Nicephorus cried out, 'Help me Mother of God.' John, sitting on the imperial bed, directed the conspirators to drag Nicephorus over to him. Nicephorus was writhing in pain on the floor. John grabbed his beard and yanked his head up, saying, 'I put you on the throne and you sent me like some peasant into the countryside.' Nicephorus just continued to call upon the Mother of God. The conspirators smashed at Nicephorus' mouth, knocking his teeth out. John kicked him in the chest and then cleft his skill with a sword stroke, while another drove a pick through Nicephorus' back into his heart.

The New Reign

The band of conspirators dragged Nicephorus' bloody body into the courtyard and left it in the snow. They proceeded to the *Chrysotriklinos*, the Golden Audience Hall. This was a round building, constructed during the mid sixth century. The Church of San Vitale in Ravenna and Charlemagne's royal chapel at Aachen copied the design of the Golden Hall. The crowd that came into the building with John, for many came running from other parts of the palace, acclaimed John emperor. He put on the scarlet buskins and sat on the throne. As John began making changes to personnel, imperial guardsmen demanded entrance to the hall, thinking they could rescue Nicephorus. John directed his compatriot, Theodorus the bodyguard, to bring Nicephorus' body into the hall. Theodorus went to the courtyard, cut off the bloody head, and thrust it through a window so the guardsmen could see it. When they saw it, the guards put their swords away and hailed John as emperor. It was about 3:00 am, 11 December, 969.

As dawn broke, bodies of chosen men marched through the streets of Constantinople, proclaiming John as emperor along with the sons of Romanus II, Basil II and Constantine VIII. Basil the Bastard, son of Romanus I, organized a unit of his household troops and also marched through the streets in support of John. Basil had joined the conspiracy but became ill when the plans were to happen. When he heard that Nicephorus was dead and John proclaimed emperor, Basil suddenly recovered. As the morning progressed, Basil went to the Golden Hall to congratulate John on his assumption of power. John received him with gratitude, confirmed his title of *parakoimomenos*, and sat down with him and other advisors to settle the administration. The first order of business was issuing a decree that forbade any disturbance, violence or looting on pain of immediate death. Imperial troops proclaimed the decree throughout the city and kept the peace, unlike the disturbances that broke out when Nicephorus assumed power. Nicephorus' brother, Leo the *kouropalates*, accepted the removal and death of his brother without any effort to subvert the new Emperor. Rather, he ran straight to the Great Church to find sanctuary.

As the morning continued, John and Basil the Bastard began changing the administrative heads of the imperial bureaucracy. He dismissed Nicephorus' appointments and sent new men to take over the positions of praetor, *droungarios* of the fleet, of the city watch, and the prefect of the city police force. They removed all the governors of the imperial provinces sending men to replace them. The Emperor ordered all the removed officials to reside in their country estates. He gave assurances to Leo the *kouropalates* and to his son, the Patrician Nicephorus, that he would respect their persons and property but ordered that they reside on the island of Lesbos. He also removed the Duke and Patrician Bardas, another son of Leo the *kouropalates*, from command of the frontier army in the province of Chaldia. John ordered Bardas to report to Amaseia, capital of the Armenian theme, where he was to reside for a time. In a few days the state of affairs clarified; John Tzimiskes had seized the throne with a minimum of disturbance. Only two people were killed, Nicephorus and one of his guards. The city remained quiet and those who would normally support Nicephorus' cause were, for the moment, satisfied with the change of regimes. John, who was now forty-five years old, was a vigorous and popular person. His close kinship with Nicephorus meant that he was related to most of his potential rivals. His ability to deal with people fairly and his moderation were well known. After Nicephorus' harsh manners and arbitrary ways, John Tzimiskes seemed to most people, even his rivals, as a good choice for the imperial office.

On the seventh day after he gained power, John organized a procession from the palace to the Great Church. Since the new reign successfully handled affairs, it is fairly clear that Basil and John stage-managed the following imperial drama. John, in imperial regalia, marched to the main door of Hagia Sophia, in order to ascend the ambo and receive the imperial crown from the patriarch. But the Patriarch Polyeuctus met him at the main door and told him not to enter the church. A man, he said, whose hands dripped of the blood of a slain kinsman needs to show repentance in order to earn the privilege of walking on the floor of the Lord's House. The patriarch then announced that the Augusta had to leave the palace, that John had to identify the murderers of Nicephorus, that John must abrogate the laws that Nicephorus had imposed, giving the Emperor veto power over decisions of the holy synod. John humbly accepted the patriarch's instruction and promised to perform the penance. After he returned to the palace, the Emperor announced that Leo Balantes and Theodorus the bodyguard did the actual killing of Nicephorus and they did so at the order of the Augusta. The patriarch ordered them exiled. The Emperor sent Theophano to Prokonnesos, the Islands of the Royal Dowry. Just what sort of understanding developed between John Tzimiskes and Theophano prior to the coup is unknown but certainly Theophano should have known that accused, unjustly no doubt, of poisoning one emperor and now involved in the murder of a second emperor, her presence in the palace would raise many questions from many points of view. Evidently, however, she felt cheated. Sometime later, she left Prokonnesos and sought sanctuary in the Great Church. Basil the Bastard had her apprehended and sent away but not before she punched him in the head and raised quite a bruise. She found herself residing at the Damideia monastery, newly founded by John in the Armenian theme. When Theophano went off to Armenia, her mother, Maria, was relegated to the Mantineion monastery in the Bucellarion theme.

John Tzimiskes demonstrated his willingness to atone for the sins committed while gaining the throne. In addition, he distributed his own private property because as emperor he had a claim on all property. He distributed his landed property to the neighbouring estates. He donated his liquid wealth to the hospital for the care of those with the holy disease (leprosy), refurbishing old buildings and constructing new ones. John was sincere about his concern, taking the time when he could of caring for the patients with his own hands. He also released the Armenian theme, his original home and military base, from paying taxes. With these accomplishments, John marched in state to the Great Church on the Day of the Nativity and received the anointing and crown of the emperor. The Patriarch announced that the act of anointing removed the taint of murder as baptism removes sin.

John Tzimiskes Takes the Empire in Hand

The Emperor clearly saw the problems pressing against the Byzantine state. John said it was like being at a triple fork in a road; the problem was to decide which problem to tackle first. First, the famine had gone on for three years and was weakening the fabric of the empire. Second, Nicephorus had taken a great deal of land in the east and conquered great cities but these seethed with unrest and the Muslim powers were getting ready to recover the lands. Third, the Rus were threatening the Bulgarians with conquest and if they succeeded, they would soon be at Constantinople's gates. John immediately dealt with the food crisis. He sent agents around the eastern Mediterranean and Black Sea areas and bought copious supplies of wheat; he sold the wheat at normal market prices or donated it as charity. He stopped the practice of forced sale of wheat to the government at low prices and abolished the parity of the *tetarteron* with the *numisma*, which restored confidence in the coinage. By spring, the famine had abated and the harvest looked, and indeed would be, plentiful.

The affairs of the east pressed upon John. Since the Muslims of Antioch had killed the patriarch of the city, John needed to ensure that his successor would follow sound imperial policy. He chose an ascetic monk, Theodore of Colonia, abbot of the monastery of Kyra Antonius in the Armenian theme, as his nominee. Abbot Theodore was in Constantinople at this time. He came before the Ecumenical Patriarch and the permanent synod, a committee of all bishops in or near to Constantinople. After examination, they decided that while Theodore was weak in secular knowledge, his knowledge of Christian doctrine was sound. Therefore, Polyeuctus anointed Theodore as Patriarch of Antioch. Unfortunately, within a few days, Polyeuctus died and now John had the difficult task of finding a new Ecumenical Patriarch who would support him but also hold the confidence of the Church hierarchy. John had already decided just who he wanted in the office. The day after Polyeuctus died, John summoned the permanent Holy Synod and the Imperial Senate to an audience in the throne room. Here, from the throne he pronounced to the assembled magnates the following: 'I recognize One Authority, the supreme and primary, which brought into existence from non existence the edifice of the visible and invisible universe. But I know that in this life and in the worldly realm here below, there are two authorities: priestly and the royal rule.' As he proceeded, the Emperor made it quite clear that while the Church guided people's souls, it was the imperial state that looked after the physical universe. He then presented his choice for Ecumenical Patriarch, a famous ascetic monk, living the solitary life, Basil. John proclaimed Basil a miracle worker and seer. The Emperor requested Basil come to the Patriarchal palace the next morning. On that day, which was Sunday 13 February 970, the Feast for the Commemoration of the Restoration of Orthodoxy, the Holy Synod anointed Basil and proclaimed him Ecumenical Patriarch.

The Byzantine capture of Antioch invigorated many Muslim warriors in the east. They joined together under the new rulers of Egypt, who the Byzantines called Carthaginians and modern history knows as the Fatimid regime. Under their commander, Jawhar, they advanced into Syria and invested Antioch. The city was well garrisoned and the walls were in repair. The Byzantines held out, but they could not defend Antioch indefinitely. When John had received word that the Carthaginians had laid Antioch under siege, he reacted quickly. He sent orders to the general of the new Mesopotamian theme, who oversaw the Trans-Euphrates Cities Command, to collected a large body of troops and relieve Antioch. The Emperor also dispatched his household servant eunuch, the Patrician Nicholas as supreme commander, with a body of elite *tagmata* soldiers. The two forces joined and marched toward Antioch. They met a large Muslim force under the Carthaginian general, Foutou, and repulsed them. With the arrival of a strong Byzantine force and the outbreak of unrest in Palestine, the Fatimid forces pulled back to solidify their hold on lands closer to Egypt.

References

Nicephorus as others saw him: Liudprand of Cremona, 'the Embassy of Liudprand to the Emperor Nicephoros Phocas on behalf of the August Ottos and Adelheid', in the *Complete Works of Liudprand of Cremona* (English Translation): Washington DC, 2007, pp. 238–82.

Ottos: Because the Western Emperor Otto I associated his son, Otto II, with himself on the throne, Liudprand refers to the rulers of the Western Empire as 'the Ottos'.

The Reign Fails: Nicephorus' administration, Skylitzes, pp. 274, 275, 278.

Nicephorus' murder, Leo, 5, 5–8; Skylitzes, 279–81.

For events unfolding in the Great Palace see Appendix IV The Great Palace.

Epitaph of Emperor Nicephorus:

> *Who once sliced men more sharply than the sword is victim of a woman and a dagger. Who once held the whole world in his power now small, is housed in a mere yard of earth. Who once it seems by wild beasts was revered, his wife has slain as though he were a sheep. Who chose to sleep but little in the night now sleeps the lasting slumber of the tomb.*
>
> *A bitter sight; good ruler, rouse yourself! Take infantry, cavalry, archers to the fight, the regiments and the companies of your hosts — for Rus, fully armed, assail our ports. The Scythes are anxious to be slaughtering while every people does your city harm that once was frightened by your stony face before the gates of your Byzantium.*
>
> *Do not ignore these things; cast off the stone, which now detains you here and stone the beasts, repel the gentiles; give us, built in stone a firm foundation, solid and secure, or if you would not leave your tomb a while, at least cry out from the earth against the foe-for that alone might scatter them in flight. If not, make room for us there in your tomb for death, as you well know, is safety and salvation for the entire Christian folk, Nicephorus, who vanquished all but Eve.*

John of Melitene inscribed these words on Nicephorus' sarcophagus.

(Skylitzes pp. 282–3, based on John Wortley's translation with changes, p. 170.)

The New Reign: Leo, 5, 9; 6, 1–2; Skylitzes, 284–5.

For detail on rooms mentioned in the account of the murder of Nicephorus II and elevation of John I, see Appendix IV The Great Palace.

Imperial processions were statements about the position of the emperor and his relation to the Byzantine state and people. See the example in Appendix IV The Great Palace.

The Orthodox Church remains under the direction of the Patriarch of Constantinople in Istanbul. For a fine survey of Orthodoxy, see Timothy Ware, *The Orthodox Church*: New York, 1993.

John Tzimiskes Takes the Empire in Hand: Leo, 6, 4–5; Skylitzes, 285–287.

The relation of the civil and military government in Byzantium to the highly organized ecclesiastical institution was always a matter of shifting priorities and personalities. For a dynamic discussion, see Gilbert Dagron, *Emperor and Priest, the Imperial Office in Byzantium*: Cambridge UK, 2003.

The emerging Muslim power, the Fatimid regime, which came out of Tunisia and occupied Egypt, destabilized the Near East as far as the Byzantines were concerned. But the imperial court never bothered to consider how different the Fatimids were compared with their older enemies in the wreckage of the Abbasid Caliphate.

For background on the Islamic states of the time, see Marshall Hodgson, *The Venture of Islam*, vol II: Chicago, 1974, for detailed political history, the best remains, Stanley Lane-Poole, *A History of Egypt in the Middle Ages*: London, 1925.

Chapter 6

John I Tzimiskes: War with Svyatoslav in Bulgaria, and Rebellion in Asia

The War in Bulgaria

While John Tzimiskes dealt with eastern matters, he was still concerned with the problems to the north. For a time in late 969, the Rus pressure abated because the Patzinaks had swept into the Rus land around Kiev and Svyatoslav had to return in order to deal with them. But, having patched up a peace, Svyatoslav returned to the Bulgarian lands in early 970 and his forces began to establish permanent settlements. The Rus brutally smashed any opposition. When Svyatoslav captured Philippopolis, he had twenty thousand Bulgarian men fastened to stakes. This policy of frightfulness compelled the local population's submission to the Rus.

The sons of the former Bulgarian Tsar Peter, Boris and Romanus, had lived in Constantinople. Now the Tsar's daughters were living in the palace, promised to the young Emperors. Through these children, the Byzantines intended to make the Bulgarian realm a dependency of the empire. The depredations of the Rus had damaged significant portions of the Bulgarian lands but John and his advisors believed that with a little pressure, Svyatoslav would return to his Dnieper realm. However, when John's envoys contacted Svyatoslav, they saw that the Rus found the Bulgarian lands were rich and productive. Moreover, they discovered, so the Byzantines said later, that Svyatoslav had an understanding with Nicephorus's agent, Kalokyres son of the Prince of Cherson, to set Kalokyres on the Byzantine throne and in return, Kalokyres would surrender all the Bulgarians lands to the Rus and also pay them the promised subsidies in full. Emperor John saw that he would have to go to war to defend the empire against the Rus.

The Emperor had begun restructuring the military forces. Collecting soldiers for their ability and loyalty, he organized a new *tagma*, the *Athanatoi* (the Immortals), both an elite battle unit and personal guards of the Emperor. In late winter, John sent orders to the Magister Bardas Skleros, brother of John's deceased wife, Maria, to collect Asian thematic troops and bring them to Europe. The Patrician Peter, the Camp Commander who had participated in the conquest of Antioch, also received orders to join and support the Magister Skleros. Together, they were to hold the Byzantine frontier with Bulgaria. The Emperor intended to march from Constantinople with *tagmata* forces when spring came. Information reached Svyatoslav that the Byzantines had begun to concentrate forces near Constantinople. He called for warriors to come to kill and plunder the Byzantines. Besides his force of Rus warriors, he convinced many Bulgarians to follow him. Even better, a number of Patzinak tribes rallied to his banners along with many Magyars, who had suffered defeat at the hands of the Western Emperor Otto I in 955, but now were recovered sufficiently to join the Rus in their war against the Eastern Empire. The conglomerate force number myriads of people, with about thirty thousand warriors.

Svyatoslav led his massive force across the Haemos Mountains, plundering Thrace. He moved past Adrianople to besiege Arcadiopolis, on the road from Adrianople to Constantinople. Bardas Skleros, with only about twelve thousand troops, shut himself up within the walls of Arcadiopolis, allowing Svyatoslav's people free run of the countryside. Soon, the Rus and their allies decided that the Byzantines were simply cowards and stopped paying them much attention. During the day, they scattered across the landscape, at night they held revelry, drinking, playing flutes and cymbals, with wild dancing. This is just as the Magister Skleros planned. Leaving about two thousand men to guard the city, Skleros led some ten thousand soldiers out of Arcadiopolis. At night, he hid corps of men in ambush. The next day, the Magister ordered the Patrician John Alakaseus to reconnoitre the enemy. The Patrician had a small but select group of horsemen. Since Alakaseus was of Patzinak descent, Skleros believed he could accomplish the difficult assignment he had set out for him.

John Alakaseus' assignment was to contact the enemy force: attack them but retreat before he lost any men. Through a series of attacks and retreats, the Patrician was to draw the enemies toward Skleros' soldiers, lying in ambush. The three groups making up Svyatoslav's host kept separate from one another. The Rus with their Bulgarian subjects were one group, the Magyars in another, and the Patzinaks in the third. Alakaseus' force hit the body of Patzinaks and retired. The Patzinak's vanguard gave pursuit and chased after Alakaseus. The Byzantines turned to fight and then retreated again. The Patzinaks charged the Byzantines, who retreated in full flight, back toward where Skleros' ambush hid. The Patzinaks followed, strung out in disorder. Suddenly, one body of Skleros' army appeared in front of them. The Patzinak vanguard pulled up and prepared to attack, not seeing another body of Skleros' force form up behind them. The Patzinaks were smashed as the two wings closed on them.

A prisoner pointed out to Skleros that the main Patzinak forces, both cavalry and infantry, followed and he could see that after initial confusion, they began forming battle order. Skleros marshalled the Byzantine forces into formation as the Patzinak's cavalry rode toward them. The Byzantines met the Patzinak attack and repulsed their forces. The Patzinaks recoiled onto their infantry, reformed and waited for the Byzantine attack. The battle lines merged into a series of melees. As the fighting continued, a massive Patzinak horseman charged Skleros while he was reforming ranks, and swung a huge sword at Skleros' helmet. The blow glanced off but Skleros turned and swung in a downward motion at the Patzinak's helmet. Skleros' sword smashed through his opponent's head, cutting him in half all the way down. As Skleros smote his enemy, more Patzinaks rushed at him. His brother, the Patrician Constantine, not yet twenty years old but large and strong, charged a fierce Patzinak who threatened Skleros. Constantine swung his sword at the head of the attacker who quickly pulled up his horse so the swing missed the Patzinak and instead struck the horse's neck, slicing off its head. As the horse fell, dumping the Patzinak on the ground, Constantine dismounted, grabbed the enemy's beard with his hand and slit his throat. Because the melee turned against the Patzinak force, their cavalry fled the field, leaving their infantry. The Byzantine cavalry reformed, rode down the infantry and pursued the cavalry. They broke and scattered the Patzinak force, winning a notable victory.

Rebellion in Asia

The Byzantine army had begun reforming, repairing equipment, cleaning weapons and armour when an imperial dispatch arrived for Bardas Skleros. The Emperor ordered the Magister to immediately come to Constantinople. Once there, John Tzimiskes told Bardas Skleros that Bardas Phocas, the son of Nicephorus II's brother, had raised the standard of rebellion in Cappadocia. The Emperor ordered the Magister to take a powerful army to Asia and put down the rebellion with a minimum of bloodshed. The rebellion had started sometime earlier, when Duke Bardas escaped from Amaseia, capital of the Armenian theme, where John had banished him. Using prearranged relays of horses, Bardas Phocas soon reached Caesarea, the main military base for the *themata* centring on Cappadocia. The brothers Parsakountenos, Theodore, Bardas, and Nicephorus cousins to Bardas Phocas, had helped him escape and set up his camp at Caesarea. His family rallied to the Duke and he was joined by all sorts of adventurers and malcontents. The brothers Parsakountenos and an obscure but imposing soldier, Symeon the Ambelas (vinedresser), mustered the volunteers into military units and saw to their training. When the Duke Bardas saw his troops exercising in an efficient manner, he decided that his time had come. He removed his military boots and pulled on the scarlet buskins. At that, the rebels lifted him on a shield and proclaimed him emperor.

John Tzimiskes was well informed about these events. Furthermore, he discovered that similar treachery was happening much closer to Constantinople. The Bishop Stephen of Abydos was acting as an agent for Leo the *kouropalates*, banished to the island of Lesbos, who was supporting the bid of his son, Bardas for the throne. Stephen was promising money and position to members of the elite *tagmata*, trying to subvert their loyalty to the sitting emperor. John had him swiftly arrested and brought to Constantinople. Stephen was convicted of treason and removed from his office of bishop. The court also convicted Leo the *kouropalates* and his son, Nicephorus, of treason with the sentence of death. John commuted their sentence to blinding and banishment and then, evidently, countermanded the order to blind them. John's problem in all this was only too clear: one of his bases of power was his membership of the large interconnected family that centred on the House of Phocis. He could destroy the leaders of House of Phocis but that would weaken his relations with other focus points of interests upon which he depended. John had to carefully balance his need for security for his person and power and his dependence on the great houses of Asia Minor.

The Emperor John sent a letter to Duke Bardas Phocas. He requested that the Duke step down and surrender to imperial direction. John offered him limited amnesty. The Duke refused even to replay but sent his troops to plunder and ravage the lands of John's supporters. When John heard of these depredations, he had sent for the Magister Bardas Skleros and his elite *tagma*, and appointed him supreme commander in Asia. His orders were to end the rebellion. The Emperor told the Magister that he still desired as little blood be shed as possible. John gave him signed chrysobulls to appoint commanders, governors, and patricians to subvert Bardas Phocas' supporters. Magister Skleros marched his soldiers to Dorylaion, the main base of the Opsikion theme. He called up the *themata* forces and began building a large army. He exercised his soldiers, forming tactical units and trained his units to manoeuvre in formation. When he was confident that his soldiers could meet an enemy on equal terms, he sent a letter to the Duke. Just as John Tzimiskes had married the Magister Bardas Skleros' sister so the Duke Bardas Phocas' sister had married the Patrician Constantine, the Magister Skleros' brother. So the Magister wrote to the Duke as a relative and friend, offering him amnesty for himself and his supporters if they would submit to the Emperors John, Basil, and Constantine. The Duke considered the Magister's offer but rejected it because, he said, the repulsive murderer killed a sleeping man and harshly oppressed his family, including himself. The Duke went on: he would ascend the imperial throne or he would die, either way, he would no longer have to deal with the unholy tyrant.

The Magister was ready for the answer he expected. He drew his army into marching order and advanced toward Caesarea, the Duke's base. Setting up camp near the rebel base, Skleros sent trusted men, disguised as beggars, to the Duke's leading men. Their message was clear: abandon Bardas Phocas and receive full pardon. They would receive offices and honours as the lords of the Asian *themata* as was their due. Stay with the rebel and their fate would be his fate. The rightful emperor's forces would defeat them, strip them and their families of property, and kill them. The message struck home. At night, small groups of men deserted the rebel base and came to pledge their loyalty to the Magister. These included Diogenes Adralestos who was Bardas Phocas' nephew, the brothers Parsakountenos, and the general Symeon Ambelas, all of who had helped Bardas Phocas start the rebellion. When the Duke found out about these desertions, he was most upset, calling his lieutenants together and pointing out that they could defeat the forces of the Emperor John but only if they stayed united. The next night, even more deserted his base. Seeing that obviously his army was not going to hold together, Bardas Phocas joined by about thirty well armed trusted followers left his base in the middle of the night. They made their way deeper into Cappadocia, toward the Citadel of the Tyrants, a castle set in a fertile valley amidst great mountains. Understanding the vagaries of fate the Duke had a trusted garrison in the castle along with ample food and fodder.

In the morning after the Duke left his base, his force surrendered to the Magister except for some holdouts who fled following Bardas Phocas. The Magister gave chase, capturing some of the fugitives and blinding them as traitors. The Duke and his party made haste toward their refuge but the pursuers were right behind them. Bardas Phocas turned his mount to act as rear guard as his follower made for his castle. A young brave horseman, Constantine Charon, was in the lead of the pursuers and approached the Duke. Phocas warned him to stay back but the youthful Constantine charged at him. Phocas spun his horse and struck Constantine's helmet with his mace. This blow smashed Constantine's helmet and his skull. The young man silently fell from his mount and the Duke continued toward his castle. Soon Magister Skleros arrived and put the castle under blockade.

The Magister sent messages to Bardas Phocas. He pointed out the hopelessness of his situation. Many of the rebels had their families with them, including the Duke's wife and children. If the Magister's army stormed the castle, everyone was at risk. The Duke asked the Magister for assurances of personal safety for himself, his family, and followers. The Magister referred the matter to the Emperor, who quickly replied that the Duke must accept Holy Orders and banishment of him and his immediate family to the island of Chios. The Duke accepted and the rebellion was over. John included orders for Bardas Skleros to return to Europe with his elite *tagmata* and take up winter quarters. In the spring of 971, his army would have to face the enemy in Bulgaria.

The War in Bulgaria Continues

While the elite army units and their commander suppressed the rebellion in Asia, the Rus and their allies continued to harass and plunder Byzantine settlements in Macedonia and Thrace. In the fall of 970, Magister John Kourkouas held command but his forces were too weak to accomplish much against the invaders. The Emperor began preparing for a major offensive in the spring by sending many provisions for men and horses to Adrianople and strengthening the fleet. The fleet commanders refurbished the fire shooting projectors, installed them in ships, and began production of their fuel.

Emperor John I Tzimiskes also began strengthening his position on the throne by winning support from the Byzantine citizens in the Great City. In November 970, he married Theodora, daughter of Constantine VII Porphyrogenitus and Helena Lecapena, daughter of Romanus I. This connection with the Imperial House pleased many supporters of Orthodoxy and safeguarded the rights of the young Emperors, Basil II and Constantine VIII. During winter 970–971, the Emperor displayed remarkable qualities as God elected ruler of the Holy Empire, yet, affable and personable mentor and judge. He organized entertainments and sports in the Hippodrome for the people of the city and these were well received. All the time, however, he oversaw the training and drilling of his new *tagma*, the Immortals. They marched and counter marched, practising battle deployment manoeuvres, advancing, retreating, turning front, wheeling from one formation to another, fully armed, perfectly synchronized.

With the arrival of spring, 971, the Emperor set in motion the Byzantine war machine to settle matters in Bulgaria. In full procession, he left the Great Palace through the Brazen Gate, entering the Church of the Saviour, right by the gate. This church commemorated the restoration of Orthodoxy by the Empress Theodora, wife of Theophilus and mother of Michael III, in popular mind, the mother of the Imperial House. The Emperor declared that the church was much too small and hard to enter through the maze of streets. He immediately announced that he was going to build a larger and more imposing edifice. Then the procession proceeded to the Great Church.

Here, he beseeched the Divinity for direct guidance in the coming campaign. Leaving the Great Church, the procession continued through the Forums of Constantine and Theodosius, taking the street through the Forum of Macian to the Church of the Mother of God at Blachernae. When the Emperor appeared at the window of the palace there, the imperial *dromones*, bearing fire projectors, manoeuvred across the waters of the Golden Horn, racing and turning about. In all, the fleet consisted of 300 ships, some the massive bireme battle *dromones*, others, *galeas* with a single level of oars, and many still smaller light craft. The Emperor awarded the sailors and soldiers of the fleet donatives and honours. He oversaw the fleet's departure, following his orders, to the north. They were to base themselves on the mouth of the Danube and intercept any attempt of the Rus on the Dnieper or the sailors from the Crimea to attack the Byzantine lands and to stop any effort of the Rus in Bulgaria to retreat to the Dnieper.

With the dispatch of the fleet, John marched his army out of Constantinople and headed to Adrianople where he already stockpiled supplies. He joined Bardas Skleros and his forces together with his own. Scouts had reported that the route through the narrow mountains and across swift rivers to the centre of the Bulgarian domains were unguarded. John decided to advance immediately against the Bulgarian capital, Preslav. The Emperor reasoned that the Rus and Bulgarians would not expect the Byzantines to mobilize their army until after Easter. Many of his officers opposed such a precipitous offensive but John overruled them and led his army forward. Emperor John I Tzimiskes, in shinning gilded armour, riding a spirited horse, carrying a long lance, rode in front of his personal *tagma*, the Immortals, resplendent on fierce horses in gold and silver armour. He was followed by fifteen thousand well appointed, well trained heavy infantry and behind them, thirteen thousand well practised cavalry. The trains moved slower, bearing supplies, extra weapons and the important parts of siege machines. Basil the Bastard commanded the logistic troops and ran a well organized operation. The battle units drove over the mountain passes and through the narrow defiles without so much as sighting an enemy soldier. The Emperor called a halt when the army reached the heights overlooking the lush valley and walls of the Bulgarian capital, Preslav. There, the army set up a hidden but secure camp and rested briefly.

As first light, the Emperor roused his army. They formed up into the great march square and advanced down into Preslav's valley. Trumpets sounded the orders and drums beat the pace. The Byzantine army evolved its formation from square into battle line. The heavy infantry, marshalled deep, formed a centre with echeloned right and left wings. The cavalry formed two groups, guarding each flank. The Emperor and his Immortals were behind and to the right of the right wing. As the Byzantines deployed with trumpet, cymbals, drums and cheers, the Rus and their Bulgarian allies suddenly woke up to the fact that a massive enemy army was bearing down on them. The Rus infantry hurried out of their camp, quickly forming up into battle line. Their large shields locked together into a wall, with their long spears pointing out to the front. The Byzantine infantry in deep formation advanced with steady steps toward their enemies. The lines met with a great clash of weapons and yells as the two sides engaged. The battle front waivered back and forth. Judging the proper point in time, the Emperor launched his heavy cavalry Immortals around his own right wing and charged the enemy. The Rus left wing wheeled about to receive the Immortals but the wedge formation of lance carrying horsemen smashed into the Rus battle line. Whether the Rus shield wall flinched before the charging armoured juggernaut or simply broke apart trying to hold back the Immortals is unclear. What did happen was that the Rus shield wall folded, rolled up and collapsed. The Rus soldiers started to flee and the Byzantine infantry lunged forward, slaughtering their enemies. Many of the Rus made their way into Preslav but they left eight thousand five hundred dead on the field.

The garrison of Preslav manned the city walls. They allowed the defeated army back through the gates and closed them against the Byzantines. They hurled missiles against John's army whenever they approached the walls. At that time the Patrician Kalokyres, the agent Nicephorus II Phocas had sent to the Rus to convinced them to attack the Bulgarians, was inside the town. He knew that if the Byzantines captured him, the Emperor John would see to it that his end would be most unpleasant. In the middle of the night, he found a way out of the city and through the Byzantine lines. He went to Dorystolon, toward the Danube delta, where Prince Svyatoslav and his army camped. The next day, Basil the Bastard and the trains arrived. Catapults, ballistas, and supplies of missiles had arrived in the trains. The Emperor decided to assault the walls and see if his army could carry the city by escalade. He ordered the throwing machines set up and emplaced, ammunition passed out to the archers, and had ladders built to fit the wall. In the city, Svyatoslav's commander, Sviatold, encouraged those inside the town to hold off the Byzantines. The defenders lined the walls and shot at any Byzantines within range of their arrows or catapults. The Emperor oversaw his assault units manoeuvring in front of the point of attack. The throwing machines began to sweep the walls while groups of archers rushed forward, shooting at anyone they saw exposed on the wall. John gave the order, the trumpets sounded and heavy infantry, carrying ladders, rushed toward the walls. A young man, Theodosius Mesonyktes, mounted the first ladder. Protected by his shield held in his left hand, with his sword pointing before him, he scrambled up the ladder. A defender suddenly appeared with a long spear set to impale Theodosius. But the valiant Byzantine swung his sword, catching the defender in the neck, and lopped his head off. The head, helmet and all, bounced on the ground at the foot of the wall.

Mesonyktes gained the wall top, and was quickly followed by large numbers of the assault troops. They cleared the wall of defenders, throwing a fair number off the wall on to the waiting assault troops who finished them off. The Defenders broke and fled to the inner citadel while the Byzantines forced the city gates, entered, and slaughtered the inhabitants. The Rus and their Bulgarian allies secured the palace citadel while the Byzantine solders and camp followers looted Preslav. Numerous solders tried to break into the palace in a disorganized manner. As they forced their way into the palace gate area, the defenders slew them, one at a time. When the Emperor arrived at the scene, he put an immediate stop to these useless efforts. John stationed Bardas Skleros and his unit of well trained solders in the square in front of the palace. Then he ordered archers to shoot flaming arrows into the palace. Soon, the building was burning nicely. The defenders rushed out into the square where they meet Bardas Skleros' troops. The Rus and Bulgarians refused to surrender and the Byzantines killed them all, to the number of seven thousand. However, Sviatold and a small group of attendance escaped. In two days the Emperor and his troops had captured Preslav.

References

The war with Svyatoslav: Leo, 6, 11–13; Skylitzes, 288–91.

Svyatoslav's assumption of power at Kiev and battles with enemies, see also Samuel Cross and Olgerd Sherbowitz-Wetzor *The Russian Primary Chronicle*: Cambridge Mass, n.d., pp. 58–68, The Russian Chronicle's account is not very consistent with the Byzantine accounts.

Byzantine-Bulgar enmity: influences from Mediterranean areas had brought wealth to landowners but poverty to the peasantry. The Paulicians, a dualistic egalitarian sect, came with transplanted prisoners and emerged in a Bulgarian form, the Bogomil sect. This dualistic sect was later an influence in the emergence of the Albigensians in southern France. The Byzantine authorities saw this sect as very dangerous and determined to wipe it out. See Dimitri Obolensky, The Byzantine Commonwealth, Eastern Europe, 500–1453, New York, 1971, pp. 126–8. For details on Dualistic sects in the European Middle Ages, see Steven Runciman, *The Medieval Manichee*, London, 1960.

Rebellion in Asia: Leo, 7, 1–6, 8; Skylitzes, 191–294.

Byzantine army: see appendices.

Problems of Eastern Houses with the imperial government: see appendices.

War in Bulgaria continues: Leo, 7, 9, 8, 1–7; Skylitzes, 295–98.
    See also, Russian Chronicle, pp. 69–75; Stephenson, *op. cit.* 51–5; Fine, *op. cit.*, pp. 187–9.

Byzantine large scale military operations: on training see George Dennis editor and translator, *The Taktika of Leo VI*: Washington DC, 2010, Constitutions 6 and 7, and on organization and tactical manoeuvre, see Constitutions 12, 13, and 14; also, see the *Praecepta militaria*, sections 1 and 2, in Eric McGeer, *Sowing the Dragon's Teeth*: Washington DC, 2008, pp. 13–33.

Byzantine siege operations: see Leo VI, Constitution 15.

Chapter 7

John I Tzimiskes: War with Svyatoslav and Battle of Dorystolon

The Emperor Fights in Bulgaria

E mperor John I Tzimiskes celebrated the day of Holy Resurrection, 16 April 971 in Preslav. With him was the young Tsar Boris, son of Tsar Peter, rescued (captured?) in the fall of Preslav. John recognized the young man, educated in Constantinople, as ruler of Bulgaria and treated him, his young wife, and two infant children as royalty. The imperial army received deserved rewards and honours. The men refitted their equipment, resting up for a new effort. John freed a number of the Rus prisoners and sent them off to Svyatoslav at Dorystolon. They took with them a message from Emperor John. This informed the Rus leader that Preslav had fallen with the destruction of the Rus defender force. The Byzantine emperor gave Svyatoslav a choice: either accept the Byzantine dominance of the lands south of the Danube or prepare to fight. The Byzantines mobilized their army and began the march to Dorystolon on the lower Danube. As they marched through the Bulgarian lands, towns and fortresses surrendered to them, including the important centres of Pliskova and Dineia.

When Svyatoslav realized that the Bulgarians were supporting the Byzantine, he decided that he needed to convince the Bulgarians that he would not tolerate treason. He had some three hundred noble Bulgarians in his camp. He ordered them all arrested and thrown into chains. Those who appeared less than absolutely coward had their throats slit. The Rus leader mobilized his forces, collecting some 60,000 men. He marched his army to a plain a few miles from Dorystolon where his warriors camped. At the same time, some more enterprising men split off from the Rus main body and moved toward the advancing Byzantines, looking for a good site for an ambush.

The main body of the Byzantine army followed an advanced guard that reconnoitred the road to Dorystolon. This advance guard ran into an ambush and many soldiers perished. When the main body of Byzantines found the dead bodies of ambushed soldiers, the Emperor ordered his troopers to spread out and find those responsible. The soldiers quickly returned with many Rus they found in the area, chaining them together. When John saw them, he ordered their immediate deaths and the soldiers hacked the prisoners to pieces. The Byzantine army arrived at Dorystolon and began to deploy. Seeing the Byzantines taking the field, Svyatoslav ordered his men to form a shield wall, with spears pointing out from their body covering shields. The Rus formation stood their ground as a living fortress. They faced the Byzantine battle line of heavy infantry, which was backed up by archers and slingers. On the Byzantine army's wings sat the ironclad horsemen, ready to charge the enemy.

The Byzantine infantry engaged the Rus. The battle lines waivered one way and another, as the forces fiercely fought to kill each other. The Rus forces gathered up a reserve force and then thrust a wedge deep into the Byzantine line. The Byzantine units pivoted and struck the Rus wedge on its sides, pushing the Rus back. Amidst the surging spears and swinging swords, the soldiers stumbled over the dead and wounded. The lines continued to engage until the sun began to set. Then on the left flank, the Emperor John gave the order: the trumpets and drums sounded the attack; the iron horsemen lunged forward against the flanks of the Rus formation; the infantry gave a great shout and heaved at the Rus and the Rus battle line shattered. The Rus soldiers fled toward the Dorystolon fortifications. Many did not make it; the Byzantines slaughtered them. The Byzantines spent the night on the battlefield.

With first light John led his men in a service of thanksgiving to the Ever Triumphant Witness of Christ, St George, for the victory took place on the saint's feast day, 23 April. The Byzantines marched to a low hill near Dorystolon where they pitched their tents in an orderly manner. Around the hill, the soldiers dug a deep trench, piling up the spoil to make a barrier between the ditch and camp. On top of the mound, the soldiers set up outward-pointing spears, held together by shields bound to them. This was the normal method of fortifying a military camp and indicated to the Rus the imperial army intended to stay. This took a day. The next day, the Byzantines army deployed in front of Dorystolon and sent light troops to test the walls: the Rus responded with a shower of arrows and stones. The Byzantines responded with counter fire but neither side did more than demonstrate their willingness to continue fighting. As the evening began to set, the Byzantines withdrew back into their camp for their meal. Seeing that the Byzantines intended to attempt the capture of the city, the Rus decided that the many thousands of Bulgarians accompanying them were a danger. They chained many and locked up the rest.

After a short time, the imperial fleet appeared in the Danube opposite Dorystolon. The great fire projecting warships led the supply ships into an anchorage. The Rus, remembering the defeat inflicted on the fleet of Igor, Svyatoslav's father in 941, pulled their transport dugouts up on shore under the city walls. Now John had the Rus force trapped between his army with its well fortified camp and his fleet dominating the Danube. The Rus frequently opened the city gates and attacked the Byzantines but except as spectacles these attacks accomplished little. After one such attack, as the evening began to set, the Byzantines withdrew back into their camp for their meal. Two of the city gates suddenly flung open, the one to the west under the watch of Peter the *Stratopedarches*, commander of the Army of the West and the other to the east, under Bardas Skleros, commander of the Army of the East. Out charged the Rus warriors, infantry but also mounted Rus, attacking the disordered Byzantine troops while they entered the camp. The Byzantines were surprised that the Rus were mounted because they had not used horses before in the war and they believed that the Rus did not really know how to ride. Nonplussed, the Byzantine officers gave the proper orders; the infantry took immediate defensive posture and the heavy cavalry put on their armour, mounted their warhorses, grabbed their lances and rushed out of camp into formation. The Rus horsemen rode here and there, their mounts not well managed. The Byzantine cavalry formation tore down upon them, breaking up whatever unity the Rus may have had, killing many of them. The rest of the Rus retreated back into the city. The next morning the Emperor summoned all the garrisons he had left in the Bulgarian towns and fortresses. Clearly, the Bulgarians were not going to ally with the Rus and the Byzantines could trust them with the maintenance of their lands. Indeed, envoys came to the Emperor from Constantia and nearby fortresses, requesting amnesty and offering loyalty. The Emperor received these communities back into his good graces and sent officials to re-establish the imperial order.

On a following evening, the city gates flung open and the Rus army deployed into deep infantry formations, the men protected by mail shirts, standing in ranks behind their tall shields. Seeing the Rus offering battle, John committed his infantry to the attack. The Byzantine armoured foot deployed against the Rus and both sides engaged. The battle line swayed to and fro, until a Byzantine soldier cut down a large Rus warrior whom the Byzantines believed was a commander. Another Byzantine soldier, Theodore Lalakon, a large and strong man, a descendent from an old military family, slaughtered many of the Rus with his massive iron mace, which crushed both helmets and the skills within them. The Rus were not able to break through the Byzantine battle line but they held their ground all night and through the next morning. The Emperor sent strong detachments to cut off the Rus from the city gates. This broke the Rus effort to hold the ground in front of Dorystolon. Those who could make it back to the city did so, the rest spread out in the hills where the Byzantines tracked many down. That night, Svyatoslav organized a labour and military force, which dug a trench around the city walls to keep the Byzantines from directly attacking the fortifications. However, this left the Rus with a serious strategic difficulty. Dorystolon was a city full of warriors and prisoners under strict siege. The Byzantine camp dominated the land routes in and out of the city and the imperial fleet controlled the Danube approaches. Many of the Rus were wounded and supplies were short. The Rus had to find a solution to these problems or be destroyed.

The Rus soon began facing the problem of short supplies and the possibility of starvation convinced Svyatoslav to take action. The windswept stormy night was moonless. Rain and thunder drowned out all other sounds. Svyatoslav and some two thousand men embarked in their boats. They sailed down the river to open farmland. There, the men spread out and collected supplies, bringing them back to the boats. They collected together and began sailing up river toward Dorystolon at dawn. They saw a large group of soldiers' servants watering horses and collecting fodder. Quietly approaching the shore, the Rus disembarked, attacked the servants, killing many, and took what they could find. Then they returned to their boats and sailed to Dorystolon. The Emperor was furious when he found out that a large force had left and returned to the city without anyone being aware of it. The Byzantines decided that rather than trying to attack the Rus in the city, they would blockade the city until the Rus starved. They cut all routes, posted sentries, and kept close watch on the river front.

As the siege ground on, a particular stone-throwing device caused great trouble to the city defenders. The Rus decided to try to destroy this machine with a quick but powerful attack. A strong unit of Rus warriors marched out of a city gate, defending themselves with their large shields and long spears. They advanced toward the throwing machine with torches and combustibles to burn the engine. The Magister John Koukouas, son of the former Domestic of the West Romanus Koukouas, commanded the guards of the batteries. Leo the Deacon had a low opinion of this commander, portraying him as both a drunk and despoiler of churches. Still, Koukouas, in gleaming armour and gilded trappings, ordered his troop to mount their horses and rode against the Rus. In this charge, the Magister's horse fell into a hole and threw Koukouas. The Rus, seeing the gold gleaming accoutrements, thought he was the Emperor. The warriors mobbed him, slashing at him with all their weapons. They cut the Magister apart, stuck his head on a spear and waived it about, proclaiming to the Byzantines that they had killed the Emperor. Then they set the spear up on a main tower, proud of their accomplishment.

Their confidence restored, believing that now the Byzantines had no supreme leader, the whole Rus army marched out of the gates in the morning of the following day. They deployed their army ready to advance. The Byzantine army marched out from their camp, deploying to face the Rus. The Rus infantry advanced, engaging the Byzantines. At the point of the Rus attack stood the famous warrior, Ikmor, a huge powerful man, resplendent in Rus armour and helmet. He advanced at the head of a band of fierce warriors who slew many Byzantine soldiers. The Emperor and his entourage were sitting on their horses, overlooking the battlefield. They saw Ikmor and his following cut into the Byzantine battle line. An imperial bodyguard, Anemas son of the last Arab Emir of Crete, now a trusted companion of the Emperor, drew his sword as his horse turned about, gave spur, and charged Ikmor. Swiftly coming up to the Rus warrior, Anemas slashed at his head. The blade sliced into Ikmor at the neck, cutting off his head and right arm, which flopped onto the ground. As Ikmor's remains slid off his horse, a cry of horror rose from the Rus army. The Byzantines cheered and struck harder. Their momentum gone, the Rus force shouldered their great shields and retreated back through the gates.

That night, under the full moon, many of the Rus came out to collect their dead. They built pyres to burn bodies. On the tops of the pyres, they killed men and women as sacrifices to the spirits of the dead and then set the fires. On the other side of the city, the Rus drowned suckling infants and chickens in the Danube waters. Leo the Deacon saw these sacrifices as examples of the ancient Greek pre-Christian religion, and in some sense he was right, but what he was probably actually seeing was the sacrifice of Ikmor's sworn brothers and their households, Ikmor's 'comitatus'. After the completion of the funeral ceremonies with the coming of dawn, Svyatoslav called a war council to consider their position. They had, Svyatoslav believed, three choices. They could attempt to sneak out of Dorystolon, either crossing the river at night or taking to their boats and race the Byzantine ships to the sea; or they could negotiate with the Byzantines and agree to leave on terms; or they could make one more supreme effort to defeat the Byzantine army. The decision was made: they would fight.

The Final Battle

After spending the rest of the day and most of the next in preparation, the Rus army marched out of the gates at sunset, 24 July 971. Their large shields and spears at the ready, they waited for the Byzantine attack. The Emperor John led his army out of their camp, deployed his troops and engaged the Rus. The infantry fought in two wings, the right wing under the command of the Patrician Romanus, son of Prince Constantine who was son of Romanus I and the left wing under Peter the *Stratopedarches* – Romanus was also in overall command.

The Rus line stood firm; special Rus archer and javelin units positioned behind the battle line targeted the horses of the Byzantine cavalry, bringing them down and spilling their riders. The Immortal bodyguard, Anemas, saw Svyatoslav encouraging his men and cutting down Byzantine soldiers. He gave his horse the spur, and charged at Svyatoslav. Meeting the Rus leader, Anemas swung his sword, smashing Svyatoslav on the upper chest, throwing the Rus off his horse. But Svyatoslav caught part of the swing on his shield and the sword could not cut through his mail armour. Bruised, Svyatoslav got up to the cheers of his men. The Rus soldiers surrounded Anemas, killed his horse and, despite the fight the Byzantine put up, they cut him down. The survival of Svyatoslav and killing of Anemas heartened the Rus, whose battle line pushed the Byzantines back. The Byzantine infantry retreated before the Rus battle line who charged forward to slaughter the Byzantines. Seeing his troops being pushed together into a confined area, the Emperor passed orders to the file officers, to give ground so the whole army backed into a wider formation. The disciplined units retrogressed slowly, holding their lines but moving backward. The Rus believing that the Byzantines were retreating because of their attacks, strove forward, losing their organization. When the Byzantine line had reached a certain point and had widened out, the Emperor set his spear and yelled, 'Now!' The drums and trumpets sounded: the infantry dug in their left foot and struck back at the Rus and the cavalry launched against the Rus. The commander, Theodore of Mistheia, charged at the head of the cavalry. A Rus lance brought down his horse and the Rus soldiers rushed him, thinking to make short work of him. He grabbed a Rus soldier by the belt, swinging him back and forth, using him as a shield. The Byzantines rushed to his aid and he successfully backed into the Byzantine line.

The Emperor saw that his soldiers, fighting as hard as they were, still were not defeating the Rus. When a lull settled on the field, he sent his challenge of individual dual to Svyatoslav. The Rus leader strongly rejected the Emperor's challenge but the time this took allowed the Byzantines to organize an elite cavalry strike force under the Magister Bardas Skleros. Bardas' orders were to lead his strong cavalry unit against the now exposed rear of the Rus line, turning it. When he set off, the sky opened with wind and rain. And lo! Suddenly a marvellous apparition appeared. A horseman, dressed in white riding a white horse, broke through the battle, giving heart to the Byzantine forces. The white rider had not been seen before nor was he seen again. The Rus battle line collapsed. The Byzantine army pushed up to the city walls, killing many of the Rus soldiers. Svyatoslav just managed to escape into the city, wounded by arrows. The Byzantines counted some fifteen thousand five hundred Rus dead while admitting three hundred fifty dead and many wounded.

Later, the Emperor and Church leaders identified the white rider as probably the Saint Theodore Stratelates whom the Emperor had beseeched for aid. This found support in a vision of a young nun in Constantinople on the night before the battle. She dreamed that the Theotokos appeared to her, accompanied by Holy Seraphim. The Mother of God said to her companions, 'Summon for me the Holy Witness Theodore.' Suddenly, a young beautiful man in armour appeared. And the Mother of God said, 'Lord Theodore, your John, who fights the barbarians at Dorystolon is now in trouble. With haste help him! Danger assails him now!' The Lord Theodore saluted the Theotokos and left. Then the young nun woke. Of course, manufacturing miracles on medieval battlefield was not unknown. Finding a trusted chevalier to dress in white and sweep about a battlefield during an anticipated crisis would certainly raise morale. Then follow-up tales just grow by themselves. This too, was part of Byzantine strategy.

Svyatoslav and his war council discussed their position late at night. Clearly, they were not going to defeat the Byzantines but their fighting capacity remained strong. Rather than dissipating their strength tying to hold out against the Byzantines, they would ask for terms. At dawn, Rus envoys asked to speak to Emperor John. The Rus, they offered, would leave Dorystolon and its peoples untouched, handing it to the Byzantines; the Rus would evacuate the Bulgarian kingdom surrendering all their captives. In return, the Byzantines would allow the Rus to leave on their boats without attacking them with the shooting fire, would supply provisions so the Rus would not have to forage, and the Byzantines would renew the trade privileges of the Rus in Constantinople. The Emperor agreed, treaties were signed and sealed. The Byzantines gave two bushels of wheat per man in the Rus force, the total amount representing twenty-two thousand people.

After the treaty was made and the Rus began evacuating the city, Svyatoslav asked to speak to the Emperor. John agreed and rode, in his golden decorated armour, surrounded by his mounted Immortals in their gilded armour, to the banks of the Danube. To the Emperor came a Rus light boat, with Svyatoslav rowing a paddle just like the others in the craft. The Rus chieftain stood and talked with the Emperor. Svyatoslav was of medium height, muscular and strong, with grey eyes, thick eyebrows, and clean shaven on the chin but with a long bushy moustache. His head was shaved bald except for a lock of hair hanging down on one side, as a sign of nobility. His clothes were white, just like all his men, except his was sparkling clean. In one ear, he had an earring, made from gold with two pearls flanking a red ruby. He looked angry and wild. After he and the Emperor finished, Svyatoslav returned to his boat, took the helmsman position and shoved off into the Danube.

Trouble at Constantinople

The Emperor and many of the important imperial officials spent months on the distant Bulgarian frontiers. In the imperial absence, the Great City presented an inviting vulnerability to those whose interest was to claim supreme power. John was well aware that imperial absences were dangerous. He appointed the Patrician Leo, *Droungarios* of the Fleet, Eparch of Constantinople. Similar to a modern mayor, the eparch oversaw the city's civic services and was responsible for security. John gave Leo unlimited powers of discretion to maintain order. Of course, if Leo failed to preserve the city for John, he would find his career significantly shortened. Events were to prove John's suspicions were well founded as was his choice of eparch.

The rebellion that John had suppressed, hoping leniency would heal all wounds was still smouldering. On Lesbos, in the town of Methymna, Leo the *Kouropalates*, brother of the Emperor Nicephorus, and his son, Nicephorus, lived in exile. The sentence that John had originally decreed, blinding for the both of them, was not actually executed. Leo, however, thought that John's leniency was weakness and the absence of the army in Bulgaria was opportunity. He bribed his guards with gold. Sailing away from Lesbos on a light ship, the *Kouropalates* and his son landed on the Asian shore opposite the Great City, at an estate called Pelamys. Once situated, the father and son sent an agent into the city to contact the main people of the Phocas faction. These people received the news of Leo's new attempt to seize the throne with enthusiasm. They promised to gather a strong force of armed men and decided to steal keys to allow them to enter the imperial palace. They bribed an imperial key-keeper to make wax impressions of the keys, which they then used to manufacture a new set. Their plans succeeding as they hoped, Leo's conspirators asked him to come into the city, so that they could set in motion their *coup d'état*. Leo and his son sailed across the Bosporus in the dead of night, entered the city through a little known postern gate, and made their way to the house of a family retainer in the Sphorakion neighbourhood. This house was centrally located north of the great Mese Street between the Milion and the Forum of Constantine.

Supporters of the Phocas faction spread the word of the coming change in order to widen the circles of collaborators. One of the Phocan supporters went to the imperial weaving guild where he told his friend who was guild master, that the *Kouropalates* was in the city and planning a *coup*. He requested assistance from the guild master in the uprising and that he convince his fellow guild members to come out in support of the House of Phocas. The guild master readily agreed. He immediately left his office as if to contact important fellow members. Instead, he went straight to the office of the Eparch, the Patrician Leo. He told Leo that the *Kouropalates* was in the city and was about to execute a *coup*. At first, Leo was incredulous but with a little consideration, he saw the immediacy of the danger. Calling together a force of the Watch, he marched to the house in the Sphorakion neighbourhood and entered the building. The *Kouropalates* and his son escaped through a rear window and quickly made their way to the Great Church. They supplicated the sanctuary of the church but the Eparch would have none of it. His men seized the *Kouropalates* and his son, and dragged them out of the church and to their headquarters where the officials blinded both men and then sent them off to an isolated island, Kalonymos. Emperor John approved the actions of the Eparch.

References

The Emperor fights in Bulgaria: Leo 8, 8–10; 9, 1-2, 6; Skylitzes 298–302.
  Russian Primary Chronicle: pp. 64–74 as the Rus remembered the conflict.

Modern reconstruction of the campaign: John Haldon, *The Byzantine Wars*: Charleston SC, 2000, pp. 98–105.

Byzantine mix of forces and tactics: Eric McGeer, *Sowing the Dragon's Teeth*, see particularly pp. 253–328, the chapter that draws the book together; Leo the Wise, *Taktika*, 'Constitution 14, Day of Battle'; see also commentary, John Haldon, *A Critical Commentary on the Taktika of Leo VI*: Washington DC, 2014, pp. 275–293.

The final battle: Leo 9, 7–11; Skylitzes 303–310.
  See above references for this section.
  The miraculous in Byzantine history: the Holy, Apostolic, Ecumenical, and Orthodox Faith ministered to a believing population. Miracles happened daily: loved ones recovering from sickness, death coming too close during an accident, for these and similar occurrences, people prayed to their guardian saint, through focusing on the earthly image of the sacred, the Holy Icon. That a technical ploy could increase the awesome power of faith was neither unknown nor condemned. As Napoleon said, Morale is to material as three is to one.

Trouble in Constantinople: Leo 9, 3–4; Skylitzes 303.
  To see life in the Great City, see William Hutton, *Constantinople the Story* of *the Old Capital of the Empire*: London, 1909. While much of this book describes Constantinople as it was under the Ottomans, in many ways, the city of the Padishah was not so different from the city of the Basileus.
  For discussion of the architectural structures in the city, see Cyril Mango, *Byzantine Architecture*: New York, 1985, especially pp. 108–140, also Freely and Akmak, *op. cit.* pp. 154–201.

Chapter 8

John I Tzimiskes: Victorious Emperor

Triumph in Byzantium

Emperor John I Tzimiskes liberated the prisoners of the Rus, reorganized the Bulgarian lands, and installed strong garrisons in their towns and strongholds. Then, after a total of four months of war, the Emperor marched back to Constantinople. When he approached the great walls of the city, he found crowds of citizens in ceremonial dress, welcoming him back to the capital. They presented John with gold crowns and sceptres decorated with jewels and drew forth a gilded chariot drawn by a white horse for him to ride through the city in triumph. John accepted the crowns and sceptres, returning gift for gift, but he refused to ride in the chariot. Rather, he instructed that a *Hodegetria* (an icon depiction of the Mother of God, holding the Infant Jesus and pointing to Him as the vessel of Salvation for mankind) be placed in the chariot to precede him into the city. And so the imperial triumph entered the city: the chariot with the Theotokos leading; John crowned, with sceptre in hand, riding a spirited horse; next, the victorious army in their gleaming armour and shinning weapons followed, while the way was bedecked with purple, gold cloth and laurel branches looking like a decorated interior. The procession moved down the main Mese Street to the Great Church where they offered prayers of thanksgiving. John personally dedicated the imperial Bulgarian crown as first of the spoil. The Emperor proceeded to the Imperial Palace and had Boris, ruler of Bulgaria, brought forth. John ceremoniously divested Boris of his crown, purple robe and scarlet buskins then elevated him to the rank of Magister. The former Bulgarian empire now became simply provinces of the Byzantine Empire. The Emperor issued coinage showing the Theotokos placing the imperial crown on his head. The city proclaimed the achievements of the Christ Beloved Emperor.

The New War in the East

Here, we must leave our narrative for a review of significant problems in the literary sources. Leo the Deacon, who appears to be an eyewitness of many of the events he described, and John Skylitzes, who was a careful and thoughtful compiler, give very little information about John Tzimiskes' eastern campaigns. Indeed, Jean-Claude Cheynet, author of the notes to John Wortley's translation of Skylitzes, comments that the two works are 'very unbalanced for they have little to say about the east-which was the principal field of operations under Tzimiskes'. Rather than being a simple matter of balance, this issue represents an underlying problem in the Byzantine state and society. The people of Constantinople, the merchants, shippers, craftsmen, and artisans along with the political and economic elites, the managers of the government offices, policy makers, overseers of regulations and the landowners, all were very concerned with the Great City and its hinterland. This interest extended to the accessible sea coasts towns and their hinterland. Bulgaria was important in this discussion because Bulgarian forces could easily disrupt important parts of these lands. But, the east, beyond the centre of Asia Minor was of very little interest to these Byzantines. Here were the seats of the great houses, chief among them the House of Phocas. These houses rested on great estates of horse farms, breeding and raising mounts for the cavalry and pack animals for logistics. In and among the horse farms were soldiers' properties, where individual families, actually clients, of the great houses, raised the necessary food and raw materials for the armed forces and were themselves participants in those forces. Further west and north in Asia Minor, the soldiers' properties began to intersect with the cash crop plantations of the landowning civil elite. There was, beginning from the accession of Romanus I (920) through the end of the reign of Basil II (1025), a constant struggle of the civil elite to absorb soldiers' properties into their plantations and efforts of the military emperors to preserve and extend soldiers' properties to increase the size of the army.

The Byzantines of Constantinople were not excited about either Nicephorus II Phocas or John I Tzimiskes extending the empire to the east. All they saw was more taxes, more good land going to soldiers, and less wealth coming into the city. The Byzantine Church also was unenthusiastic about the eastern campaigns. The Holy, Apostolic, Ecumenical, and Orthodox Church was in the business of salvation not empire building. The Church maintained a strong presence in the Near East. Their services continued at the Holy Sites under the protection of the Muslim civil authorities. Once in a while, disturbances erupted that upset the peace but those were rare and, usually, the Muslims authorities paid for some of the damage. Recently, riots killed both the Patriarchs of Antioch and Jerusalem but those happened because of the Emperor Nicephorus' recent campaigns. The Byzantine Church had no use for a Crusade. If the Christ Beloved Emperor, guided by the Holy Theotokos, believed that his duty was to conquer the holy places, neither the City nor the

Church would oppose him. But, by the same token, his eastern campaigns were not something very exciting.

Because both Leo the Deacon and Skylitzes give abbreviated and somewhat confused accounts of the eastern campaigns, we have to look elsewhere for an accurate narrative. Two authors lived in the lands involved in John Tzimiskes' eastern advances. They were not particularly concerned with Byzantine actions but recorded the events as part of the history of their local communities. Yaḥyā of Antioch wrote about Syria and Matthew of Edessa wrote about the Armenians. Using bits and pieces of each, the course of John's campaigns become clear. We follow the reconstruction of these events as compiled by the modern Byzantine scholar, H. Grégore.

The Events of the Campaigns

Those that the Byzantines called the Carthaginians, the Shia Muslims of North Africa, are recognized today as the Fatimid Egyptian regime. When Nicephorus II was battling in Syria, the Fatimids began expanding into Palestine, looking further up the Mediterranean coast. When John I Tzimiskes was fighting in Bulgaria, the Fatimid forces had reached Antioch, laying the city under siege. The city walls were in repair and the Duke of Antioch had both troops and supplies. Emperor John sent orders to the Strategos of Mesopotamia to march to relieve Antioch and he also sent the Patrician Nicholas with reinforcements. By spring 971, a Qarmatian incursion into Syria drew the Fatimid forces from Antioch. The reinforced Byzantine borders proved more formidable than other fields for Fatimid expansion. In Constantinople John and his court made preparations to resume Nicephorus' eastern offensive during 971. Just as Nicephorus overthrew the Amir of Aleppo so John intended to overthrow the Hamdanid Amir of Mosul and clear the Levant for Byzantine development.

In spring 972, the Emperor sailed out from Constantinople with his Immortals and select soldiers from the other *tagmata*. Marching through Asia Minor, John and his troops collected select forces from the *themata* and headed toward Mesopotamia. The Emperor strengthened the frontiers in south Armenia and Mesopotamia. In September 972, the imperial expeditionary force crossed the Euphrates near Melitene and on October 12, assaulted and entered Nisibis. There, the Byzantines massacred large numbers, burned buildings, and enslaved as many people as possible. John and his army occupied the city, threatening surrounding towns with destruction. Soon, the Hamdanid Amir of Mosul, Abu Taghlib, agreed to pay an annual tribute and John moved on toward Mayyafariqin, which he attempted but failed to sack.

As the campaign season ended, John established as Domestic of the East, an Armenian officer who had been *Strategos* of Anatolia, Mleh. He set up his headquarters at Batn Hanzith; his orders were to keep the frontier secure. John left a strong force with Mleh and returned to Constantinople. The effect of John's campaign resounded through the Near East. Crowds rioted in Mosul and Bagdad after Nisibis fell. The fact that a Byzantine army of occupation was sitting just a few miles up the Euphrates caused consternation among the Caliph of Bagdad's subjects. That the Shia Fatimids held Damascus was bad enough but to have Christian Byzantines just over the hill was worse.

During winter, 972–3, the Domestic of the East Mleh, collected a strong force of Byzantines and Royal Armenians at Hanzith. His orders were to put strong pressure on Abu Taghlib, Amir of Mosul. In spring, Mleh led his army against the fortress city of Amida. Abu Taghlib understood he either had to repel the Byzantines or lose his throne. He sent a powerful army under the command of his brother Hibat Allah to protect Amida. The Muslim forces shattered Mleh's army, killing many, capturing more, including Mleh. Abu Taghlib sent the heads of the dead to the Caliph in Bagdad. A letter appeared, purportedly written by Mleh and addressed to Emperor John, which accused John of needlessly starting war and having many people killed. By March 974, Mleh was dead, still in honourable captivity. Abu Taghlib's propaganda campaign undermined John's positions in the Near East. Mleh's defeat was significant and the Muslim potentates were making the most of it. The King of Armenia, Ashot III the Gracious, was looking for support from many sides, while the Byzantine connection was weakening. The Emperor intended to sweep away these annoyances with another expedition to the Near East. Planning and preparations took a year. John was ready to set out in spring 974. Before the Emperor left for his campaign, he had to handle a scandal that struck the Church of Constantinople. High Churchmen accused the Ecumenical Patriarch, Basil Skamandrenos recently appointed with John's approval, with the misuse of his power in favour of a certain magnate. The Imperial Tribunal called the Patriarch to answer the charges, but Basil refused to come, claiming that only an ecumenical council could remove him. The Emperor ordered Basil into exile, appointing his place of banishment to be a monastery Basil himself had founded. The new Patriarch was Antony III Stoudites, an ascetic monk from the monastery of Stoudios. With the Church question settled, John finished his preparations for the coming campaign.

A major part of the Emperor's preparations had to do with the royal Armenians. After Mleh's defeat, in 973, the Armenian nation, royal princes and chief barons, held assembly under King Ashot III, in the land of Harq, northeast of Taron. The point of assembly was useful in that a force could either descend the Euphrates and defend Armenia from the south, or move to cover the Armenian western frontiers if the Byzantine position in north Syria should collapse. John sent envoys to the Armenian assembly, who in return sent a delegation to Constantinople. The Emperor John and King Ashot III signed a treaty by which the Armenians would participate in a major offensive into Muslim Syria and Mesopotamia by providing ten thousand well armed cavalry troops, mostly horse archers, and supplying provisions for the joint Armenian-Byzantine force. In spring 974, John marched through Asia Minor, bringing with him his Immortals and select elite troops of the *tagmata*, collecting select troops from the *themata*, and joining the Armenian forces at Mus, the capital of Taron. Once the forces joined the Byzantine Emperor led it south, to begin a major effort, a crusade, to conquer the Levant and the Holy Land.

The Byzantines first approached Amida. John accepted a large tribute from the town and passed it by. Then he approached Mayyafariqin where he accepted more tribute. Marching passed Nisibis, now deserted, John encountered no significant opposition to his advance. The reason for this was the position Abu Taghlib found himself. After the defeat of Mleh, the Amir had strong disagreements with the Caliph Al Muti and his supporters in Bagdad. He saw the Byzantine invasion not as a problem to be faced but as an opportunity to enhance his own power. An agreement with the Byzantines, allowing them to attack Bagdad, would strengthen his hold over his own lands. Emperor John also saw that breaking Bagdad's power would benefit both the Byzantines and Armenians. John led his army south into Jazira.

Even as the Byzantines marched toward Bagdad, the Fatimid forces, having smashed the Qarmatian rebels, marched back through Palestine into Syria. The Fatimid Caliph at Cairo, al-Mu'izz, sent a general to occupy Damascus. During the winter, 974–75, Fatimid forces marched up the coast, taking Tripoli and Beirut from Byzantine garrisons. Informed about the Fatimid offensive, in late 974, John halted his march down the Euphrates because he saw the developing threat to Antioch and Cilicia as more serious than possible advantage from sacking Bagdad. The Byzantine army split, the Armenians returning home and John marched to Antioch. Leaving most of his troops to winter in Antioch, John returned to Constantinople with his Immortals. The Emperor celebrated a great triumph in late 974, displaying the riches he brought back. In spring 975, John and his elite troops returned to Antioch.

The Byzantine army, refitted and organized, marched out of Antioch in April, with the objective of driving 'the accursed Africans' out of Syria and Palestine. Emperor John led his forces down the course of the Orontes, arriving at Emese. Here, he found a correct reception as stipulated by the treaty of 969–70. From Emese, the Byzantines approached Baalbek, which surrendered after a short struggle. From Baalbek, John marched against Damascus. Damascus was under the control of a refugee from the upheavals in Bagdad, Amir Aftakin, who had recognized Fatimid suzerainty. But, when John and his army drew near, Amir Aftakin came to terms with the Byzantines, paid tribute, and became John's vassal. John left Damascus and marched through Galilee to Tiberias and Nazareth. The Byzantines set up camp on Mt Tabor, where delegations came to him, from Acre, which agreed to accept a Byzantine garrison, and from both Ramleh and Jerusalem, which requested that the Emperor appoint governors for their cities. Leaving Mt Tabor, John marched to and took Caesarea. This was the limit of Emperor John's and the Byzantines' advance in Palestine.

At the same time, the Fatimids were withdrawing before the Byzantine advance. They concentrated in the main fortress cities of the Levantine coast. The Fatimid commanders looked to a long term strategy. By concentrating on the coast, they ensured the delivery of supplies to their forces while threatening the Byzantine flank. The deeper into Palestine the Byzantines moved, the more exposed were their lines of supply. Emperor John specifically stated, in his letter to Ashot III preserved in Matthew of Edessa, that the Fatimid hold on the coast was what kept him from marching on Jerusalem. John decided to clear the coast of Fatimid forces before he proceeded deeper into Palestine. The Byzantines marched to the sea, attacking and taking Beirut after a fierce battle. Then they marched south and took Sidon. Turning about, the Byzantines marched north and took Byblos by assault. The Emperor appointed commanders and organized garrisons for these captured cities. But north of Byblos there sat the important fortress city of Tripoli. The Fatimid garrisons, driven out of many of the coastal fortresses, congregated in Tripoli. The Fatimid commanders decided that they had to hold Tripoli at all coasts.

John marched up the coast from Byblos to Tripoli. He forced a passage with his armoured cavalry through a defended defile to the plain before Tripoli. The Byzantines ravaged the lands around the city inducing the defenders to come out and face them in battle. The Byzantines claimed victory but marched away from an unconquered Tripoli.

John ravaged land around Tripoli and met them in battle. John said he defeated the Muslims but Muslim authors claim they defeated the Byzantines. Whatever happened, John marched away from Tripoli. Continuing up the coast, the Emperor took city after city, including Balamea and Gabala, so that, except for Tripoli, the Byzantines controlled the whole coast from Caesarea to the Duchy of Antioch. Then John advanced into the interior, mopping up strongholds that had not surrendered. In the heights of the Lebanon, he took Burzuya, held by Kulayb, secretary to the Mamluk, Ruytash. The Emperor made Kulayb a Patrician and an imperial official. The Byzantines also took Sahyun, in the Duchy of Antioch. After a campaign of five months, in September 975, John led his army into Antioch.

The Death of Emperor John

Settling the administration of the new eastern lands and establishing garrisons to defend them, the Emperor and his Immortals entourage marched back toward Constantinople. They travelled through Cilicia and Cappadocia to Bithynia, where John stayed at the estate of the Patrician Romanus *sebastophoros*. The Patrician Romanus was the son of Stephen Lecapenus who briefly had been emperor in 944–5. Romanus was castrated when his family fell. With the Emperor was Romanus' uncle, Basil the Bastard, *parakoimomenos*. One morning, John found his limbs numb and his body paralyzed. The imperial physicians were unable to find alleviation. Understanding that he was gravely stricken, John ordered that he be taken to the Imperial Palace. He directed the completion of his tomb and made large donations to the poor, particularly to the hospital for sufferers of leprosy that he had founded. His limbs were feeble and his breathing laboured. He called for the Bishop of Adrianople, Nicholas, and confessed his many sins and beseeched the Mother of God for her intersession. John died on 10 January 976.

From the beginning, rumours of poison circulated. However, the fact that the initial physical infirmity was in September or October and that John lingered on through the early part of January is consistent with the onset of some physiological breakdown, either a stroke or heart problem, or a malignancy of some kind. Nevertheless, the story grew and developed into its final form: that when the Emperor was returning from Antioch, he saw a beautiful and fertile farm at Longinus in Cilicia and another at Druze in Cappadocia. He inquired about their ownership and found out that both were in the hands of Basil the Bastard, his first minister, *parakoimomenos*. The story continues, that John was most upset at this evidence that his first minister was grabbing up the valuable properties won by the valiant soldiers of the empire. John displayed his wrath to Basil, who became frightened. So, when Basil brought John to the estate of his nephew, he had John poisoned so that he would escape punishment. This is a good tale. However, a little analysis will tell us whether it is political propaganda or a meaningful accusation. Basil the Bastard had been a major player in Byzantine politics for years. He was involved in the elevation of Nicephorus II and in his murder. Basil had supported John's elevation and worked with John on many projects. Clearly, John and Basil saw eye to eye on many issues. The fact that Basil was picking up properties and improving them was only to the empire's advantage. Basil the Bastard was a eunuch. When he died, a lot of his property would revert to the throne. There is no material reason why John would not appreciate and accept his servant's efforts at property improvement.

But, even more important: if Basil was to kill John, he would need another more pliable candidate for the throne. Here, there was a problem. There were two emperors already occupying the throne. The sons of Romanus II, the Purple Born Basil II and Constantine VIII had been emperors from their infancy. Basil was now eighteen years old and Constantine was sixteen. Both were well educated and had been involved with the court from childhood. Clearly, now that John was on his death bed, these two were going to take over. If Basil poisoned John, and these two knew about it and believed that he murdered an emperor, he created more trouble than he originally faced.

References

Triumph in Byzantium: Leo 9, 12 Skylitzes 310.

The advent of the victorious emperor: for background, see Sabine MacCormack, *Art and Ceremony in Late Antiquity*: Berkeley, 1981, especially pp. 240-66; on John I's triumph, see particularly Michael McCormick, op. cit. pp. 171–5.

New War in the East: lack of information on eastern campaigns in both Leo the Deacon and Skylitzes, Wortley, *Skylitzes*, p. 295. The best sources for these campaigns are Yaḥyā of Antioch and Matthew of Edessa.

Byzantine attitudes towards the Levant: Clearly Leo did not find the eastern campaigns very important since he made little effort to include details in his account. Since Skylitzes followed Leo for his material, he too left out a detailed account. But Skylitzes wrote in the reign of Alexius I, when Crusading armies were moving by and through the Byzantine realm, so the fact that he did not try to find an alternative source is significant. The many Crusaders thought the Byzantines really were not interested in 'freeing' the Holy Land. How right they were.

The Events of the Campaign: Leo 10, 1–6, 11; Skylitzes 311.

The events of John I's eastern campaign, based on the chronicles of Yaḥyā of Antioch and Matthew of Edessa is in H. Grégore, 'The Amorians and Macedonians 842–1025', *The Cambridge Medieval History, IV: The Byzantine Empire, part I Byzantium and its Neighbors*: Cambridge UK, 1966, pp. 163–71.

Death of the Emperor John: Leo 10, 11; Skylitzes 311.

Causes of death: When we look at the events in peoples' lives in ancient and medieval history, we need to know that those people understood life and death very differently than we do. Sudden deaths, strokes, heart attacks, hidden malignancies, all, were very imperfectly understood. Moreover, it was a very well informed person who could select a real poison from the ideas floating around. This is not to say that slick operators could not eliminate targets with poison; they certainly did. But, every strange death was accompanied with suspicions of poison, which made the possibility even more frightening.

Chapter 9

Basil II and Constantine VIII: Civil War in the East

The Two Emperors

Before Emperor John I Tzimiskes died, in December 976, Basil and Constantine assumed power over the Byzantine state. Liudprand the Bishop of Cremona and envoy of Emperor Otto I had seen them as children sitting together on a small throne behind Nicephorus II Phocas. From infancy, they dwelt in the palace among the intrigues and fights, manoeuvres and power politics. The palace and administration held no secrets from them. Growing up amidst forceful personalities and subtle plots, dealing with difficult people who were attempting to gain advantage, all this became second nature to them. The two brothers never disagreed in public. Ultimately, the two together presented the essence of stability. Some viewed Basil as a mindless soldier and Constantine as an effete voluptuary. Nothing could please them more. Basil handled the military and foreign affairs while Constantine dealt with internal matters and the city. Together, they ruled the empire for more than fifty years: not something to be expected from a mindless soldier and effete voluptuary living in that snake pit, the palace of the Byzantine Caesars.

Always cautious, the two brothers were very close. Later, Michael Psellus explained that the strong Basil simply dominated the weak Constantine but the brothers' continued harmony and political success indicate that outward appearances did not reflect reality. When supreme power descended on the young men, they had important decisions to make. Military co-emperors representing the great eastern houses had dominated the empire from 963 to 976, a total of thirteen years. The military Emperor Romanus I Lecapenus had dominated the reign of Constantine VII for twenty-five years, from 919 to 959. Now, did Basil and Constantine want to continue with this alliance of the Imperial House with the conglomerate houses of the east? If so, the man to elect co-emperor was Bardas Skleros. He had served Nicephorus II Phocas and John I Tzimiskes well. He was Domestic of the East. The army loved him and as John I's brother-in-law, he was the closest male relation of the dead emperor. However, making Bardas Skleros co-emperor would endorse and continue the policy of conquest in the Near East. This policy did not seem beneficial to Basil and Constantine for two reasons: one, such conquests strengthened the Eastern Houses as opposed to the Great Houses of the City; that meant taxes, completion for the positions of state, and trade problems with the Near Eastern markets. Two, the leading men of the City, both clerical and lay, did not see the Islamic states of the Near East as inveterate enemies. Just as with John I's attempt to conquer the Holy Land, there was no enthusiasm to create greater upheaval in the Near East than that which already existed under the competing Muslim dynasties. Such a policy would only lead to the neglect of the western parts of the empire, which were important to many in the City. Therefore, the two Emperors decided, whatever the cost, to avoid the establishment of another co-emperor.

The question remained: how were the Emperors to consolidate power to give them freedom of action without directly allying with one of the main factions? In order to ensure as much stability as possible while leaving the eastern magnates without strong influence in the City, the Emperors chose to rely on their great uncle, Basil the Bastard, *parakoimomenos*. Basil had managed the administration under the Emperor John, so leaving him in charge ensured continuity. Even more important, Basil, the Emperors' great uncle, had always paid attention to the imperial children and strong bonds of affection bound the youths and uncle together. The first act of the new administration was calling the boys' mother, Theophano, back to the palace. While Theophano returned to the palace, she lived quietly and stayed out of politics until her death in 991. The next major move was dealing with Bardas Skleros: the command he held, Domestic of the East, was suppressed, the *tagmata* recalled to Constantinople and many soldiers released. This was, no doubt, explained as a cost-cutting measure. Not desiring to let Bardas Skleros be unemployed or feeling unappreciated, the Emperors appointed him Duke of Mesopotamia, in charge of the *themata* of the frontier commands. This position was superior to a theme *strategos* if not so grand as a domestic. Moreover, the image projected from the palace was that the boy Emperors were really too young to make decisions so any unappreciated measure was made by Basil the Bastard. The palace hoped that this would alleviate any ill feelings with the thought that in just a few years, the Emperors themselves would make all things right.

The Civil War in the East I: the War Begins

The Emperors announced these decisions after John's funeral. All concerned were in the City for the imperial ceremonies ending one reign and beginning another. Besides Skleros becoming commander in Mesopotamia in charge of the main frontier with the Muslim powers, his lieutenant, Michael Bourtzes, became Duke of Antioch thus isolating him from Skleros. To replace the Domestic of the East command, Peter the *stratopedarches* became responsible for coordinating manpower and supplies for all the eastern forces. Skleros' distress at these arrangements was immediately most clear. He described this as a demotion and insult. What particularly upset him was the fact that the House of Phocas gained ascendancy when Peter, who was a creature of that house, became commander in Asia Minor. When he complained to the court, Basil the *parakoimomenos* told him in no uncertain terms that if he continued to demand more than his due, he would find himself confined to his estates. Skleros quickly took leave of the court and the City, going to his command post. On the way, beloved as he was by the eastern armies, respected by the eastern Great Houses, he informed officers and units of Peter the *stratopedarches'* forces to expect major changes in the administration. When he felt that he was far enough from Constantinople, he successfully sounded out many eastern interests and decided that the time had come to announce his elevation by the army to be emperor. Skleros' first action was to send an agent, Anthes Alyates, to Constantinople in order to escort his son, Romanus, to his father's camp and safety. When Anthes arrived in the City, rumours swirled around about Skleros' usurpation. Anthes depicted Skleros as incompetent and weak. By continually saying negative things about Skleros, Anthes appeared to support the established administration. In this way, he was able to attach Romanus to his entourage and so was able to spirit him out of Constantinople and to Skleros' camp.

The armies of the east collected around Skleros' camp. Bardas Skleros appeared with an imperial crown on his head, garbed in an imperial robe. The army, especially the Armenian contingents, loudly proclaimed him emperor. It was summer 976. As emperor, Skleros needed money more than anything else because money is the key to everything in war. His agents took over the state revenue offices in the eastern districts and seized all their money. The local officials could either join Skleros' administration or suffer arrest: some chose imprisonment rather than join the rebels. Skleros pressured some of the eastern houses to give him money while other eastern houses willingly brought him wealth with the hope of collecting more when Skleros won. The rebel command secured Charpete, a strong fortress in the Mesopotamian theme now called Harput. Into this fortress, the rebels deposited their money and supplies, securing a base in their rear in case of a reverse. Skleros also sent envoys to the Muslim states just across the Byzantine frontiers. He contacted Abu Dulaf, Emir of Amida, who held the city for the Hamdanid Emir of Mosul, Abu Taghlib. With Abu Dulaf's help, the rebels also began dealing with Abu

Taghlib himself. Skleros secured acknowledgment as emperor and friendship with these powers through marriage alliances. The emirs gave him money and a special force of three hundred Arab horsemen. From the point of view of the Hamdanids, delivery of significant aid could only help to weaken the Byzantine Empire. As the rebels' fortunes waxed, all sorts of adventurous people flocked to their standards. Skleros organized his forces and in early summer, he set out to march on Constantinople. Just as Romanus I and Nicephorus II did before, he thought that his appearance at the head of a strong army before the City walls would result in a quick about face and seat him on the imperial throne in the Golden Hall.

The swirling rumours about rebellion turned into reality for the people in the forums and halls of Constantinople. It was said that the Emperors were distressed and Basil the *parakoimomenos* was upset. Those who look forward to upheaval rejoiced. Those for whom peace and tranquillity meant prosperity moved in fear. Actually, the situation was developing as well as Basil the Bastard and the Emperors could expect. Bardas Skleros was going to try to become emperor: that was clear. That his attempt started in the eastern lands was advantageous to the Emperors. The eastern lands produced some revenue but their military forces needed subsidies from the imperial treasury. With the eastern lands in revolt, the treasury would have more money for the short run. Skleros' only real hope was to bring a powerful and loyal army to Constantinople's gates. Then, the pressures within and without the City would become unmanageable. Basil the Bastard would pay the price and the two Emperors would be relegated to the inner recesses of the palace. But, the way to avoid that happening was simple: keep Skleros away from the City.

Since Skleros was collecting troops and money in the eastern districts, he would have to take the Great Military Road across Asia Minor to reach Constantinople. The ancient fortress city of Caesarea commanded the route where the road debauched from the Armenian mountains leading to the River Halys. The Emperors sent orders to Peter the *stratopedarches* to occupy the fortress with his *tagmata* units and hold it against Skleros. The rebels might outflank Caesarea but they could not leave it in their rear. At the same time, the Emperors sent the *synkellos* Stephen, Bishop of Nicomedia, to Skleros as a personal envoy. Stephen offered absolute amnesty for all if Skleros renounced his rebellion. Of course Bardas Skleros refused to back down, extending his food to show his scarlet buskin, saying 'It is not possible for one who willingly drew this boot on to take it off. Tell your masters in Constantinople: either they willingly recognize me as Emperor or I will force them to recognize me.' But, the *synkellos*' audience was not Skleros alone. His offer was to be remembered by Skleros' supporters, when things went wrong. As King Ptolemy I once said,

'I would build a bridge of gold for a retreating enemy.' Skleros granted the *synkellos* forty days for the powers in Constantinople to come to their senses and sent him on his way. When he reported the results of his discussions with the Emperors and Basil the *parakoimomenos*, they sent instructions to Peter the *stratopedarches* not to advance against the rebels but hold the city and road against any possible attack from them.

Skleros collected his forces and began the march on Constantinople. As advance reconnaissance, he sent a strong cavalry contingent under the command of Anthes Alyates to feel out the strength of the force in Caesarea. While Alyates' force moved through a narrow pass called Cuckoo Rock, they ran into a reconnaissance force from Caesarea, under the command of the Magister Eustathios Maleinos. The two forces milled around, yelling threats and posing as attacking, but because most of the soldiers in both forces knew each other and had fought together, neither side was willing to actually fight each other. Alyates found this most foolish. Giving his horse the spur, he charged at Eustathios' soldiers. They quickly cut him down. His forces simply dispersed and returned to Skleros' camp. When the Magister told Peter the *stratopedarches* about the engagement, the commander decided that the imperial forces needed to block all the routes near Caesarea. Skleros camped just beyond the blocked routes, waiting for the situation to develop. He had heard that his commander of Muslim mercenary troops was about to defect to Peter. He brought the man to a hearing but simply scolded him. However, he instructed some loyal mercenary troopers kill the commander. As the mercenary commander passed by his troopers in broad daylight, some pulled out their swords and killed him. Skleros waited some weeks, his men questioning why he did not move. Then he received a visitor to his camp.

The visitor was an imperial general of Armenian origin, Sachakios Brachamios, who was defecting to Bardas Skleros. He brought information about a route around Caesarea that would allow Skleros to bypass Caesarea without besieging the fortress. The rebel army set out. Brachamios led the vanguard followed by Skleros with the main body along a byway for three days. They reached Lapara, also called Likandos, in Cappadocia, well in the rear of Peter the *stratopedarches*. Peter, when he discovered that the rebels were moving past his forces, made a night march to catch up to Skleros' army. Approaching the rebels, Peter set up his camp opposite Skleros' camp. But, just as before, both sides knew each other and were not eager to fight. Both forces delayed any moves to engage in combat. Bardas Skleros, very practised in the ways of war, devised a tactic to overthrow Peter's army. In the morning, he posted his usual sentries to guard his front while bringing in to his camp wagons loaded with food. Peter and his officers saw this and assumed that Skleros was planning a celebration for his forces. They allowed their own forces to relax and take care of needed personal cares. In a few hours, Skleros ordered the trumpets to sound the attack and his army, already armed and ready, launched an assault against Peter's camp. Surprised, Peter's force still managed to arm and to form up, successfully holding off Skleros' onslaught. Skleros understood that neither force was going to push the other side to extremities. He had another tactic ready. While the main forces danced around each other without much effect, Skleros sent his Muslim mercenaries around the battlefield, to fall on the rear of Peter's camp. There, they found the baggage train. Unlike the two Byzantine forces, the mercenaries had no compunction about killing their enemies. They slaughtered the camp followers in the baggage train, capturing officers' families. Peter's main commander, Michael Bourtzes Duke of Antioch, was one of the first to understand what was happening. He pulled out of the battle and surrendered to Skleros. With that, Peter's army broke up and either fled or surrendered.

Gathering up the plunder from Peter's camp, the rebel army moved on, bypassing Caesarea to the south, to the city of Tzamandos, a strong fortress set in a rich area. Skleros' financial and supply circumstances became favourable. The breaking up of the Emperors' position in Caesarea sent many to Skleros pledging their loyalty and willingly providing money and goods. With Michael Bourtzes came the Duchy of Antioch, and this pushed down a row of dominoes. Skleros sent Michael Kourtikios to the Kibyrrhaiote Theme, which was the main source of men and supplies for the fleets. The main city Attalia threw the high admiral who supported the Emperors in chains and welcomed Kourtikios. The result was that the south coast of Asia Minor fell to the rebels along with a strong fleet.

The loss of Caesarea and of the coast from Antioch to Rhodes disturbed the Emperors, the *parakoimomenos*, and the imperial council. Yet at this point, the original strategy had not collapsed. Skleros was still stuck in the east and while he held more of it, he really was no closer to Constantinople. The usurper would have to advance along the old Great Military Road and the next choke point was at Kotyaeon.

The Civil War in the East II: Round Two

The imperial court decided to try to undermine the usurper yet again. They conferred on a high-ranking courtier, Leo the *protovestiarios* (a position second only to the *parakoimomenos*) the power to speak with the Emperors' voice. He was empowered to grant pardons, amnesties, and grant honours as he saw fit and his actions would have the force of law. As his spokesman, the

Walls of Constantinople.

Imperial Byzantine architecture interior of the Great Church, Hagia Sophia.

Crowning the Emperor Byzantine.

The Byzantine Army.

The Emperor in court.

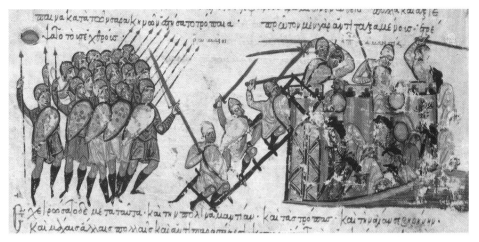

Emperor Nicephorus II's forces assault a city.

Fighting between Byzantines and Arabs.

Byzantine soldiers.

Silistra (Dorystolon).

Ecumenical patriarch of
Constantinople in full
regalia; Emperor's
regalia similar only
more colourful.

Presentation cross of
Justin II, given to the
Pope.

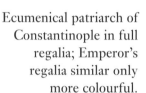

Chrysobull, Byzantine
legal document.

Great Hall of Charlemagne
at Aachen, copied from
Byzantium's Golden Hall.

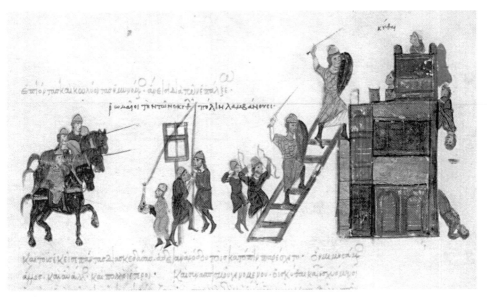

Byzantine assault of Preslav.

Seraphim defending
the Holy Empire in
Hagia Sophia.

The heart of Byzantium,
Theotokos in apse of Hagia Sophia.

St Achilles Island, stronghold of Bulgarian Empire.

Early Bulgarian building from the time of the First Bulgarian Empire.

Entrance of Emperor Nicephorus II into Constantinople.

Coronation of Basil II as a child.

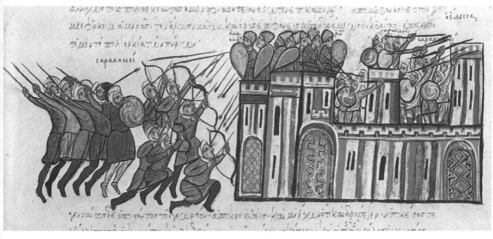

Byzantine siege.

Empire Basil II interviews Skleros.

Battle of Phocas and Skleros.

Protovestiarios Leo negotiating with Skleros.

Emperors appointed the famous orator, the Patrician John. At the fortress city of Kotyaeon, Peter the *stratopedarches* had concentrated his remaining troops and received reinforcements from the western Asia Minor *themata*. In spring 977, Leo brought young recruits of the elite *tagmata*. Peter's forces made ready to resist Bardas Skleros' advance. Skleros had made camp at an imperial stud farm at Dipotamon, down the road from Kotyaeon. Leo sent messages to those of the usurpers' force who he knew, telling them of the offers of amnesty and honours. Many seemed interested (or at least willing to see who won) but were surrounded by Skleros' supporters. Skleros and his staff ridiculed these offers as signs of desperation from the corrupt administration in Constantinople. Leo saw that Skleros' camp was holding together but not very strongly. Selecting an elite force of heavy and light cavalry, Leo left Kotyaeon, passed Skleros' camp at night and marched east up the Great Military Road toward the eastern themes. The security Skleros promised for his followers' property and families suddenly was at risk. Many of the usurpers' officers and soldiers were ready to ride east to protect their homes. If that happened, the usurper's strength would blow away like dust.

Skleros did not want to lose his position, pressing the Emperors' forces against the Opsikion theme, but his forces threatened to disintegrate. He organized a unit of elite light cavalry under the command of the Magister Michael Bourtzes, Duke of Antioch, and the Patrician Romanus Taronites, a member of a prominent eastern house. Their orders were to harass Leo's force, cutting off stragglers, attack foraging parties, and in general, use hit and run tactics. They were, however, strictly instructed to avoid a general engagement. The dispatch of this strike force assuaged fears for the settlements in the east. This was a good plan but was quickly thwarted. As Leo knew and Bourtzes discovered, a caravan coming from the Muslims in the east was bringing the gold tribute owed to the empire. On a certain day the caravan was going to pass between the two armies. When the caravan reached the fortress of Oxylithos, both Leo's forces and Bourtzes' charged in to gather up the gold. The two forces collided in a melee, in which Leo's force, backed up by heavy cavalry, crushed Bourtzes' light cavalry, putting many to flight. Leo's force, from the elite *tagmata* stationed at Constantinople, had no compunction about killing their enemies and they slew most of those who tried to surrender. They particularly sought out Armenian soldiers whom they blamed for the insurrection.

Skleros was distressed at the collapse of his effort to counter Leo the *protovestiarios'* strategy. The only good news was that Leo and his soldiers had to return to Peter's camp to guard the gold shipment. Skleros immediately mobilized his army and drew up in battle formation at a place called Rhageas, which blocked Peter and Leo's communications with Constantinople. Peter and many experienced commanders thought that the best option for their army was to do nothing. Skleros would not attack their fortified camp. They had sufficient supplies for the while. Let Skleros, they reasoned, simply sit there. Eventually he would run short of supplies and would have to withdraw to his camp. This would make him look weak. But the younger soldiers looked forward to battle. They impressed Leo with their zeal and he ordered the army to make ready for battle; it was fall 977. Quoting Sophocles, our historian says, 'He who urges haste follows the path to misfortune.' The two armies assumed battle formation: Skleros' forces formed the usual tripartite formation; a heavy infantry centre, commanded by him; a heavy cavalry right wing, commanded by his brother, Constantine; and a left wing of heavy cavalry commanded by Constantine Gabras. Light infantry screened the front and light cavalry protected the flanks and rear. Peter's force formed along similar lines. Leo gave the order to attack, trumpets and drums sounded and the Emperor's army launched against the usurper's battle line. In the clash of both wings, Skleros' men cut through Peter's younger forces, smashing Peter's heavy cavalry and killing many of the soldiers who stood their ground. This included Peter the *stratopedarches*, struck by a spear and thrown from his horse, also the Patrician John, and many of their bodyguards. Leo the *protovestiarios* and many officers surrendered to Skleros. The usurper imprisoned Leo and dealt harshly with defectors from his own camp. He made a public demonstration in front of his whole army of blinding the brothers Hagiozacharites, Theodore and Niketas. With his naval forces blocking the Dardanelles and his overwhelming victory on the field, Bardas Skleros appeared to have isolated Constantinople and so had victory at hand.

References

The Two Emperors: Skylitzes 814–316; Psellus 1, 1–4.

The brothers: both Skylitzes and Psellus wrote their histories some fifty to seventy-five years after the death of Basil II. The two historians were in the centre of political and cultural life in the Great City and had access to what information was available. Basil and Constantine, however, kept their endeavours close to their chests. This makes understanding their reign difficult; difficult for the Byzantine historians and difficult for us. Skylitzes and Psellus wrote their accounts in order to make the events of past time comprehensible. They used the sources available to them. They were not pushing this or that policy because, as perceptive Byzantine historians, they knew that policies and personalities could significantly change in a day, and a day was coming when they would. 'My history is an everlasting procession, not a prize composition which is heard and forgotten' said Thucydides (I, 22, end). The efforts to atomize medieval historians and over-intellectualize the results only lead to more confusion and the intrusion of modern concerns alien to the ancient authors.

The Civil War in the East I: Skylitzes 316–320; Psellus 1, 5.

For the routes and stations of the Byzantine military roads in Asia Minor see W. M. Ramsay, *The Historical Geography of Asia Minor*, London, 1890, reprint, Cambridge UK, 2010 (also e book, Elibron Classics) pp. 197–221.

The Civil War in the East II: Skylitzes 320–324.

Deployment of an army on the field of battle: see discussion in the 'Anonymous Byzantine Treatise on Strategy', in George Dennis, *Three Byzantine Military Treatises*: Washington, 1985, sections 31–7.

Chapter 10

Basil II and Constantine VIII: Wars in the East and West

The Civil War in the East III: the Emperors at Bay

The city of Constantinople was nearing panic. Not only had Bardas Skleros wintered near the fortress of Kotyaeon, now spring 978, he was marching toward Nicaea. All Skleros had to do was cross the Bosporus and he would be at the City. But far worse, Skleros' fleet that had come to him when his forces gained the Kibyrrhaiote theme, under the command of his admiral Michael Kourtikios, had worked through the Aegean Sea, plundering islands, seizing merchant ships, and halting grain shipments to the City. The mob in the City could explode at any time, particularly because Skleros' agents were ready to ignite riots at just the right time to destabilize the administration. The Emperors and the *parakoimomenos* understood that they needed successful action soon or the *parakoimomenos* would find an unpleasant retirement and the Emperors would become scholars. They had a weapon at hand. They had best use it effectively. The target was Skleros' fleet.

The rebel fleet was sailing up to the Dardanelles. For the most part, the force consisted of a number of smaller ships, galeas, used for suppressing pirates. These were open-decked long boats, propelled by a single row of oars with lateen-rigged sail. Leading them was a strong squadron of the main battleships of the Byzantine navy, dromons. These were large decked ships, propelled by two rows of oars with lateen-rigged sails. The main armaments were, of course, the sailors and marines operating the ships but all the ships carried a variety of throwing machines. The main projectiles shot from these machines were different incendiary devices. They also carried hand-held machines that shot streams of fire that adhered to what it touched and engulfed it in flame. This was the famous Greek fire.

Skleros' fleet threatened to blockade the City. Already, unrest spread among the merchants and in the grain market. The answer to this threat was in the upper reaches of the Golden Horn, where the great Theodosian Wall met the waters of the inlet. Here, the Emperors kept their private fleet: ships used in imperial ceremonies, pleasure craft for sailing in the waters around

Constantinople, and a special squadron of some ten warships. These imperial warships were the most terrifying and destructive weapon system of the Mediterranean world. These ships were purpose-built platforms for projected Greek fire. Dromon style ships, the crafts were stronger with reinforced bows able to carry heavy equipment and with special ballasted sterns to counter the weight in front. Set in the bows, a large furnace heated a boiler in which the Greek fire mixture heated under pressure. A pump mechanism propelled the hot mixture through a nozzle with a connected ignition. The result was a steady jet of flaming oil that held fast to whatever it struck: sails, hulls, and people. This was a weapon system with one purpose: to manoeuvre into position in order to deliver an annihilating sheet of flame. Princess Anna Comnena in her history of her father, the Emperor Alexius I (r. 1081–1118), described the projector ships as having a large animal head on the bow made from bronze or iron and covered in gold leaf. Their mouths were open, and out of their mouths shot the stream of destructive fire. Vulnerable to all sorts of attack, the projector ships needed a strong defensive guard in order to deliver their attack. The Emperors ordered a fleet to assemble at Constantinople, drawn from the ships in the Black Sea and those that could made their way from the Aegean.

The projector squadron sailed out from the Golden Horn under the command of the Magister Bardas Parsakoutenos. The collection of ships making up the imperial fleet, under the command of Theodore Karantenos, masked the projector squadron so that the ships appeared to be just another war fleet that did not impress Michael Kourtikios as being particularly dangerous. Kourtikios had landed at Abydos in the Dardanelles, planning to both seal his blockade of Constantinople and provide a crossing to Skleros' troops. This would be one of the final moves of Skleros' campaign for the throne. If Kourtikios succeeded, Constantinople would riot and the people would receive Skleros as a victorious emperor. Karantenos brought the imperial fleet to Abydos. Kourtikios sent out a powerful force to repel him but Karantenos unmasked Parsakoutenos' projector squadron, which proceeded to destroy the rebel squadron and burn all their ships in reach. The rebel fleet fled from Abydos, leaving their landing parties vulnerable to the imperial marines. With the citadel of Abydos and many prisoners captured, Karantenos pursued what remained of the rebel fleet to the small port of Phocaea. The rebel fleet dispersed and remained scattered.

Skleros was still advancing up the military road to Nicaea. The Emperors sent the Patrician Manuel Erotikos of House Comnenus with a select unit of elite troops to reinforce the city. He arrived at Nicaea just before Skleros led his army into the Nicaean district. Skleros burned all the villages around Nicaea and then attacked the city by escalade. Setting up throwing machines, the rebels attempted to clear the walls of defenders and then sent forward assault troops with ladders. Erotikos' troops pushed the ladders down and machines hurtling Greek fire bombs destroyed the throwing machine. Skleros understood that without a far more massive effort, no assault would succeed. Rather, the rebels dug in and began to besiege Nicaea. They blocked all shipments in and out of the city. The supply of provisions within Nicaea was actually very low because the imperial government had recalled most of Nicaea's grain after Skleros' fleet interrupted grain shipments to Constantinople. The city was very vulnerable to blockade. Erotikos, his elite troops, the city garrison, and Nicaean nobles all faced either starvation or surrender to the rebels, neither alternative being a positive outcome. However, Erotikos filled the granaries with sand. On top of the sand, he ordered some grain spread so the granaries looked full. Then, he brought a prisoner rebel officer and showed him the granaries. Erotikos told the prisoner that although they had supplies enough to last two years, he really supported Skleros' cause. If Skleros, he went on, would agree to let him and his troops leave the city, they would surrender Nicaea and go to Constantinople to build support for Skleros. He freed the prisoner who immediately told Skleros about the offer. Skleros agreed to the terms. Erotikos, his elite troops, the city garrison and some nobles marched away and Skleros entered the city. He soon found out that Erotikos had made him a fool and was very angry. Nevertheless, it was too late.

The Patrician's escape from Nicaea with his troops was clever but a retreat is no victory. The Emperors and *parakoimomenos* faced a difficult problem: while the Greek fire fleet repelled the naval threat, they needed a powerful weapon to push Skleros away. Such a weapon was available but they thought it best not to use it unless necessary. Now it was necessary. Bardas Skleros achieved eminence by his defeat of Bardas Phocas during the reign of John I Tzimiskes. Bardas Phocas' father and brother had renounced the easy banishment offered by John I and were blinded and locked up but Bardas was merely banished to Chios as monk in monastery. Here was the weapon to undo Bardas Skleros. Phocas had no love for Skleros but still held the respect and allegiance of many important people of the eastern *themata*. True, he might attempt to become the 'military' emperor once he defeated Skleros but, if worse came to worse, such an emperor was better if he was the court's choice. Bardas Phocas received the imperial summons probably without too much surprise. He promptly appeared at court, took the oath of loyalty to the emperors, received back his estates, and received the title Magister along with the post of Domestic of the Scholae. Selecting men for an elite unit of cavalry, Bardas Phocas set out to overthrow Bardas Skleros.

The Civil War in the East IV: Bardas Phocas

Moving his small force to the Thracian side of the Dardanelles, Phocas crossed to Abydos where he drew the attention of Romanus Skleros and his forces that were blockading Abydos. With that, Phocas withdrew back to the Thracian side of the Dardanelles and counter marched past Constantinople to the northern part of the Bosporus. Here he managed to cross to Asia without Skleros' forces knowing anything about it. Moving by night and keeping out of sight by day, Phocas soon reached the fortress city of Caesarea. The leaders in the city received Phocas and his mission with enthusiasm. The Magister Eustathios Maleinos, a local magnate, and Michael Bourtzes, who had been Duke of Antioch, both changed sides and threw in their lot with Phocas. Phocas began gathering an army, collecting those who had fought with Peter the *stratopedarches*, and new recruits eager to fight under the banner of House Phocas. Once the force was organized and armed, Bardas Phocas led them west to the fortress city of Amorion. News of Phocas' seizure of Caesarea quickly reached Skleros in Nicaea. He understood that he faced a challenge in Phocas unlike the court eunuchs and careerists that he had swept away. With Phocas' occupation of the eastern districts, Skleros could easily find that he was isolated from supplies and support. He immediately mobilized his main army and marched toward inner Asia Minor.

The strategy that the Emperors and the *parakoimomenos* had implemented worked. Skleros was gone from Nicaea and he was chasing back to the eastern districts. He and Phocas could fight for years and the court at Constantinople would simply ignore the struggle. Skleros understood that he could not ignore Phocas because even if he took the City, Phocas could march against him as he had done against the current regime. Skleros marched to Amorion to destroy Phocas' forces. On 19 June 978, the armies met on the plain of Pankaleia. The troops were no more interested in killing each other than they had been at the start of Skleros' revolt. Skleros' heavy cavalry charged Phocas' line but Phocas' troops gave ground rather than stand and fight. Phocas was not interested in presiding over a blood bath of friends and relatives on both sides. As a living legend, Bardas Phocas rode around the battlefield. Some chanced to cross weapons with him but as more of a respectful homage than an effort to overthrow him. His soldiers did not panic but withdrew in an orderly and measured way. As his army dispersed, Phocas rode as rearguard, keeping Skleros' troops at a distance. A captain of Skleros' forces, Constantine Gabras, sought glory by capturing Phocas. He charged his horse with full might at Phocas, who turned his horse to see who was coming. Recognizing Gabras, Phocas turned toward him, letting him get to arm's length, swung his great battle mace striking Gabras on the helmet and unhorsed him. As Gabras lay stunned on the ground, Phocas turned away and trotted on after his soldiers.

Phocas led his main force to the fortress of Charsianon, a stronghold of House Phocas to the north of Caesarea. Many local magnates and common people came to pledge their support and simply to see this hero of battle. Skleros led his army toward Charsianon. He set up camp at the local hot springs and called on Phocas to fight. Bardas Phocas immediately led his household force out of the fortress and prepared to engage Skleros' army. While each side swirled around each other, trading blows and coups, Phocas rode across the battlefield, joining in combat with any who dared. Swinging his massive mace, he unhorsed and laid low any who tried to engage him. His problem: he had a strong loyal army at hand; he had a dedicated following spread throughout the eastern districts. If his followers killed large numbers of Skleros' followers, the resulting feuds would last generations and weaken the position of the eastern houses in their dealings with Constantinople. Rather than engage in all out combat, Phocas left his secured fortress and rode off further east leaving the field, for the moment, to Skleros. He went to David of House Bagrationi, Prince of Tao-Klartjetie. The Prince received Phocas as a friend, recalling the time when Phocas was Duke of Chaldia, the neighbouring Byzantine district. He gave Bardas Phocas a strong cavalry force unit under the command of John Tornik (Tornicius), a soldier monk. (Tornik was to end his days at the Georgian monastery, Iviron, on Mt Athos.) This force would willingly kill Skleros' men and would not incite local blood feuds.

Soon, Phocas returned to the eastern districts around Caesarea with his reassembled army. He marched against Skleros' camp nearby. Skleros immediately mobilized his force and marched out to meet Phocas' force. The basic situation had not changed. Neither army was willing to enter into real battle. When the armies engaged, they swirled and twisted about, some warriors choosing to exchange blows, others displaying their riding dexterity. Judging the time right, Bardas Phocas gave spur to his mount and rode into the milling mass, straight through Skleros' forces, who gave way in consideration of Phocas' reputation as a mighty warrior. He and his massive mace challenged Skleros. Resolving a battle and a political struggle by a champions' single combat offends modern sensibilities. Many current historians do not believe Skylitzes' narrative of the end of this war in the East. We need, however, to look at a number of specific circumstances in this war between Bardas Phocas and Bardas Skleros: while the struggle, in this instance, started because Skleros was aiming at the throne in Constantinople, the actual prize was primacy among the eastern houses who dominated the eastern *themata*. If Skleros achieved his objectives, this would diminish the power of the House of Phocas. If Bardas

Phocas prevailed, then the House of Phocas would dominate the eastern section of the empire and, in the fullness of time, might regain the throne. The question for the eastern soldiers was simple: who was the better man. Since they all were warriors, the answer to this question was equally simple: let the mightiest warrior prevail. When Phocas charged Skleros, the would-be emperor held his ground and returned blow for blow. Soldiers from both sides stopped moving and watched the combat between the heroes. Skleros' great sword blade sliced off the bridle and ear of Phocas' horse. Phocas returned the blow with his massive mace, striking Skleros' helmet full on, knocking Skleros senseless so that he just managed to stay mounted by grabbing his horses' neck. Phocas rode back toward his main force and took a position on a height, making the sign of victory.

Skleros' men brought him to a spring to wash his wounds. His horse, a magnificent creature called the Egyptian was frightened and in pain; he escaped his handler and raced through Skleros' lines. Skleros' soldiers, believing their leader slain, began to disperse, each going from the battlefield. Phocas, on the height, saw Skleros' army breaking up. He ordered his solders to advance to gather up prisoners. He also sent his mercenary unit forward, with instructions to eliminate certain of the rebels who might prove dangerous in the future. Groups of the rebel forces tried to cross the Halys River but the currents caught many. Skleros was taken by his close companions off the field (did Phocas really want to deal with him?) and across the border to the Amir Marwanide. Reorganizing his much shrunken fortunes, Skleros set up camp at Marwanide's seat, Martyropolis. He sent his brother, Constantine, with a letter for the *Amermoumnes* (Amir of Amirs) Adud ad-Daula at Bagdad. Skleros asked for support and an alliance, offering to serve the Buyid warlord. Adud ad-Daula did not refuse him but did not offer anything. Rather, he gave the impression that Skleros needed to come to Bagdad to see him face to face. Skleros and his party soon found that they were staying in Bagdad as honoured guests or valuable hostages; it was not quite clear.

Bardas Phocas sent an official letter to the Emperors and the *parakoimomenos* announcing the defeat and flight of the rebel, Bardas Skleros. The imperial government received the victorious general and rewarded him with honours. Learning that Skleros had sought refuge with the ruler of Bagdad, the Emperors sent a trusted personal servant, Nicephorus Ouranus, as envoy to the Amir of Amirs. Just what the terms suggested and offered remains a mystery, if they were not confused at the time. Certainly, the Emperors did not want to see Skleros again, at least for a while. They may have offered the revenue of the vassal state of Aleppo or perhaps the offer was the sovereignty of Aleppo. However, Ouranus also carried a patent of amnesty for Skleros and his followers if they would submit to the imperial court in Constantinople. When the Amir of Amirs, ad-Daula, found out about the patent of amnesty, he became concerned that the whole thing could turn out to his detriment. He had them all, Skleros and his followers along with Ouranus and his followers, incarcerated. The Amir soon released Ouranus but Skléros and his men remained in tight and uncomfortable confinement. Meanwhile, a group of Skleros' followers who had escaped capture seized a number of fortresses in the Thrakesion theme: Leo Aichmalotos, Christopher Epeiktes and Bardas Moungos took Armakourion and Plateia Petra, from which they raided the countryside until they accepted amnesty in early 980.

The War with Bulgaria I

After he occupied Bulgaria, John I Tzimiskes divided the realm into a number of military districts. Some districts began with a theme structure and others were merely garrisons of occupation. The most developed districts were those of the Paristrion, the lands south of the Danube from its mouth to the Iskur tributary, including the fortress towns of Dorystolon, Pliska, Preslav, and Sardica. South of the Paristrion, over the Haemos Mountains were the rich Thracian plains in the theme of Macedonia. To the west of Macedonia and west by south of the Paristrion, were the ancient lands of Lynkestis, Orestis, and Epirus. Under the Later Roman Empire, these lands were in the provinces of Macedonia, Epirus, and Dardania as part of the well ordered imperial administration. However, with the collapse of the Danube frontier during the reign of Maurice (582–601), Phocas (602–610), and Heraclius (610–641), these lands became home to communities of clan farmers and tribal herdsmen. The old road, the Via Egnatia, reaching from the Adriatic to Constantinople, ran through the middle of this area maintaining some elements of urban structures, but just beyond the road the world was little different from what it was before the Romans. Here, John Tzimiskes' conquests were superficial at best. After John died, a strong anti-Byzantine movement swept across this land. Leaders of this movement included the four sons of a Count Nicholas, perhaps a Bulgarian official under Tsar Peter.

The four brothers, called the *Cometopuli*, 'Sons of the Count', were David, Moses, Aaron, and Samuel. Brigands killed David early on; Moses died fighting the Byzantines; and Aaron dealt with political matters. Samuel was a charismatic valiant warrior who constantly took the fight to his enemies, the Byzantines. From their base in the region of Ohrid and Prespa, Samuel's forces spread out, pushing away any Byzantine forces in front of him, slowly consolidating a new Bulgarian realm. Shortly after John Tzimiskes died, the two sons of Tsar Peter, Boris and Romanus, eluded their guards and left Constantinople. Frontier guards killed Boris, thinking he was a Byzantine but Romanus, whom the Byzantines had castrated, found a welcoming reception. Romanus could not become Tsar because of the castration but remained an honoured figurehead.

While the war with Skleros occupied the time and resources of Basil II and Constantine VIII, anti-Byzantine war bands spread out from Ohrid and the Prespa lake country raiding manors and occupying as much territory as possible. Many of these bands recognized Samuel as their ultimate leader. The bands swept through valleys and mountains, north to the Morava River and east to the valleys of the Vardar and Aliakmon Rivers. The bands reached the Iskur River and seized Sardica. They also blockaded Thessalonica, and raided settlements in Thessaly, Hellas and the Peloponnese. Samuel took Larissa in Thessaly from which he took the relics of St Archillios, bishop of Larissa during the reign of Constantine I, and translated them to the church he was building near his palace at Prespa. With the conclusion of the war with Skleros, the Emperors and their advisors decided that they needed to end the Bulgarian threats to Thessalonica and the Paristrion. The question of who should command the army in the west was resolved with the decision that Basil II, now in his late twenties, would become the 'military' emperor. Basil had already demonstrated the determination and dedication needed to be a forceful emperor. No longer would he depend on overly powerful subordinates to manage his armies.

Basil organized his army to suit the conditions of the country in which he planned to operate. His elite Immortals, mainly Armenian, were mounted but the rest were infantry, consisting of select *tagmata* soldiers reinforced by the western *themata*. His chief subordinates were the Magister Leo Melissenos, who was in charge of logistics along with the forward bases and the Domestic of the West, Stephen the Short. In high summer, 986, Basil advanced into Bulgaria north of the Rhodope Mountains to follow the Hebrus River (today the Marica River). The Emperor marched to the north of Sardica, planning to blockade the fortress town against reinforcements coming from Ohrid. He set up an armed camp at Stoponion, planning to storm Sardica from that vantage point. However, he understood that there were Bulgarian forces spread through the hills and valleys nearby, so he sent solders out to ambush the Bulgarians. Basil believed his plans were succeeding when suddenly, in the middle of the night the Domestic Stephen came to the imperial tent and upset everything. An elaborate cover story obscures our understanding of what went on, a cover story that is clearly contemporary with the events. The story tells that when the Domestic Stephen came at night, he informed Basil II that Leo Melissenos was marching on Constantinople to seize power. He advised Basil to immediately break camp and return to the capital. In reality, the Domestic probably told Basil that an overwhelming force of Bulgars was about to attack the Byzantines and cut them off from their communications. Certainly, there was a failure of strategy and intelligence as the sequel showed. Basil II did immediately break camp. Samuel and his Bulgarian army attacked just as the Byzantines started out and swept them away, captured the camp, the imperial tent, and the imperial insignia. Basil II and his Immortals bodyguard escaped on horseback, winding through the valleys and mountains with the Bulgarians in pursuit. The Emperor and his guards managed to reach Philippoupolis. There, the story continued, Basil discovered that Leo Melissenos had not moved. On the other hand, perhaps, here is where the cover story originated. Basil II's first campaign was a sad failure.

References

The Civil War in the East III: Skylitzes 322–324; Psellus 1, 5–6.

On Greek Fire, see comments of the Princess Anna Comnena, XI, 10; modern understandings: J. R. Partington, *A History of Greek Fire and Gunpowder*: Baltimore, 1999, reprint, original edition, 1960, 'The Book of Fire of Mark the Greek', pp. 42–90; John Pryor and Elizabeth Jeffreys, *The Age of the ΔΡΟΜ ΩΝ*: Leiden 2006, appendix 6, 'Greek Fire', pp. 607–631.
      Of particular interest, see photograph in Pryor et al., figure 61, 'Greek' or liquid fire siphon pump built by Colin Hewes and Andrew Lacey under direction of John Haldon, p. 629.

The Civil War in the East IV: Skylitzes 324–238; Psellus I, 6–9.
      The late tenth-century series of civil wars comes to a culmination when the struggles ends up three sided: Skleros, Phocas, and the emperors. Skylitzes gives an extensive and detailed account, to a great extent from the point of view of the horse lords themselves. Skleros, particularly, receives sympathetic treatment at Skylitzes' pen. I imagine that a main source for his narrative is a member of Skleros' family or close supporter who lived through the wars. (Any supposition along these lines is simply conjecture when all is said and done.)

Nature of battle in this war: Holmes, in *Basil II and the Governance of Empire*, pp. 453–7, questions Skylitzes' account of these wars, particularly the personal dual between dual between Skleros and Phocas. I think this author looks for things in Skylitzes' text that simply aren't there. For a discussion of Skylitzes, as a historian see Appendix II Sources.

The War in Bulgaria: Skylitzes 328–331.

Cometopuli, 'Sons of the Count' and the rise of a new Bulgarian state: see Fine, *op. cit.*, pp. 191–197; Paul Stephenson, *The Legend of Basil the Bulgar-Slayer*: Cambridge UK, 2003, pp. 11–8; Paul Stephenson, *Byzantium's Balkan Frontier*: Cambridge UK, 2000, pp. 58–62.

Chapter 11

Basil II and Constantine VIII: Wars in the East and West II

The Civil War in the East Reignites

Basil II Porphyrogenitus knew that scholarly emperors survived defeat. That was because some victorious general was military emperor. Defeated military emperors did not last long. His defeat infuriated him. Clearly, he trusted in subordinates who did not do their job. The particular example was the Domestic of the West, Stephen the Short. The cover story served to deflect criticism from Basil but did nothing to change the fact of defeat. The idea of the story came from an incident in 985, when Leo Melissenos as Duke of Antioch was besieging Balanea. He heard a rumour that there had been a *coup* in Constantinople and withdrew from the siege. Basil, never easy going, ordered Leo to take Balanea or pay for the campaign out of his own pocket. Leo accomplished his objectives and retained imperial favour but a reminder was in order. Stephen, on the other hand, was deeply at fault. Hoping that the cover story would protect him, Stephen came to the Golden Hall expecting Basil, at least, to acquiesce with his remaining at his post. When Stephen appeared in the audience hall, Basil yelled that he was a great liar and the cause of great trouble. Stephen the Short, not one taken with humility, stood his ground, telling Basil that he had given good advice. Basil was so wroth that he leaped down from the throne, grabbed Stephen by the hair and beard and threw him on the floor. Presumably, Stephen now understood that he was unemployed. However, he was not punished either. Whatever happened, Basil accepted some of the blame. Further disaster struck. In October of that year, a strong earthquake hit Constantinople, damaging the Great Church, causing much of the dome and western apse to fall.

Basil's defeat and troubles echoed in Asia Minor. The eastern army commanders were upset that they were not included in the Bulgarian campaign, no doubt explaining that they could do the task so much better. In his estate near Caesarea, the magister Eustathios Maleinos assembled a group of commanding officers together and proclaimed Bardas Phocas emperor on 25 August 987. Their objective was not to dethrone Basil and Constantine but to establish Phocas as military emperor. However, they were not the only people looking to assume that office. In Bagdad, the Buyid Amir Samsam al-Daula became involved in a civil war with his brother. He decided that Byzantine heavy cavalry could destroy his brother's army. He called Bardas Skleros out of prison and negotiated an agreement by which he would free and arm Skleros' men and other captive Byzantines to the number of some three thousand. Once Skleros eliminated the Amir's brother, he and his men could return to the Byzantine Empire but Skleros would act favourably to the Amirs' interests in the future. The Byzantine heavy cavalry easily overthrew the rebel force and killed the brother. Bardas Skleros and his cavalry returned to the empire. On arrival, they found Bardas Phocas claiming the imperial office. They began reminding people that Bardas Skleros was already emperor.

Bardas Skleros was ever the careful man. The situation could not be more confused. Basil held the capital, the bureaucracy, and was of the Imperial House. Phocas was a brilliant, driving commander but likely to go too far. Skleros himself, beaten down by his captivity, was the weakest of the three. He and his associates decided to play both sides of this game. Skleros' son, Romanus, broke away from his father and went to Constantinople, to pledge loyalty to Basil and Constantine. If Phocas lost, Romanus could intercede for his father. Indeed, Basil II did receive Romanus and made him an advisor. Skleros then sent a message to Phocas offering to support him if he agreed to share power after he won. Phocas, after some time, sent letters to Skleros accepting his support. Phocas offered to let Skleros control Antioch, Phoenicia, Coelo-Syria, Palestine, and Mesopotamia while he would rule the rest of the empire from Constantinople. The letters included Phocas' sworn oaths to uphold the agreements. Skleros trusted the oaths and agreement. He set out to meet Phocas at his base in Cappadocia. Once Skleros entered Phocas' camp, guards seized him, stripping him of the imperial regalia. Phocas sent him to imprisonment in his fortress of Tyropoion. Now, the Emperor Bardas Phocas was ready to advance on Constantinople.

Basil II Takes Control

Basil suddenly began to distrust his subordinates, not so much their loyalty as their competence. After the defeat in Bulgaria, he decided to change the way he had administered the imperial government and military. He had studied the military manuals that underpinned Byzantine tactical practice. He had watched the imperial government in operation for almost thirty years. Now, he was ready. By spring 987, Basil had removed important people from their posts and started major changes to the military organization. First, he removed the chief minister who had served four emperors, Basil the Bastard, the *parakoimomenos*. We need to look at this event carefully; Basil the Bastard was in his early sixties at this time and was ill. According to Psellus, just before he died Basil was emaciated and trembled ungovernably. These symptoms suggest a chronic disease that started years before. When powerful older men realize that their physical and mental faculties are fading, they become irascible and unpredictable. Basil had acquired vast holdings in lands and wealth. He had used these resources in the interest of the state and imperial family, of which he was a member. Since he was a eunuch, he had no heirs of his body. When he died, the property would revert to the imperial family. The Emperor planned meticulously. In one day, in one hour, Basil the Bastard went from powerful first minister to imperial pensioner and prisoner. Nevertheless, the former minister was still uncle and beloved father figure of the Emperors. They treated him gently. After they defeated Bardas Phocas, they send him to a comfortable exile in the Crimea where he soon died of the disease that was consuming him. His property added to the imperial treasury. The Emperors also reviewed all of Basil the Bastard's chrysobulls, looking at awards, grants, and decisions. If they still profited the empire or imperial family, they remained in force. If, on the other hand, there was no imperial benefit, the Emperors annulled them. Finally, Basil II decided to reform the monastery that Basil the Bastard had founded. This was the monastery of St Basil the Great. Basil the Bastard had built a magnificent building with great luxuries for noble monks. Basil II removed the luxuries, saying according to Psellus, 'he had made of this place of meditation, a place where no more than the necessities of life would intrude upon thought.'

Having taken the administration into their hands, the Emperors changed the appearance of power. Putting aside fancy clothing, Basil II dressed in simple everyday outfits but maintained an attitude of authority and competence. Later historians talked about the way Basil dominated Constantine and relegated him to powerlessness. In some ways, this is very true but on the other hand, while Basil II led armies, handled diplomacy, and managed the military, we hear nothing of the affairs of the City. Here is where Constantine did his work. He did it so well, enjoying the beauty of displays, the delights of bathing, the excitement of gambling, that later historians heard nothing. Like Louis XIV's revels at Versailles, Constantine used social events to manage the city while his brother defended and strengthened the empire. The two brothers were very close from their infancy; they always agreed.

Beset as he was by military pressures in the Balkans and by revolt in Asia, the Emperor Basil needed allies. During the wars of Tzimiskes, the Rus warriors had impressed the young Emperor. He saw in them the solution to a number of problems. The question was how to approach them? One of the sons of Svyatoslav, Vladimir, now ruled the Rus from his main base at Kiev. He had firmly held power since 980. Evidently, during a dispute over the fortress city of Cherson in the Crimea, Basil and Vladimir opened contact with each other. Together, they found common ground on which to build a firm alliance in September 987. Later tradition tells us that Vladimir desired to improve the life of the Rus folk. He had sent envoys to the main religious groups near the Rus lands. They investigated Islam, Latin Christianity, and the Byzantine Church. Vladimir, the tradition continues, was most impressed with the Byzantine Church. He requested that Basil II send him missionaries and a Byzantine princess to be his wife. Basil responded by sending his sister, Anna the *Porphyrogenita*, and the Bishop Theophylaktos with a large staff to Kiev in 988. Vladimir received baptism on Epiphany and the multitude of Kiev on Pentecost. Vladimir married Anna in the summer. In return, the Grand Prince dispatch a *družina* of six thousand armed and trained men along with the right to hire more as he needed. They arrived in spring 988.

Here, we may stop a moment and consider Princess Anna. She was about twenty-six years old in 988, rather old in Byzantine society for a first marriage. Usually an imperial princess married a member of a powerful family allied to the Imperial House or a high bureaucrat at fourteen or so. Since a humble retiring manner was not a characteristic of the Imperial House, there is an interesting question about what Anna was doing in her early adult years. This is unknown but whatever she was doing, the Emperors had no problem sending her to Vladimir. Perhaps she gave her favours too freely or maybe she wanted to be a nun. While tradition tells us that she dreaded going to Kiev, it is also possible that she preferred being the queen of a barbarian court than a fixture in a gilded cage in Byzantium. She had at least two children by Vladimir and lived another twenty-three years. We need to note whatever the case may be here, that the conversion of the Rus is the most important event of Basil II's reign because of the future developments that came out of that event.

Of more immediate importance, the six thousand soldiers received by the Emperor changed the military structure of the empire. Basil organized them in a single *tagma*, eventually called by the Norse-Germanic term, *vár* (vow of fidelity), and *várar* (plural) thus, Proto Norse, *váringr*, hence Varangian Guard. Basil II paid the Varangians well, saw to promotions, and awarded fine pensions. They were heavy infantry, well armoured and bearing a long shafted axe as their primary weapon, but also swords and maces. They trained to fight as tight units; able to break through opposing infantry; able to withstand even heavy cavalry. Recruited outside the empire, their only loyalty was to the person of the emperor. Their reward was good pay and status. If any one of them failed to meet the standards of the emperor, he no longer had employment. Basil II's new *tagma* significantly strengthened the Emperor's position in the matrix of Byzantine society. Basil personally practised manoeuvring their tactical units. No longer was he at the mercy of over powerful subjects who could subvert soldiers' loyalties or, given his control over conditions of service, was he at the mercy of his own guard. In many ways, the emerging Varangian Guard was similar to the slave soldier systems in the Muslim lands. Now, the Emperors were ready to attack their enemies and establish their unquestioned authority.

The Emperors End the Civil War in the East

After he imprisoned Skleros, Phocas was ready to assault Constantinople. In summer 988, he sent an advanced force under Kalokyros Delphinas to Chrysopolis, the town on the Asian shore opposite Constantinople. Phocas led his main force to the fortress town of Abydos. He blockaded the town and began to set up siege works. Once he captured Abydos, he would blockade Constantinople, and with his supporters in the City causing trouble, he would take the City and throne. The Emperors sent personal messages to Delphinas, pleading with him to withdraw from Chrysopolis, not to set up a military base threatening Constantinople. Delphinas had his men continue establishing a fortified base. At night, the Emperor Basil launched a fleet of transports, loaded with his Rus troopers, fully armed and trained. Basil personally led his men in the attack on Delphinas' camp while the rebel soldiers were at breakfast. Completely surprised, Delphinas' troops broke and ran, hotly pursued by Basil's Rus warriors. For the same reason Skleros had recruited Muslim soldiers to fight Byzantines who did not want to kill each other and Phocas recruited Georgians, so Basil's Rus made short work of those enemies in their power. Basil had Delphinas tied to a gallows set up where his tent stood and let him perish in the sun and rain. Basil imprisoned Bardas Phocas' brother, Nicephorus the blind, and dealt harshly with other noble prisoners. The surviving men, he recruited into his army.

Phocas intensified the efforts of his siege of Abydos but the fortress town held out because of the assistance and supplies delivered by Kyriakos, admiral of the fleet. The Emperors launched a counter attack against Phocas' supply lines by sending a fleet with the Immortals to Trebizond. The Immortals disembarked and attacked south toward Phocas' home base. Phocas sent his son to his Georgian allies who ably defended the bases under attack. At the news of Basil's successful attack at Chrysopolis, the Georgians withdrew. Basil spent the rest of the year training his new soldiers and ensuring that Abydos held out. In April 989, Kyriakos' fleet brought a heavy cavalry force, landing those forces on the coast near Abydos. The Emperor Constantine VIII in full armour holding a great lance commanded the cavalry. They took up position on the shore opposite Phocas' camp that was in the hills. Soon, another flotilla landed the Rus warriors with their long-shafted axes. Basil II led these soldiers.

Neither army was excited about the idea of a great bloody clash in which both sides were Byzantine soldiers, relatives, friends, and neighbours. When Phocas saw Basil II riding back and forth, marshalling his troops, he thought that a quick strike similar to his personal attack on Bardas Skleros some years before would give him victory. His advisors and astrologers advised him against launching a personal attack but Bardas Phocas was not one to turn away from a fight. Even as his face turned purple, he became dizzy, and his horse slipped twice: still Phocas persevered. Marshalling his personal bodyguard of heavy infantry, Phocas rode toward the Emperor's battle line. His infantry guards were all tall strong young Georgians who had no qualms about slaughtering their opponents. Surrounding Phocas on his horse, under one standard, the unit moved to the attack. Basil II, seeing their advance rode out in front of his army. Constantine VIII also rode out in front of the cavalry, brandishing his great lance. Cresting a small hill, Phocas suddenly stopped. He dismounted and sat on the ground. Both armies, facing each other, waited for him to get up and continue but he did not move. Eventually the Emperor Constantine and some men went to see him. Without a wound, he was nevertheless dead. Constantine took credit for killing him but the rumour quickly spread that Phocas was poisoned. Phocas' army broke up and dispersed while the Emperors' army moved forward scattering the Georgian bodyguards. They dismembered Phocas' body and took his head to the Emperor Basil II.

The Emperors celebrated a great triumph, marching their victorious troops down the Mese, through the forums to the Hippodrome. The officers and nobles who supported the revolt rode asses in the parade so the populous would know who was defeated. Only Leo Melissenos avoided this spectacle because he had readily accepted Basil's pre-eminence. However, in the east, when Phocas' wife received news of her husband's death and defeat, she immediately freed Bardas Skleros. Many who had supported his original revolt returned to loyally follow him again and many who had adhered to Phocas joined Skleros. His forces avoided direct combat with the imperial army using minor raids and ambushes to maintain their strength. However, the Emperors were not very concerned about this revolt. Skleros was nearly seventy; his son and heir, Romanus, was a favoured advisor to Basil II and not likely to switch sides. Skleros as emperor had no future. Basil II sent a letter to Skleros promising good treatment and the rank of *kouropalates* if he would submit to the Emperors. Skleros, reassured by his son that Basil II would honour the agreement, surrendered to Basil in November 989 at an imperial estate in Didymortika in Thrace. The Emperor sat on a throne in the imperial tent. The guards led Skleros on foot up the path to the tent. Skleros was a very tall man but aged. The guards on each side had to support him. Seeing him come up the path, Basil remarked to his court (everyone knows the story, says Psellus) 'He whom I feared and dreaded is now led to me.' Skleros had not removed his purple buskins, although he had no other imperial trappings on. Basil saw this from a distance, closed his eyes in annoyance and said, 'He must be clothed like a citizen!' Skleros caught the drift and kicked the buskins off before he entered the tent. The Emperor rose to meet him and they embraced. When a servant offered a cup of wine to Skleros, Basil took the cup and drank a little, in order to demonstrate that there was no poison. Basil appointed that estate in Thrace as residence for Skleros and his brother Constantine. Skleros died on 31 March 991 and his brother, five days later.

Basil II Attacks East and West

While the news of Basil II's victory at Abydos cheered his supporters in Constantinople, more news quickly followed, that the Bulgarians had just captured Verria (Berroea). The fall of this fortress town threatened Thessalonica's supply lines. The Bulgarian threat in the west was serious but Basil II was also concerned about the eastern frontier in the Caucasus. The defeat of his expeditionary force sent to Trebizond by the Georgian Prince of Tao, David, worried the Emperor. After the victory at Abydos but while Skleros was still in rebellion, he sent a strong force under the command of John Chaldia to deal with Prince David. In 978, Phocas, fighting Bardas, had surrendered the frontier districts of Phasiane, Harq, and Apachounis to Prince David in return for military aid. Since this was done on behalf of Basil II and Constantine VIII, the Emperors did not repudiate the transfer. However, because David subsequently supported Phocas against the Emperors, they wanted reparation. John of Chaldia reached an agreement with Prince David in 990, which the Emperors ratified: David would keep the lands surrendered to him in 978; he would receive the title *kouropalates*; but when he died all his lands, including Tao, would revert to the Byzantine Empire.

With the Caucasus frontier near settlement, Basil II collected and trained an army to fight the Bulgarians. Mainly a light cavalry and infantry force with a hard core of heavy infantry, Basil's army followed the recommendations of Nicephorus II's book on raiding warfare. In the fall and winter of 990, Basil recaptured Verria and slowly advanced toward Sardica, carefully pacifying the lands he occupied. Yahiya of Antioch described Basil's methods:

During four years, 991–5, Basil made war on the Bulgarians and invaded their country. In wintertime, he marched upon the most remote provinces in the Bulgarian territory, assailing their inhabitants and took them prisoner. During this time he stormed a number of fortresses, retaining some and destroying others which he thought he had not the means to hold.

Basil was not a military genius, a warrior conqueror like Alexander or, indeed, like Samuel. Rather, he was a careful, meticulous, martinet. His organization of manoeuvre and supply always meant that his force held an upper hand. His demand for exact drill and perfect equipment meant that his soldiers were always ready for combat. His soldiers complained to his face but the Emperor told them that these were the ways by which they would return home and retire on their own homestead.

Besides his incessant military campaigns, Basil II launched diplomatic offensives against Samuel's state. In March 992, he finally reached an agreement with Venice in which the Venetians would protect the Adriatic from pirates and enforce trade regulations in return for lowering tolls and easing regulations for Venetian merchants in the empire. In the same year, Basil, still at his Bulgarian base, made a treaty with the Serbs that brought John Vladimir, ruler of Dioclea, into Byzantium's orbit. Basil's war in Bulgaria slowly contracted the lands under Samuel's dominion but events in the Near East interrupted concluding the war. During the early 990s the Hamdanid Amir of Aleppo, under Byzantine protection, was under pressure by the Fatimid Caliph of Egypt, al-Aziz. Receiving the Amir's requests for aid, Basil II sent reinforcements to Antioch in 994. The Emperor ordered the Duke of Antioch, Michael Bourtzes, to go to the Amir's aid. The Duke advanced down the Orontes valley, without the precautions necessary for marching through enemy country. The Fatimid commander, Manjutakin, withdrew from his blockade of Aleppo in order to attack the Byzantine Duke. On 15 September 994, Manjutakin forced his way across the Orontes River, outflanking Bourtzes, and routing his army. The Duke made his way back to Antioch and sent messages to the Emperor that Antioch was now under threat. Another urgent appeal from the Amir of Aleppo quickly followed.

Basil was setting up winter camp in Bulgaria. Waiting until early spring, he gathered a strong force of cavalry and infantry including, along with his Rus troops, newly recruited Bulgarians. Within twenty-six days, he crossed the empire by forced marches from Bulgaria to Antioch. At the end of April 995, Basil II and his army of some 17,000 men were at the gates of Antioch. When the news of his arrival spread to Aleppo, Manjutakin lifted his blockade of that city and he returned to Damascus. Basil received the thanks and homage of the Amir of Aleppo. He then turned south and led his army to Rafaniya and Emesa, continuing south as far as Tripoli, burning and pillaging. After his massive raid, Basil brought his army back to Antioch. He appointed Damian Dalassenus to replace Michael Bourtzes as Duke. Basil II ordered the new Duke to continue the annual demonstration of force, then, after installing a garrison in Tortosa, he returned to Constantinople. In less than six months, Basil II secured the eastern lands.

References

The Civil War in the East Reignites: Skylitzes 331–6; Psellus I 5–9.

Basil II Takes Control: Psellus, 1, 19–21.
Basil the Bastard *parakoimomenos*, see John Wortley, *Skylitzes*, p. 318, note 92; OBD, 270.

Anna Porphyrogenita and the Varangian Guard: Wortley, *op. cit.* p. 319, note 100; *Russian Primary Chronicle*, pp. 109–112; Janet Martin, *Medieval Russia 980–1584*: Cambridge UK, 2nd edition 2007, chapter 1, section 'Conversion to Christianity'; Raffaele D'Amato, *The Varangian Guard 988–1453*: Osprey, 2010, pp. 6–7.

Basil II's methods of government: John Skylitzes' *Synopsis* is the main narrative source for the reign of Basil II and Constantine VIII. The text appears to me to be pretty much what it purports to be, a compendium of information about past events collected by the author and presented in as straightforward a manner as possible. He can make mistakes, confuse his narrative, and be unclear but the text he presents has no hidden agenda or purposeful fictions. Holmes' *Basil II and the Governance of Empire* presents a different interpretation. This author parses the text to develop a 'revisionist' understanding not so much of Basil's rule but of inadequacies of Skylitzes' text.

The Emperors end the Civil War in the east: Skylitzes 336–9; Psellus 1, 12–18.

Basil II Attacks East and West: Skylitzes 339.

Basil's eastern campaigns: J. R. H. Jenkins, 'The Amorians and Macedonians 842–1025', *The Cambridge Medieval History, IV: The Byzantine Empire, part I Byzantium and its Neighbours*: Cambridge UK, 1966 (H. Grégore died while this chapter was in progress and J.R. H. Jenkins finished the work) pp. 181–2.

Chapter 12

Basil II and Constantine VIII: Basil Sets the East in Order

Basil II Breaks the Great Eastern Houses

A fter his victories in northern Syria, Basil began his return to Constantinople. Before moving on to the main routes to the City, however, he decided to inspect the peoples and lands of the eastern parts of the empire. What he found, he did not like. Illustrating Basil's investigation was the story of his reception at the estate of the old rebel, Eustathios Maleinos. The Emperor found that Maleinos' holdings occupied a significant amount of land in Charsianon and Cappadocia and that, the best land. Maleinos appeared almost as an independent prince and clearly, he was not alone. The great eastern houses had taken over as their own property vast tracts of land originally dedicated to soldiers' property or imperial estates. Basil II had suspected this and now he knew that a main reason he could not depend on the *themata* armies was that the soldiers were no longer citizens of the empire but rather subjects of local princes.

The Emperor decided to uproot these houses. He issued an edict on 1 January 996 that required each property owner to submit documentary proof of his title to all the land he occupied. If he could not satisfactorily demonstrate his right to the property, previous owners or their heirs could file suit for restitution without paying any compensation for the land or any improvement placed upon the land. While previous emperors had issued such orders before, Basil II's decree was significantly different because he revoked the established forty-year statute of limitations on property recovery. In the decree, Basil also restated with emphasis, the ban on gifts of lands to the Church. Viewed by the imperial government as a tax dodge, the Church was not supposed to collect vast holdings of properties. In addition, the Emperor demanded proof that those who occupied imperial estates had legal reason to do so. The decree made the case that all titles to imperial properties went back to the time of Caesar Augustus and any grants from the imperial properties was the product of corruption. Moreover, property owners who depended on documentation issued in the years 976–85, which would be in the name of the *parakoimomenos*, needed to resubmit the documents to the Emperor to ensure that his personal endorsement appeared on the document. Of course, since Basil II had recalled all of the *parakoimomenos*' official documents during the time of rebellion, many of the former rebel's title would not have such endorsement.

The effect of Basil II's decree was hard on the eastern houses. Maleinos lost all of his lands and his freedom for life. The House of Phocas lost vast holdings. Real poverty descended on some houses. Others ended up with only soldiers' holdings. Basil had no qualms, he said that the members of houses that became poor were an example, '... so that the powerful may take note of it and not leave this sort of inheritance to their children'. Not quite satisfied, Basil II issued further decrees in 1003–4 that established the principle that the amount of taxes assessed to a community be paid by the larger property holders in that community if the lesser owners were unable to pay. This fell heavily on the Church and monastery lands. Basil also supported the practice of charistikion (*charistike dorea*, donation) by which the financial management of a monastery and its property was granted to a layman. This had the result of channelling resources from the Church to the laity and thus allowed the state to tax the monastery. In 996, Basil appointed a member of the laity, the physician Sisinnios, as Patriarch. Sisinnios tried to protest the application of charistikion by the Emperor but Basil rebuffed him. His reign lasted only three years and in 1001, the Emperor appointed Sergios II. This Patriarch protested Basil's legislation in 1004 and 1016, but the Emperor simply dismissed these actions.

The War with Samuel Continues I

For the two years, January 996 through midsummer 998, Basil II remained in Constantinople, presiding over the applications of his legislation. During the time that Basil was in the east and remained in the City, Samuel rebuilt his forces and mounted an offensive against the Byzantines. Advancing against Thessalonica, his forces consisted mainly of light troops, infantry with some cavalry in a dispersed formation to raid and ambush. He sent a small but powerful force right up to the walls of Thessalonica, to draw the Byzantines' attention from his real objectives. The Duke of Thessalonica, Gregory Taronites, sent out his son, Asotios, with a reconnaissance vanguard and proceeded to follow him with his main body of heavy cavalry. Asotios and his light force collided with Samuel's vanguard; the Bulgarians took flight and Asotios followed. Suddenly, he found his force struck by a cleaver ambush and the Bulgarians captured him. Hearing of his son's defeat, Taronites led his force in a spirited attack against the Bulgarians. However, Samuel's forces remained in ambush. Taronites' force hit thin air only to fall into the Bulgarian trap. The Bulgarians killed the Duke and most of his soldiers. Taronites' immediate successor, John of Chaldia, likewise fell into an ambush and captivity. Samuel sent his forces further south, allowing them to raid and plunder the Theme of Hellas all the way to the Isthmus of Corinth. While some of Samuel's armies pushed against the Byzantines in northern Greece, others extended his powers in the north and west. The Byzantine client king of Croatia and guardian of the Dalmatian coast, Stephen Druzialav, died. Samuel occupied his lands, took Dyrrachium, invaded Dioclea, and took its prince, John Vladimir prisoner. Samuel advanced up the Dalmatian coast. The towns repulsed his light forces but he took hold of the hinterland, extending his control into Bosnia. He proclaimed himself Tsar.

The Emperor, during his negotiations with the Muslim states, had paid a ransom and freed his trusted favourite, Nicephorus Ouranus. To recover from the military collapse near Thessalonica, Basil II sent out Ouranus as Duke with a force of heavy infantry and cavalry. In late 997, Samuel and his forces continued to raid the Theme of Hellas and even into the Peloponnese. Operating from the firm base of Thessalonica, Ouranus led his force across the Olympic range and marched to Larissa. Information came telling him where to find Samuel and his men. Deciding that he needed a swift offensive, Ouranus set up an advanced base at Larissa, which protected his baggage and moved quickly by forced marches across Thessaly, the plain of Pharsalus, and the River Apidanos. He set up a fortified camp on the banks of the river Spercheius, opposite to where Samuel had already set up camp. Rain was falling heavily and the River Spercheius was in flood. Samuel believed that he was safe from attack. Ouranus, however, sent scouts up and down the river, looking for a possible ford. At night, he awakened his soldiers, quietly had them arm themselves, and led them to a crossing. They attacked Samuel's camp with the Bulgarians still asleep. The Byzantines killed very many and the rest fled. The prisoners the Bulgarians had captured, they freed. The great amount of plunder the Bulgarians had collected, they seized. Samuel and his son Romanus were both wounded in the attack but they played dead until they could escape, running into the mountains. They fled through the Aetolian Mountains, crossed the Pindus range and found safety in Bulgaria. Ouranus returned in triumph to Thessalonica.

Basil decided that the time had come to launch major offensives against the Bulgarians. He used both diplomatic and military forces. Since the collapse of the Croatian kingdom with the death of Stephen Druzialav, Basil had started negotiations with the Doge of Venice for the Venetians to assume the protection of the Adriatic and Dalmatian Coast. During 997–8, Giovanni

Orseolo, eldest son of the Doge, Peter II, remained in Constantinople to hammer out the agreement. They concluded the treaty in 998, with Orseolo returning to Venice with the treaty and the promise of an imperial princess bride. During that time, the situation in the Adriatic began to change. When Tsar Samuel returned to his capital, his daughter, Miroslava, told him, so the story goes, that she was deeply in love with Asotios, son of the Duke Taronites, whom Samuel held captive. She would kill herself, so she said, unless she could legally marry him. After the wedding, Samuel sent the couple off to Dyrrachium, to keep them away from the Byzantines. However, after some time, Asotios convinced Miroslava to escape from Dyrrachium with him and go to Constantinople. They made a connection with a Byzantine ship captain who took them to Constantinople, to the Emperor. Basil II received them with honours, raising Asotios to the rank of Magister and Miroslava to that of Woman of the Patrician Order. Asotios brought with him a letter from a leading man in Dyrrachium, Chryselios, saying that if the Emperor raised him and his two sons to the rank of Patrician, he would deliver the town to the Byzantines. He meaning, of course, is that his family would then be governors of the town. Basil readily agreed, with letters patent signed and sealed, the Patrician Eustathios Daphnomeles, accepted the homage of the town for the Emperor and awarded Chryselios' two sons the rank of Patrician, their father having died.

The Emperor led strong military offensives against the Bulgarians, beginning in 998. Setting up a base camp at Philippopolis, Basil's forces surrounded Sardica, occupying or building forts to blockade the town. This action put the main routes along the Iskur to the Danube and from Pernik and Radomir to Skoplje under Byzantine control. Basil's generals, the Patrician Theodorocanus and the *protospatharios*, Nicephorus Xiphias with a strong force, advanced beyond the Haemos Mountains and captured Greater and Lesser Preslav. By dominating the central position, the Byzantines could quickly move their forces to block any Bulgarian advance along the main routes from the Adriatic to the Black Sea, with the result that the Byzantines split the Bulgarian Kingdom. While his forces overran central Bulgaria, Basil II sent his fleet up the Danube, re-establishing the line of fortresses along the river to block any reinforcements that might come to Samuel from Hungary or the Patzinaks (Pechenegs). In summer 999, the Byzantines finally captured Sardica. In the year 1000, Theodorocanus and Xiphias reduced the Dobrudja, securing the lower Danube. By 1001, the Byzantine army had secured Macedonia and the Paristrion.

This campaign was a struggle of sieges and negotiations rather than a series of battles. Basil II's objective was to settle the land under Byzantine administration in order to have peace and order. He was not interested in displacing local potentates or eliminating local populations. Even those groups he removed to another part of the empire he did not treat as slaves but rather the imperial administration awarded them as citizens with lands and helped them to become taxpaying farmers and loyal soldiers. During the Emperors' advance north of Thessalonica, the Bulgarian governor of Berroea, Dobromir, who was married to a nice of Samuel, surrendered his town to the Byzantines and Basil rewarded him with a confirmation of his position and the title of Proconsul. The commander of the fortress of Kolydros, Demetrius Teichonas, agreed to allow Basil take the fortress if he and his men could leave with the honours of war. Basil agreed so those Bulgarian troops returned to Samuel while the Byzantine occupied the fort. The Emperor was ready to come to agreement with any Bulgarian leader who would recognize his rule. He even forgave some who returned to Samuel after they received pardon.

The Emperor Returns to the East

Following the Emperor's instructions, the Duke of Antioch, Damian Dalassenus raided Muslims lands once a year to maintain Byzantine prestige in the area. In July 998, during a march near Apama, the Duke fell into an ambush. The Muslims broke and routed his troops and killed him. Basil II saw the significance of this event. He handed the Bulgarian war to the new Duke of Thessalonica, David Areianites, taking Nicephorus Ouranus with him and began to marshal a force to go east. The Emperor arrived in Syria in September 999 with his faithful Rus infantry. Within three months, he cleared up the military situation to his satisfaction, although he was unable to reduce Tripoli. He appointed Ouranus as Duke of Antioch and took up winter quarters at Tarsus in January 1000. Basil had gone east, not only to avenge the death of Dalassenus but also to keep an eye on events in the Caucasus Mountains that appeared to be coming to a head. He waited in his Tarsus camp into April 1000.

News suddenly came that a disaffected party had murdered David the *kouropalates*, Prince of Tao. Basil was waiting for some such event and immediately began marching to occupy the lands that now fell to the empire. He marched northeast through Melitene, Hanzith, and Erez, settling various matters in those places while he was on his way. He met the assembled Armenian and Georgian potentates at the Hafjij fortress on the south bank of the River Phases. A riot broke out in which Basil's Rus warriors beat a group of Iberian soldiers. While the Emperor deplored the needless violence, he could not be but pleased with the outcome. Bagrat, King of Abasgia and Prince of Karthli led the Caucasian princes. King Bagrat's southern frontier ran along the lands of Tao, now imperial territory. Basil and Bagrat defined their joint boundary to the satisfaction of both; the Emperor then awarded Bagrat the title *kouropalates*. The Emperor inspected his new lands north of Lake Van and Tao, returning to Constantinople through Theodosiopolis. While Basil dealt with the Caucasian princes, Ouranus faced an upheaval that disturbed the Levantine lands. A leader of the Noumerite Arabs proclaimed that he was the Mahdi and his followers began plundering villages in Coelo-Syria. The Duke fought a number of battles against them and pushed them away from Byzantine lands. Peace descended on the Byzantine east in 1001 after Basil concluded a ten-year truce with the Fatimid Caliph.

Basil's War with Samuel Continues II

In the spring of 1001, Basil resumed his war against Samuel. Fighting short, sharp campaigns, his forces took the fortress towns of Verria and Servia. In autumn, he cleared Thessaly of Bulgarian forces. In early winter, Basil returned to Constantinople to finalize the marriage agreement between the Western Emperor, Otto III, and an imperial niece. Unfortunately, in January 1002, after the princess landed in Bari, she found out that the prospective groom had died.

In the spring of that year, Basil marched his army to the Danube. Advancing to the northwest, he invested the fortress town of Vidin in April. The fortress repulsed Basil's attacks, using large earthenware jars to extinguish the Byzantine Greek fire bombs. Samuel, thrust on the defensive by Basil's attack, mobilized a light cavalry force and raided deep into Byzantine territory. Out of nowhere, his forces attacked the imperial sponsored fair under the walls of Adrianople. Sweeping up an immense booty, he plundered plantations and villages before returning to his capital near Ohrid. Basil, however, did not react. Rather he settled down to besiege Vidin until it fell. After eight months, Vidin fell to Basil. In November, as he marched his army back to Constantinople, Basil overthrew every Bulgarian stronghold he passed. On his way, Basil and his army came to the Bulgarian fortress town of Skopje, which dominated the route down the Vardar to Thessalonica. He found, much to his surprise, Samuel and his light forces camped on the other side of the River Vadar. The rains had come and the river was high and swift. Samuel thought his camp was perfectly safe from any enemy because of the high water and bad weather. One of his scouts brought news to the Emperor of the location of a ford where the Byzantines could cross the Vadar. Basil launched an assault on Samuel's camp, and took it to the surprise of Samuel and his men. The Bulgarian warriors jumped on their horses, if they could, and fled with Samuel leading the way.

The Byzantines cut down those who failed to escape. Samuel's tent and a large amount of plunder fell to Basil. The fortress town of Skopje surrendered to Basil without incident. Samuel had appointed Romanus, son of Tsar Peter, brother of Tsar Boris, as governor of the town and Basil received him with great honour as he presented the town to the Emperor. Basil elevated Romanus, now calling himself Symeon, to the rank of Patrician and the office of *praepositus* (an office reserved for eunuchs) with a command at Abydos. From Skopje in the winter, the Emperor marched northeast to Pernikos. This fortress, under the command of Samuel's loyal lieutenant, Krakras, commanded the route from Naissos (Nish) to Sofia. Basil was attempting to cut Samuel's communications with the Danube. The Byzantines besieged Krakras' fortress but failed to take it despite numerous casualties. Basil gave up the effort as winter deepened and withdrew to Philippopolis where he disbanded his army and he returned to Constantinople.

With the conquest of Vidin and Skopje, Basil broke the back of Samuel's power. He cordoned off the Paristrion and Macedonia from Samuel's incursions; he blocked Samuel's expansion north of the Danube, isolating Samuel's kingdom from possible allies to the north. While Samuel had his son, Gabriel Radomir, marry a daughter of St Stephen, King of Hungary in 1000, the Hungarians would have to fight the Byzantines to aid Samuel. Moreover, the alliance with the Venetians came to fruition in summer 1004, when the eldest son of the Doge, Giovanni Orseolo, married the imperial princess, Maria Argyroulina. The Venetian fleet patrolled the Adriatic and blocked any major communications that Samuel might have with the west. For the moment, Basil could let Samuel simmer in his mountain fastness around the lakes near Ohrid. The Byzantine fortress along the Danube and Vardar confined Samuel to the east; the Venetians held him on the west and only more mountains were in the south. By maintaining pressure on Samuel's frontiers and allowing any defector to find a safe haven in the empire, Basil intended to strangle Samuel's empire. To think that the Byzantine Emperor would ever make a treaty with Samuel the hill bandit is to misunderstand Basil's concept of the nature of his empire. Armenian princes and kings who recognized Byzantine hegemony were within the imperial system. The spawn of Satan Muslims, as the Byzantines saw them, were an unpleasant fact that needed a pragmatic approach. Samuel was simply a despicable brigand. From 1004 to 1014, Basil allowed low intensity local warfare to harass Samuel, sending reinforcements as necessary but allowing local potentates to increase their holdings at Samuel's expense. All the while, Byzantine forces improved roads and fortified centres so when the war with the Bulgarians heated up, the imperial forces could strike swiftly and with strength.

Basil II and Constantine VIII Manage the Empire

In the first years of the second millennium, Basil and Constantine had personally ruled the Byzantine Empire for twenty-five years; they would continue to rule for another twenty-five years. This is a long reign for any medieval state. They both were elevated to imperial status as infants and had sat on the throne for almost fifteen years before their personal rule began. We need to recall the image that Liudprand, Bishop of Cremona, gives us of the two little boys sitting on a small throne behind Nicephorus II Phocas. We can be sure that the children made appearances during major holiday celebrations or important audiences. They understood the job of Byzantine emperor both as practical matter and as an image to project. The brothers were deeply concerned about any action they took at a given point of time; they were very careful in their decisions. However, neither brother cared about their future image. They did not encourage nor support any contemporary writer to record their history. Because of this, their image, as it appears to us, is the result of later memory and reminiscences of people who were not directly involved with the two Emperors. While these images certainly reflect the experiences of some, they do not reflect what really went on at the heart of the palace and camp, in which both brothers were private and secretive. This fact hides the reality of their personalities and the character of their rule. While we have followed Basil II, we need to consider Constantine VIII, in order to see the brothers' methods and motives.

As pointed out previously, the two brothers were brought up in the midst of Byzantine politics. Constantine was born two years after Basil, in 960. Romanus II crowned both brothers in 962. Only a year later, with the death of their father, turmoil engulfed the palace and the City with the strife that preceded the accession of Nicephorus II Phocas. The boys were then under the direction of the stern and formidable soldier emperor. Then, only about seven years later, this stern father figure met a gruesome end and his killer threw their mother out of the palace into a convent. Basil was about nine and Constantine was around seven. In 976, Basil at eighteen and Constantine at sixteen became the ruling emperors under the direction of their subtle and crafty uncle, Basil the *parakoimomenos*, and so began their graduate course in applied political science. Constantine immediately married Helena, daughter of Alypios. There is only one brief note of this fact, which is in the work of Michael Psellus. He says that her father was a City aristocrat and not from a great house. There was no obvious political advantage to the match. However, Helena was beautiful and loyal. We may speculate that this was a love match. Both brothers were interested in maintaining their power and tranquillity within the City. While

Basil fought wars against their enemies, Constantine entertained and pleased the City with the result that there are no notices whatever in the sources about urban unrest in Constantinople. Even more important, there are no notices whatever in the generally hostile sources that there was disagreement between the brothers. The Byzantine Empire enjoyed more than fifty years of governmental continuity and military success without great strain on the fabric of society. Clearly, the imperial brothers knew what they were doing.

The imperial administration ground on, the men and women of the City and the empire lived their lives growing and processing food, clothing, and goods, amidst the successions of births, marriages, and deaths. In 1009, the Fatimid Caliph al-Hakim ordered the destruction of the Church of the Holy Sepulchre on account, so some say, of the fraudulent practice of the 'Miracle of Fire'. Moreover, the Caliph ordered the destruction of many monasteries in Fatimid lands. Significantly, the Emperors did not react with war. In the next year, an unusually severe winter froze even the Black and Aegean seas. An earthquake that damaged buildings in Constantinople followed. The Emperors had the damage repaired as soon as practical. Besides the ongoing, low intensity war with the Bulgarians, disturbances ripped through Byzantine Italy. The Emperors sent reinforcements as necessary but for the most part, they let the Italian lands fend for themselves.

References

Basil II breaks the great Eastern Houses: Skylitzes 340.

For details about imperial protection for small holders, see Appendix III Land and Soldiers.

The War with Samuel Continues I: Skylitzes 341–4; see also, Obolensky, *op. cit.*, 132–3; Fine, *op. cit.*, pp. 192–7;Stevenson, *Basil*, pp. 16–8; Stevenson, *Byzantium*, pp. 58–60.

Battle tactics: Eric McGeer, *Sowing the Dragon's Teeth* gives an extended discussion of Byzantine battle tactics, see especially part II chapter 4, pp. 253–328.

The Emperor returns to the East: Skylitzes 345; see also, J. R. H. Jenkins, *op. cit.*, pp. 186–7.

Basil's War with Samuel Continues II: Skylitzes 346, 348; Fine, op. cit., pp. 197–201; Stevenson, *Basil*, pp. 18–25; Stevenson, *Byzantium*, pp. 66–72.

Basil II and Constantine VIII manage the empire: Skylitzes 347–8; Psellus, 2, 4.

Chapter 13

Basil II and Constantine VIII: Basil Battles in the Balkans

The War with Samuel III

B y 1014, the repeated Byzantine incursions and nibbling away at Samuel's lands had forced the Bulgarian Tsar back to his core holdings around Ohrid. Samuel had no force that could withstand the heavy Byzantine infantry and Basil's constant attacks, small as they might be, ground down his light forces. Samuel, grown old and feeling the claws of mortality, understood that either he had to have a singular victory or his state would collapse under Byzantine pressure. Gathering up a strong cadre of veteran and loyal soldiers, the Bulgarian Tsar led them over the Vardar River down the valley of the Struma River that connects the valley of the Vardar with the valley of the Strymon River. Here there is a long valley three to four miles wide, that from one direction provided a route to block the communications to Skoplje and pointed north or threatened Thessalonica to the south. From the other direction, there is a route to the rich plains of Thrace. Basil II had often used this route during his campaigns against Samuel's kingdom. Samuel's army constructed a strong fortified camp that dominated the valley and had room to hold strong fighting forces. In this way, he both blocked Basil's route of attack and opened routes for his own forces to hit the Byzantines. Samuel's camp backed up against the mountains to the south at the village of Kleidion. The rough ground provided sufficient cover for supplies and water to enter the camp even though under siege.

Basil saw the threat to the complete Byzantine strategic structure in the Balkans. He reacted strongly. Marching up the Strymon River to the Struma River, Basil advanced up the valley to Samuel's camp. Basil launched his Rus infantry against the fortified barricades fronting the camp but since the camp extended up a steep hillside, Samuel's combatants rained down missiles that broke the Byzantine impetus of attack. The casualties were so high that Basil gave up his attempt to take the camp by assault. The Byzantine commander of Philippopolis, Nicephorus Xiphias, advised the Emperor to maintain pressure on the enemy camp. While Basil stayed and drew Samuel's attention with his heavy infantry, Xiphias would lead a large force of light infantry to get behind the Bulgarians. After a number of days, retracing his steps out of the valley, finding goat paths up steep hills, marching through deserted landscapes, Xiphias found himself above Samuel's camp. On July 29, 1014, after agreed signals passed between the Byzantine forces, both Basil and Xiphias threw their solders at the Bulgarians. Ready to face Basil's Rus, Samuel and his men recoiled from Xiphias' attack in their rear, as the Byzantines yelled and showered missiles at the Bulgarians from above them. The Bulgarian force panicked, broke, and fled the camp. Basil broke up the abandoned camp and spread out, trying to capture as many prisoners as possible. Samuel's son saved the Tsar by grabbing a horse for his father and led him away from the defeat to the fortress of Prilapon on the way toward Ohrid. The Emperor destroyed the Bulgarian camp and took many prisoners.

Analysis of the Events at Kleidion

We must stop here and consider not so much the events of this day but how future Byzantines saw these events in sixty to seventy years and the effect this has on our understanding of Byzantine history. The difficulties revolve around Basil's treatment of the Bulgarian prisoners. John Skylitzes tells us that Basil took some fifteen thousand prisoners, who he ordered blinded except for one man in every hundred, they would lose only one eye. Basil ordered those blinded in only one eye in order to lead the prisoners back to Samuel. Further, the account continued, the sight so shocked Samuel that he fell to the ground and was dead two days later. This image is both distressful and awesome. Out of this image came the later legend of Basil the Bulgar-Slayer. However, while the propaganda value of the story of the blinding of the Bulgarians is high for many purposes of the future, for Basil II and his problems, the story meant something quite different. First, the number is faulty. Let us work on reconstructing the battle to see why. The area between the Belasica Mountains to the south and the Ograzden Mountains to the north, the Belasitsa-Osogovo Valley, maintains a consistent three and a half mile width for much of it length around Kleidion, the assumed site of the battle. Fifteen thousand men might be able to draw a cordon across the valley to block it but this manoeuvre would fail for two reasons: first, an attacker, even with significantly fewer troops can always break through such a cordon by feinting at one spot and concentrating at another. Second, in this distant and wild land, as it still is, the logistics to support fifteen thousand men becomes overwhelming and the defence of the logistical structures will become more important than the defence of the place. Therefore, there was no cordon across the valley and far fewer than fifteen thousand men. We need to look at the source text carefully.

The synopsis historian John Skylitzes (xvi, 35) says that Samuel intended to block the route through the 'long valley' at the 'key' (or is it to construct the 'key' to the long valley?). Samuel built a significantly wide fortification manned by able defenders to keep Basil out. I assume that Skylitzes' military narratives come from the reports filed in office of the Domestic of the Scholae in the Great Palace (see appendix on sources). Therefore, I assume that these narratives are technical in nature and use typical military shorthand descriptions. We need to consider this fortification. Since a wall across the valley is not a tactical possibility, Samuel's fortification was something else. Pre-gunpowder forces blocked routes by building a fortified base on one side of the route, high enough in at least one part to be able to scan the landscape in order to see any group approaching. We are familiar with such structures in medieval European castles, many of which blocked routes. These castles are both defensive, in that they block an enemy, and offensive, in that they provide a base from which forces could spread out to raid and plunder. Skylitzes says that the fortification was *significantly* (or very) wide. Romano-Byzantine camps were square or nearly so. Tribal camps were generally round. The reason for this was so that forces from the centre could reach any boundary as quickly as possible. (Romano-Byzantine camps were square to accommodate animal drawn carts that had to turn at right angles, hence the grid pattern.)

Samuel's camp was, however, noticeably 'wide'. Here, we need to look at the description of the Basil's initial attack: (Basil) *arrived and attempted to force a way in* (or *enter*). *The guards* (or *defenders*) *strongly resisted by killing and wounding the attackers by means of throwing from above.* This is clearly a tactical not a strategic description. Basil was attempting to force a way into the fortification, not into Bulgaria. The Emperor formed up his men against a face of the camp and pushed forward. However, a bombardment from above stopped his forces. This was not a wall, because if it was and Basil intended to take it by escalade, his force would clear the top using arrows. Rather, the Byzantines were pushing into something that rises by itself: hence a hillside. Now the situation becomes clear: Samuel's fortification was a camp built onto a hillside so only one face was accessible from the valley floor and the defenders were not holding the parameter but were staggered up the hillside, throwing rocks and sharpened wood missiles against the attackers. While, in normal circumstances, the attackers would simply form a shield wall turtle, here the broken ground, over which they must advance, broke their formation. This was how the camp was 'wide'. The fortification, probably a ditch and barricade, ran along the face of a hill and presented only one front to the attacker, the rest of the camp being inaccessible to formed units because of broken ground.

The strength of Samuel's fortification was his men's ability to throw missiles that caused wounds and death. We may be correct in assuming that these missiles were simply rocks thrown or slung at Basil's soldiers. A baseball pitcher can throw a hardball at around a hundred miles an hour and place that ball in a selected spot. A rock thrown with the same force would seriously dent a helmet or amour and easily kill a disabled soldier. Moving over broken ground would not only disrupt military formations but would expose vulnerabilities on armoured men's bodies. When Basil had captured Samuel's men, he had a number of options to ensure they did not oppose him again. He could kill some or all of them; he could cut off their throwing hands; he could blind them. Basil ordered them blinded but this was not as simple act as it might appear. The Byzantine blinded people using a number of methods but the preferred procedure were the use of red-hot iron to burn the eyeballs of the victims. Depending on the intent of the executioner, the blinding could be complete and final but also might just blind temporarily. Presumably, Basil's executioners made quick judgments in their actions, really blinding some, injuring others. Basil's war with Samuel was not a battle of populations or effort at genocide. Rather, Basil's objective was to turn the Bulgarian population into Byzantine taxpayers and soldiers.

This takes us to the question of numbers. Skylitzes gives the figure for blinded Bulgarian prisoners as fifteen thousand. However, following Herodotus' method, he offers the figure attached to a 'they say' rather than vouching for it. If the number of prisoners was fifteen thousand, then Samuel's whole army was at least twenty thousand men. The logistics of moving masses of men through the Belasitsa-Osogovo valley strongly disagrees with such a magnitude of men. The Byzantine numerical structure might explain this problem. Using the Classical Greek numerical system, the Byzantine expressed numbers with letters of the alphabet. Digits 1 to 9 were the first nine letters, 10–90 were the next nine letters, and 100–900 were a third set of nine letters with some unused but remembered archaic letters to make the numerical system of twenty-seven figures. Thousands resulted from making a stroke in front of and lower than the first letter-number (ODB 1501). So increasing a figure from hundreds to thousands was rather easy.

Basil II had a problem with the engagement at Kleidion. Since 976, the Byzantines had been fighting the Bulgarian insurrection. After 1004, almost thirty years later, the war finally simmered down into local and minor incursions. Now, however, in 1014, the war suddenly flamed up. The City had enough of the war and its taxes. Basil and Constantine did not look good, being unable to master a pack of stinking barbarians. While the battle at Kleidion was a fine tactical victory, the need for the battle was a strategic defeat for Basil. His long-term strategy ended up looking faulty. We may imagine that Basil actually captured some fifteen hundred of Samuel's toughest warriors. He blinded those who looked the most vicious, singing the eyes of the rest, and only blinding one eye of one out of ten to lead the rest back home. That way the prisoners, excellent throwers, would cease to be a problem. This was a way of turning fighters into taxpaying farmers. To convince the City that he was doing all that could be done in the war, the Emperor saw to it that the figure of fifteen hundred became fifteen thousand and increased the magnitude of his victory from a rather nominal tactical exercise to a great strategic triumph. No doubt, many knew the truth of the matter and the figure manipulation might appear as an 'honest' mistake but what made it real was the fact that Tsar Samuel died on 6 October 1014. Since Samuel was the heart and soul of the Bulgarian revolt, his death meant that Basil would eventually take over Samuel's kingdom. In the ever-popular methods of political theatre, *post hoc ergo propter hoc*, the blinding of the fifteen thousand soldiers directly caused Samuel's death. The Ever Victorious Emperor, the harsh and militant Basil II, conquered his enemy with harsh and brutal attacks. In some ways, this was true but Basil's winning manoeuvre was simply to outlast Samuel.

The Bulgarian War after Samuel

The battles at Kleidion did not end Basil's campaign. When Samuel began marching toward Kleidion, he sent David Nestoritzes, a Bulgarian chieftain, with a strong striking force to raid Thessalonica. At that time, the Byzantine general, Theophylact Botaneiates, was Duke of Thessalonica. With his son, Michael, the Duke met the Bulgarian raiders and smashed them, taking many prisoners and much booty. The Duke sent both prisoners and goods to the Emperor, while Basil was still involved with Samuel at Kleidion. After the Emperor cleared Samuel's forces from Kleidion, he advanced against Stroumbitza (Strumica FYRM) and took the fortress that dominated the area. By that time, Botaneiates had arrived at Basil's camp. The Emperor ordered the Duke to take his forces south, clearing out all the Bulgarian strongholds in his way and open the route to Thessalonica. Botaneiates marched through the Bulgarian lands toward Thessalonica without hindrance. Thinking that the Bulgarians had withdrawn from the route, he started to quickly march back to Stroumbitza. As his forces marched through the defile of the Kosturino Gorge, he fell into a massive ambush. Gabriel Radomir, Samuel's son, had surrounded Botaneiates' forces, blocking the pass at both front and rear of the Byzantine soldiers. They rained rocks and other missiles down on them. The press of men was so great that the army was unable to attack up hill at their tormentors. Most of the Byzantines died, unable to fight. Gabriel himself disembowelled Botaneiates with his spear. Very few soldiers escaped the trap.

When the Emperor found out about this defeat, he was very concerned. He turned his forces around, intending to clear the lands behind him. This is probably when he decided to blind and release his prisoners. Basil marched across the mountains to the east and came to the Bulgarian fortress of Melnik in the upper Strymon valley. This was a large series of structures defending a broad hilltop and surrounded by deep ravines and high rounded mountains. The local farmers and landowners had collected in the fort, not because they supported Samuel's kingdom but so they might avoid marauders in a time of upheaval. Basil understood their position and he sent an eminent chamberlain, the eunuch Sergios, to negotiate with them. The terms were simple: accept Basil's rule, surrender the fort, and Basil would support the current power structure with titles and honours. The terms accepted, Basil garrisoned Melnik and moved on. His next destination was Mosynoupolis, a stop on the way to Thessalonica. While he was at Mosynoupolis, Basil heard about Samuel's death on 26 October. Now, the Emperor and his advisors generated the story connecting together the victory at Kleidion, the maiming of Bulgarian prisoners, and the death of Samuel. Not necessarily an accurate picture of events, Basil's story nevertheless turned a rather grinding war of attrition war into an unforgettable conquest. Basil and his army then marched to Thessalonica. He clearly saw that Samuel's death provided an opportunity to mop up his kingdom.

In Thessalonica, Basil rested and reorganized his forces. Leading a small but very effective force built around his faithful Rus infantry, Basil marched north to Pelagonia, a fortress town near the Ohrid lakes. On his way, Basil ensured that his troops did not plunder the local inhabitants or destroy property other than burning Gabriel's palace at Voutele. From Pelagonia, the Emperor sent out detachments to occupy the fortresses of Prilapon and Stypeion. Basil struck deeper into the mountain fastness near Ohrid, his army passing a swift mountain river on rafts and inflated bladders to demonstrate that his army could go anywhere. Securing the centre of Samuel's domain, Basil marched to Edessa-Vodena, receiving the town into his graces. From there, he returned to Thessalonica on 9 January 1015. In the spring, he again marched to Edessa-Vodena because the leaders of the fortress town had repudiated the agreement that they had concluded in the winter. Basil laid the town under close blockade and made it clear that he was not going away. Negotiating with the towns people, the Emperor secured their surrender with assurances of personal safety. He transported the fighting men to the fortress of Boleron and settled in Edessa a unit of light infantry whose reputation for brutality was well known. Basil also oversaw the construction of two small but strategically important forts in the valley near Edessa.

He returned to Thessalonica to oversee the occupation of Samuel's kingdom. The Emperor received in audience a certain Roman the One Armed, who claimed to represent Romanus Gabriel, now Tsar. The representative claimed that Tsar Romanus wished to lay aside his title and become Basil's subject and administrator of Bulgaria. Basil trusted neither the envoy nor the offer. He reckoned that the centre of Romanus Gabriel's power base was near Moglena (Almopia), northwest of Thessalonica. The Emperor sent the Patrician Nicephorus Xiphias seconded by Constantine Diogenes with a strong army to Moglena. After he had settled matters at Thessalonica to his satisfaction, Basil followed. When he came, his generals had already plundered and destroyed the farms in the area and had begun to besiege the fortress town. Basil ordered his soldiers to dig a new channel for the river that flowed under the town walls. The diverted water exposed the foundations of part of the town wall. Shoring up the wall with wood blocks allowed the Byzantines to remove significant sections of stone. When done to their satisfaction, the Byzantines fired the shoring and down came the wall. The breach was so wide that the defenders surrendered, with prayers and lamentations. The Byzantines captured important members of Romanus Gabriel's court; among them was Domitianus Caucanus, a local potentate (the name *Kaukanos* is the title of the ancient Bulgarian *khagan*'s second in command), and Elitzes, the Tsar's governor of Moglena, along with a large number of veteran fighting men. The Emperor transported the fighting men to Asprakania (Vaspourakan), a frontier district to the southeast of Lake Van in Armenia. The Emperor had the remainder of the men mutilated so that the Byzantines could identify them in the future. The Byzantines destroyed this fortress town and other forts in the area.

Basil was settling the affairs near Moglena when Roman the One Armed came to his camp requesting an audience. With him was a bondsman of John-Vladislav, son of Aaron, brother of Samuel. The Tsar had killed his brother, Aaron, years before. John-Vladislav's bondsman delivered a letter to Basil saying that John-Vladislav had killed Romanus Gabriel and now held supreme power in Samuel's kingdom. John-Vladislav's letter announced that he recognized Basil as emperor and offered to pay proper respect to the empire. Basil officially accepted the letters, confirming his appointment of John-Vladislav as leader of the Bulgarian area of the empire with signed and sealed chrysobulls. In a few days, Roman the One Armed returned with official letters from John-Vladislav and his subordinate rulers of Bulgarians that recognized and accepted Byzantine hegemony. The Bulgarian leaders, captured with the fall of Moglena, also accepted Basil's majesty, including Theodore Kpachanes, brother of Domitianus Caucanus. In effect, the Bulgarian War was over. Basil and the Byzantines now had the job of pacifying the wild and lawless Balkan hinterlands.

References

The War with Samuel III: Skylitzes, 339, 341–2; Fine, *op. cit.*, pp. 197–9; Stephenson, *Basil*, pp. 25–6; Stephenson, *Byzantium*, pp. 72–3; Florin Curta, *Southeastern Europe in the Middle Ages 500–1250*: Cambridge UK, 2006, pp. 242–5.

Analysis of the Events at Kleidion: Skylitzes, 348–9; Psellus, I 32–3.
   Military histories need maps. But in our later day, we have something better. Following, say, Caesar in Gaul on maps is good; Google Earth is better. Here, you can see the area, the landscape, lines of sight, all sorts of things. Google Earth clarifies the events at Kleidion.

The Bulgarian War after Samuel: Skylitzes 353–5; Fine, *op. cit.*, pp. 199–211; Stevenson, *Basil*, pp. 26–31; Stephenson, *Byzantium*, pp. 73–5; Curta, *op. cit.*, pp. 245–7.

Chapter 14

Basil II and Constantine VIII: Basil Victorious in the Balkans and Asia Minor

Breaking the Bulgarians

Basil saw the utility of accepting John-Vladislav's submission but to him and the Byzantines, the tribal confederations of the Balkans remained just unruly hill bandits that required the benefits of Byzantine law, order, and management. When Theodore Kpachanes suggested that he and John-Vladislav's bondsman return to John-Vladislav and kill him, Basil offered them great rewards. Unfortunately, for them, John-Vladislav struck first, killing both Theodore and the bondsman. After reviewing the general situation, Basil decided that he did not need John-Vladislav's help to settle the Balkans. He had to launch only a few more campaigns in order to establish Byzantine administration of most of the area. Now, 1015, the eastern Balkans was secure, consisting of the imperial *themata*: Thrace, the Paristrion, Hellas, Thessalonica, Strymon and Macedonia. His tasks included extending control along the old Via Egnatia to Dyrrachium, securing the route to Skopje, and extending his control to Belgrade and Sirmium in the north to deflect incursions from that direction. The Emperor announced that John-Vladislav was untrustworthy, that he had gone back on all of his agreements, and that the Byzantines needed to subdue the lands. Basil mobilized his army of veteran Rus infantry and light cavalry. He advanced into the centre of what had been Samuel's kingdom, occupying or destroying any stronghold in his way. The Byzantines marched through the lands of Lake Ostrovos (Lake Vergoritis) into the plains of Pelagonia. The army crushed all resistance, blinding their captives. Basil occupied Ohrid, establishing a regional headquarters in Samuel's palace.

The Emperor then prepared to advance toward Dyrrachium because the western regions had erupted in turmoil. Under Samuel, Dioclea and the surrounding areas had remained peaceful under the direction of Vladimir, who was married to a daughter of Samuel. Vladimir and Romanus Gabriel also maintained good relations. However, after John-Vladislav killed Romanus Gabriel, he sent the Bulgarian Archbishop, David, to request that Vladimir present himself to John's court. The Archbishop gave Vladimir a safe conduct oath but John-Vladislav ignored the oath, imprisoned Vladimir and then killed him. After eliminating Vladimir, John-Vladislav tried to seize Dyrrachium and the surrounding lands but the town and hill people resisted his efforts. Once Basil had started for the western regions, he had to turn around because disaster overcame his forces in Pelagonia. When he had left the Pelagonian plains, he had left a detachment of soldiers under George Gonitziates and the *protospatharios* Orestes. As this force mopped up the area, an army of Bulgarians under the command of the renowned Ibatzes ambushed and killed most of the Byzantines. Basil marched back and set off in pursuit of Ibatzes but failed to find him. The Emperor returned to Thessalonica to plan his campaign for the rest of the year. He sent Xiphias with a strong force to take the fortress of Triaditza and then to go further on and take the stronghold of Boio (in the area of Sardica). He sent David Areianites with a force to the Strumica area to wipe out any resistance there. In a surprise attack, Areianites seized the fortress of Thermitza. The Emperor himself marched to Mosynoupolis, clearing out enemy forces as he marched. Pleased with his accomplishments in the Balkans, the Emperor returned to Constantinople in January 1016.

After spending the spring and summer dealing with business in Constantinople, Basil mobilized his Rus infantry and attendant cavalry in September. He marched out from the City and went in the direction of Sardica. Near the fortress of Triaditza, a Bulgarian force still held the fortress of Pernicus. Basil blockaded the fort and tried to break in but the garrison resisted strongly and repelled the Byzantines. For eighty-eight days, Basil maintained the siege, all the while plundering and laying the lands around the fortress to waste. He then gave up the siege and returned to Mosynoupolis. In spring 1017, Basil led his army out of Mosynoupolis and marched into lands not yet under Byzantine control. He besieged and took the fortress of Longos. From Longos the Emperor advanced to the fortified town of Kastoria. Finding that forcing the defences would cost more than he wanted to pay, the Emperor methodically plundered the area. At the same time, Basil had sent David Areianites and Constantine Diogenes to the plains of Pelagonia to plunder any locality that did not immediately accept Byzantine rule. The Byzantines collected a great deal of plunder on these expeditions. Basil divided the loot, a third went to his Rus troops, a third went to the Byzantine *tagmata* and *themata* troops, and the Emperor kept a third as the imperial share.

The Emperor received a letter from the Duke of Dorystolon, Tzotzikios, son of the Patrician Theudatos the Iberian. The Duke informed the Emperor that the Bulgarian potentate, Krakras, had organized a large force and joined with John-Vladislav. Krakras was trying to form an alliance with the Patzinaks, the nomadic tribes living on the shore of the Black Sea near the lower Danube. When John-Vladislav, Krakras, and the Patzinaks joined forces, they would descend on the Byzantine Empire. Basil was deeply worried about this possibility. He decided to clear the area to the west of Thessalonica and north of Thessaly, slowly concentrating his forces to meet the expected attack. He overthrew local strongholds and took the town of Berroea (Veris). Basil evidently sent secret envoys either to the Rus Prince Vladimir, his brother-in-law, or to contacts with the Patzinaks because all of a sudden they refused to deal with the Bulgarians. Concentrating his forces in the Pelagonian plains, having devastated the lands of any possible supporters of John-Vladislav, Basil descended on another of Samuel's palace fortresses, at Setena. This was a main depot for John-Vladislav's forces, holding a great deal of grain. Adding the supplies to his army's baggage train, Basil fired the settlement.

John-Vladislav's forces were hovering about. Basil decided to see if he could trap them. The Bulgarians avoided direct confrontations; they preferred hit and run ambush tactics. Basil sent out a strong force under Constantine Diogenes consisting of the western *tagmata* followed by the Thessalonica *themata* that marched in the general direction toward the Bulgarians. Scouts located the site where John-Vladislav and his men were planning to ambush the Byzantines. When Basil learned where this was, he leapt into the saddle, calling out, 'Every true warrior! Follow me!' He personally led his Rus troops towards the Bulgarians at the gallop. When John-Vladislav's scouts saw the imperial force charging toward them, they rushed back to their camp, crying, '*bezeite ho tzesar*' (Beware! The Caesar comes). As Basil advanced from one side, Diogenes gave the order and attacked from the other side. The Bulgarian camp and ambush broke up amidst panic and flight. John-Vladislav managed to escape with a group of his officers but his equipment and nephew fell into Byzantine hands along with two hundred of John's best warriors, complete with their horses and armour. The Byzantines had killed many of the Bulgarians and Basil had the nephew blinded. Basil had cleared the Bulgarian lands around the lakes to his satisfaction. He marched his forces to Edessa Vodena, dismissed his soldiers and marched with his Rus back to Constantinople, arriving there on 9 January 1018.

Making the Balkans Byzantine

With the coming of spring, John-Vladislav brought his forces against Dyrrachium. Expelled from the Bulgarian heartland, John-Vladislav was desperate to capture a new power base. John attempted to lay Dyrrachium under siege but Basil's commander, the Patrician Niketas Pegonites, brought the battle directly to John-Vladislav with a cavalry sortie. John-Vladislav fell in the engagement, his entrails ripped out by two Byzantine foot soldiers mixed in the melee. When Pegonites officially reported the death of John-Vladislav, the Emperor mobilized his Rus troops and set out to settle matters in the Balkans. On arriving at Adrianople, the Emperor met the brother and the son of the powerful potentate, Krakras. They immediately surrendered their strong fortress of Pernikos and thirty-five other fortresses that Krakras held. The Emperor received them with honour, granting to Krakras the title of Patrician. From Adrianople, Basil proceeded to Mosynoupolis. Here, he met envoys from the towns of Pelagonia, Morovisdos and Lipenios who officially accepted Basil as legitimate ruler. Advancing to the town of Serres, the Emperor received with honour Krakras along with the commanders of the thirty-five fortresses that Krakras was surrendering to Basil. After he received Krakras, Basil received Dragomouzos, Bulgarian commander of the area around Stroumbitza (Strumica), who officially surrendered the whole area. He also brought a prisoner, the Patrician John Chaldos, whom the Bulgarians had held for twenty-two years. Basil proceeded to Stroumbitza. David, Archbishop of Bulgaria, who carried a letter from Maria, widow of John-Vladislav, met him. She said in the letter that she would leave Bulgaria if Basil provided suitable residence and station for a queen. Basil indicated his agreement. Basil continued his march through the Bulgarians lands and received the submission of potentates and warriors.

Besides subduing the heartland of Samuel's kingdom, Basil sought to achieve defendable frontiers. The Danube above the Iron Gates remained a concern. The strategic fortress of Sirmium attracted imperial attention. Lost to the Byzantines for centuries, Basil sent his commander, Constantine Diogenes, to take the fortress. The fortress was very strong and beyond the Byzantine logistical web. Diogenes, however, planned to take the fortress by other means. He sent an official letter to the ruler of Sirmium, asking for a face-to-face meeting to settle some outstanding issues important to both of them. To prove his good faith, he offered to meet the ruler with only three attendants on a raft in the centre of the river. The ruler would also come with only three attendants and so they could trust one another. The ruler agreed and they met on a raft. Suddenly, Diogenes pulled a dagger out of his robes and stabbed the ruler with a jab to the heart. The ruler's army dispersed in confusion (no doubt aided by a few choice preplanned payoffs). Diogenes concentrated his troops and marched on Sirmium. The ruler's wife was distraught and accepted Diogenes' promises. She surrendered Sirmium and went to live in Constantinople. The Emperor appointed Diogenes commander of the fortress town. In Skopje, the Emperor appointed the Patrician David Areianites as *katepan* of Bulgaria, commander of all military forces in the Bulgarian lands.

As the Emperor marched past important and strong Bulgarian fortresses, the population came out and acclaimed him with processions and hymns. Basil marched back south, then turned right unexpectedly, and marched into Ohrid, Samuel's capital. The people of the capital came out to meet the Emperor with paeans of praise, clapping of their hands and acclamations. Basil seized the Bulgarian treasury. There were about ten thousand gold coins, not a very great amount, which the Emperor gave to his soldiers. Basil appointed Eustathios Daphnomeles governor of the city and its region and gave him a strong force to garrison the town. Soon, guards brought John-Vladislav's widow, three sons, six daughters, a bastard son of John, along with two daughters and five sons of Radomir Gabriel. Three other sons of John-Vladislav and Maria had fled into distant mountains. The Emperor received those of John-Vladislav's family who surrendered themselves in a gentile and benevolent manner. He then ordered all of them detained in safe places. Many important and powerful Bulgarians came to the Emperor to submit and accept his rule. His agents even brought in the commander, Ibatzes, already blinded. Basil had smashed Samuel's kingdom and now his only tasks were to stamp out embers and strengthen frontiers. Basil settled Bulgaria, setting up *themata*, large provinces, and self-governing dependencies. The heartland of Samuel's kingdom, around Ohrid, he organized as the province of Bulgaria. He confirmed the establishment of the province of Paristrion on the lower Danube, north of Macedonia and Thrace. He also established a strong military unit and theme at Sirmium on the upper Danube. Serbia and Croatia remained self-governing under Byzantine hegemony. Basil's treaty with Venice protected the Dalmatian coast.

The Blinding of Ibatzes

The story of how Basil's agents seized and blinded Ibatzes is instructive in that the incident illustrates Byzantine methods. When Basil instituted the Byzantine administration in the Bulgarian lands, Ibatzes left imperial territory and went to the mountains south of Ohrid where he found a refuge at a beautiful settlement called Pronista. Warriors who were not interested in submitting to the Byzantines collected around him. Soon, Ibatzes had dreams of reconstructing the Bulgarian Kingdom. Basil marched to Diabolis (Zvezde, Devoll District, Albania). Setting up a base near to Pronista, he wrote to Ibatzes, requesting that he come and surrender. Ibatzes responded to Basil's letters with respect but kept making excuses about why he could not submit at a given time. Basil came to believe that Ibatzes was playing for time to build up his forces. The Emperor told his governor of Ohrid, Eustathios Daphnomeles, that it would be good if the threat from Ibatzes disappeared.

The unspoken order was clear: Daphnomeles took two of his most able guards and, in anticipation of the Feast of the *Koimesis* ('Falling Asleep of the Virgin' Assumption Day in the western liturgy – 15 August), made his way to Pronista. Ibatzes celebrated the feast with a great banquet, not only for his neighbours but also for many people coming from great distances. Daphnomeles showed up with just his two attendants and told Ibatzes' guards to announce who he was and that he had come for the celebration. Ibatzes was amazed. Even though Daphnomeles was an enemy, Ibatzes welcomed him and received him with open arms. In the late morning, after Holy Service had concluded the celebrants retired to refresh themselves for the afternoon. Daphnomeles approached Ibatzes and told him that they needed to discuss a matter in private. Ibatzes thought that Daphnomeles wanted to join his incipient rebellion and so sent away his personal guards and taking Daphnomeles by the hand, he led him to a cul-de-sac in his garden where they could talk unheard. Daphnomeles, who was a large strong man, suddenly grabbed Ibatzes, gagged him, threw him to the ground and signalled his two associates to come. The plot was prearranged and they were just on the other side of the hedge of the cul-de-sac. The three bound Ibatzes and then blinded him.

Daphnomeles and his men hustled Ibatzes out of the garden and into the central palace building. Bounding up the stairs, his two men drew their swords and stood over Ibatzes while Daphnomeles stood in the loggia overlooking the courtyard. A mass of men came running into the courtyard, armed with swords, rocks, spears, and firebrands. They yelled for the Byzantines' blood, threatening to burn the building. Daphnomeles faced them from the second story loggia. He showed them that Ibatzes was still alive. He told them that he was an agent of the Emperor and was from Asia Minor. He was not a personal enemy of Ibatzes or of the Bulgarians. They could kill him, he continued, but then the Emperor would come and he would take revenge. Wiser older men in the crowd toned down the upset. Some then came forward and pledged loyalty to the Emperor. Daphnomeles took his prisoner and presented him to the Emperor who rewarded him with the command of Dyrrachium and all of Ibatzes' movable property. Ibatzes, the Emperor imprisoned.

Basil II Porphyrogenitus' Triumphant March

Basil II's reign carried him across the expanse of the empire fighting enemies both within and without the imperial lands. We should not forget that he was able to single-mindedly devote so much time and energy to these tasks because the City and its hinterland was in the hands of his brother, Constantine VIII, of whom little is heard because he did his job efficiently and without fuss. For the most part, Basil left the local powers in place when he took over an area. He readily accepted surrender of enemies. That renegades and people who went back on their words found harsh treatment is true enough. But Basil's problems in the Balkans was to protect the more settled imperial lands and the Paristrion from raids and subversion by the people of Samuel's kingdom who were coming from lands lost to imperial control centuries before. Patience and persistent paid off as Basil kept the pressure on until Samuel died and then took over his lands. That Basil's settlement lasted longer than a century demonstrates that he knew what he was doing. Once he completed the task of bringing peace to the Balkans, Basil made a tour of the imperial west, visiting places that had not seen an emperor in generations.

Basil marched to Athens to celebrate his victory in the Holy Church of the Virgin. This, of course, was the Parthenon, still the religious centre of Athens. The building had badly burned sometime in the upheavals of the third and fourth centuries. The expense of providing roof truss across the width of the building was beyond the resources of the restorers, so they roofed just the enclosed space of the building. A new interior colonnade came from a ruined building in the Agora. With minor modifications, the structure became a church. Basil came to Athens to worship in the Church of the Theotokos, the Holy Mother of God. The fact that was in an ancient temple was incidental to Basil. However, to us, at this distance in time from these events, the worshipping of a Byzantine Caesar in Pericles' temple is evocative of the continuity of Greek culture and traditions. From Athens, Basil proceeded to Constantinople. Here, he marched in triumph through the great doors of the golden gate, crowned with a crested golden diadem, his procession led by Bulgarians, including Maria, widow of John-Vladislav and her daughters along with many notables. The procession moved down the Mese to Hagia Sophia. There the Patriarch presided over a service of thanksgiving in which the Emperor, his court, and the people filled the church. By 1019, the Byzantines had stabilized their Balkan frontier.

Basil returns to the East

In the years Basil was fighting in the Balkans, centrifugal forces swirled around the eastern frontiers. *Kouroplates* Bagrat of Abasgia died and his son, George, refused to recognized Byzantine dominion. George seized Tao and Phasiane. Basil was fighting in the Balkans but he sent a fleet in 1016 to the eastern Black Sea, to the north of George's lands. After his return to Constantinople in 1018-9, Basil began organizing an expeditionary force for the east. Built around his faithful Rus warriors but augmented by select *tagmata* and *themata* units, he marched deep into Asia Minor in 1021. Because Muslim pressures were building across Armenia and Atropatene, the small kingdoms there began to look for ways to defend themselves. The master of Upper Media (Vaspurakan to the south of Lake Van), Senacherim, brought his whole family into the empire and surrendered his lands to Basil. The Emperor appointed him Patrician and *Strategos* of Cappadocia, in charge of the towns of Sebasteia, Larissa, and other fortress cities. The Emperor sent the Patrician Basil Argyros to rule Vaspurakan but he failed to gain the confidence of the inhabitance and so the Emperor removed him. Basil then sent the *protospatharios* Nicephorus Comnenus as ruler and he brought order and peace to the land. During these events, Basil led his forces through Taik deep into Iberia. There was a major battle at Lake Palakatzio in which Basil prevailed but did not decisively defeat George's army. However, George withdrew from Tao and retreated into his own lands of Abasgia.

George intended to continue fighting. He contacted Basil's generals, the Patrician Nicephorus Xiphias, now *Strategos* of the Anatolic theme, and Nicephorus, the son of Bardas Phocas. Basil was some sixty-three years old. Clearly, he was not interested in elevating Xiphias to higher command, and not in elevating Phocas to any high command. Moreover, the Emperor was now appointing eastern potentates to high command and his main forces came from beyond the empire. Xiphias and Phocas, encouraged by George of Abasgia, launched an uprising at Podandus in Cappadocia (Pozanti, Adana province in Turkey, just on the eastern side of the Tarsus Mountains). The time had come, they thought, for a new imperial regime. It was now spring 1022. Their plan was to catch Basil's army between their rebel forces and George's Armenian armies. Basil and his staff saw the position they were in: great danger stared them in the face. Resourceful and wily, Basil designed a plan to break the pincers about to close on his forces. The Emperor wrote two letters, one to Xiphias, and the other to Phocas. The courier delivered to each a letter without the other knowing that both were recipients. The letters promised amnesty and high office to the recipient if he would surrender. Phocas immediately informed Xiphias about his letter but Xiphias stayed silent. A few days later, the two rebels met together at Xiphias' suggestion. When Phocas came, Xiphias' men grabbed him and killed him. The date was 15 August 1022. Xiphias sent Phocas' head to Basil who displayed it to his troops. Basil dispatched Theophylact, son of Damian Dalassenus, to Xiphias with orders to arrest him and assume command of the Anatolic theme. The rebellion had collapsed and loaded with chains, Xiphias entered Constantinople in the custody of John the *protonotarios*. John had Xiphias tonsured and sent him to a monastery on the island of Antigonus.

Basil renewed his invasion of George's lands. Catching George's army near the Phasis River, Basil engaged them in a hard fought battle. Both sides suffered but neither decisively. The Byzantines killed George's commander, Liparites. George retreated deeper into the Caucasus and sent envoys to Basil offering diplomatic submission and an infant son as hostage to be educated in Constantinople. The Emperor promoted George as magister and turned to other problems. He forced John Smbat, King of Armenia to surrender lands around Ani to the empire. Basil then inspected the lands of Vaspurakan he had received from Senacherim. The Emperor proceeded to march through Cappadocia. He arrested those involved in the recent uprising, confiscating their property and putting them in chains for some time. Major exceptions included the Patrician Pherses: a Georgian connected with David the *kouropalates*. Basil ordered him executed because he was one of the first advocates of rebellion and had a number of imperial officials executed, killing an imperial eunuch with his own hand. Also, an imperial chamberlain, working with Xiphias, had tried to poison Basil. Basil had him fed to lions.

Basil's Reign Ends

Vladimir, Prince of Kiev, died in 1015, his wife, Basil's sister Anna, predeceased him. A member of Vladimir's family, Chrysocheir, came to Constantinople with eight hundred men in order, so he said, to enlist in Basil's forces. Basil ordered the Rus to surrender their arms and then he would enlist them. However, Chrysocheir refused and sailed into the sea of Marmora. He attacked Abydos and defeated the Byzantine commander there. He proceeded to Lemnos and entered into negotiations with the commander of Samos, David of Ohrid and the Duke of Thessalonica Nicephorus Kabasilas. Chrysocheir trusting their offers of peace, ended up slaughtered by the ships of the Kibyrrhaiote theme. Basil, during this time, was preparing an expedition to Sicily. He had already sent an advanced force under the eunuch Orestes but in the month of December, he suddenly took ill. Basil II died on 15 December 1025.

References

Breaking the Bulgarians: Skylitzes 353–6; Fine, *op. cit.*, pp. 199–211; Stevenson, *Basil*, pp. 26–31; Stephenson, *Byzantium*, pp. 73–5; Curta, *op. cit.*, pp. 245–7.

Making the Balkans Byzantine: Skylitzes 357–60; Fine, *op. cit.*, 210–11; Stevenson, *Basil*, pp. 30–1; Stephenson, *Byzantium*, 75; Curta, *op. cit.*, 247.

The blinding of Ibatzes: Skylitzes 360–3.

Basil II Porphyrogenitus' triumphant march: Skylitzes 364.

Basil's progression through the European part of his empire illustrates the fact that Byzantium remained Hellenic as well as Christian. At Athens the Emperor celebrated victory in the Cathedral of Our Lady of Athens, the Parthenon. The Parthenon of Pericles was a church longer than the building had been a temple to Athena. See Anthony Kaldellis, *The Christian Parthenon*: Cambridge, 2009, pp. 81–91.

Basil returns to the East: Skylitzes 366–7; J. R. H. Jenkins, *op. cit.*, pp. 188–9.

Basil's reign ends: Skylitzes 367–9 Psellus 1, 37.

Conclusion

The Byzantine Empire after the death of Basil II was more powerful, had more wealth, and was better administered than the empire had been in five hundred years. The great walls of Constantinople, six centuries old, site of massive sieges and battles, were now just historical artefacts. No enemy was likely to get anywhere near the city gates. Frontiers stood guard in Italy and the Adriatic on the one hand and in the High Caucases and the mountains of Armenia on the other, holding possible enemies at bay. Peace and the ensuing prosperity meant that the fields and pastures of the Balkans and Asia Minor produced goods that filtered through the villages and towns of the empire, the profit of which ultimately reached the capital. The imperial administration had removed or weakened possible rebels in the provinces and tied the city factions to the imperial dynasty.

Yet not all was well. For centuries, Byzantium was a bastion that stood against the forces of darkness: chaos and barbarism to the west and north, the evil Islamic lords to the east and south, or so they thought. The Sacred Emperor and his imperial administration was the only legitimate government in the world. As the tenth century waned however, the conditions that allowed the utility of their worldview changed significantly. By pushing back the frontiers, the military emergencies that so often disturbed the empire diminished. Moreover, the forces standing against the empire slowly transformed from mindless barbarians into perceptive and profitable business partners. When Liudprand had come to Constantinople in the early middle of the century, he was impressed and amazed by the Byzantine world but on his second trip during the reign of Nicephorus Phocas, he found the empire and its court tawdry, conceited, and corrupt. The Byzantines looked upon Venice much as they saw southern Italy, an outlying dependency, basking in the light of Byzantine brilliance. They were unaware of the new energy and growth rising in northern Italy and in Western Europe. Moreover, many times, Byzantine people found that they had more in common with their Islamic neighbours than with their Western European fellow Christians.

All this made the basic Byzantine concept of who they were obsolete. However, what would replace the unique Imperial Mission? Was the empire to be just a Greek kingdom? If so, what of the other nations that composed the state, particularly the Bulgars and Armenians? Would continuing to pretend that they were the only legitimate state serve any purpose? Alternatively, would that simply make the empire a humbug? The masters of the empire dithered on this issue and never did come up with a viable formula. The result of this problem was that the strong bonds that held the empire together in its darker hours had loosened and slowly unravelled. Nothing replaced those bonds.

Basil II and his brother had broken the power of the great eastern noble houses. They reduced the military muscle of the eastern houses and replaced them with Basil's new elite unit, the Varangian Guard and with new military settlements in the Balkans. The military families in the east coalesced around lesser landowning families, fragmenting eastern influence in the capital. With possible opposition to Basil and Constantine divided, the Emperors ensured there was formal focus of dissatisfaction by not choosing any successor. As long as both Emperors lived and did well, this did not matter. Basil never married nor, as far as we know, had any children. Constantine as a young man married the beautiful and chaste Helena, daughter of Alypius. Her family was part of the city aristocracy, her father being one of the leading men in Constantinople at the time. While we hear very little about the Empress Helena, she presented Constantine with three daughters. The imperial princesses remained unmarried during the reign of Basil II because, we may imagine, their husbands should not threaten their father and uncle's dominion. The problem emerged when Constantine finally decided that he needed to choose a successor and marry him to one of his daughters. The women were beyond childbearing years and so the dynasty would end. While the imperial brothers had secured their rule, the future was in doubt.

Basil II placed his tomb in the church of St John the Evangelist and Theologian in the Hedomon (the seventh mile), a suburb to the west of Constantinople near the sea. He wrote his own epitaph

Other past emperors
previously designated for themselves other burial places.
But I Basil, born in the purple chamber,
place my tomb on the site of the Hebdomon [Palace]
and take Sabbath's rest from the endless toils
which I satisfied in wars and which I endured.
For nobody saw my spear at rest,
from when the Emperor of Heaven called me
to the rulership of this great empire on earth,
but I kept vigilant through the whole span of my life

guarding the children of New Rome
marching bravely to the West,
and as far as the very frontiers of the East.
The Persians and Scythians bear witness to this
and along with them Abasgos, Ismael, Araps, Iber.
And now, good man, looking upon this tomb
reward it with prayers in return for my campaigns.

Basil and his brother did well by the empire. They worked hard to maintain and expand the Byzantine state. They died old. The future of the empire rested in the hands of their successors who would either find new ways of maintaining the state or let their world crumble.

References

Basil II Epitaph: Stephenson, *The Legend of Basil the Bulgar Slayer*, p. 49.

Appendix I

Sources

Byzantine historians were the inheritors of the classical literary tradition. Their chronicles and analytic works stretch back in unbroken practice to the start of Hellenic historical consciousness, to the works of Herodotus, Thucydides, and Xenophon. The Byzantines read and studied these authors and others, from the time of the Roman Empire and the Eastern Roman Empire up to and beyond the time on which this study concentrates. We know that this is true, not only because of the reuse of obsolete terms for peoples and places inherent in Byzantine writing but because the analytic writings of Byzantine authors such as Photius' *Bibliotheca*, the *Suda*, and Constantine VII's works contain excerpts from these and other classical works. Perhaps an individual author never saw a classical book, but they knew people who did, who were acquainted if not fully familiar with the ancient works. Byzantine history is a living extension of Classical history, having many of the same themes. For those who appreciate the Athenian historians, the Byzantines provide the same fine qualities

This brings up a second feature of Byzantine history. Just as the Athenian authors collected their information from oral recollections, collecting stories and accounts from one person and then another, balancing these and then drawing them up in a dramatic narrative, sometimes sprinkling inscriptions or short documents in the narrative, so our Byzantine authors drew more from personal communications than the study of documents. However, the original narrative, once published, became the raw material for compilers to incorporate into their works which, in turn, became incorporated, either whole or as epitome, in still later works. The result is a body of literature consisting of a number of longer books that break down into component parts, each available for individual investigation. This creates an interesting series of problems that only a historian would enjoy, slowly stripping the documents apart, like an onion, to restore forgotten narratives.

Literary Sources

This study of Byzantine wars from 959 to 1025 rests primarily on three historical texts and a number of analytical handbooks. Leo the Deacon wrote a military-political narrative covering the years 959–76, with some extensions. The primary manuscript, *Parisin graecus* 1712 (P) fols 272r–322r, seems to date to the twelfth century, although some suggest the thirteenth. In the book, the pseudo-Symeon chronicle (813–961) precedes Leo's *History* and Michael Psellus' *Chronographia* (976–1078) follows; clearly the scribe constructed the three works as a single historical narrative, particularly because he makes no significant breaks between the three works. Parts of Leo's manuscript were edited and published in the seventeenth century, but a complete edition waited until 1819 when C. P. Hase, a noted philologist, published the work with an excellent translation in Latin and many significant notes. The *Corpus Scriptorium Historiae Byzantinae* (1828) simply reprinted the Hase edition. A number of modern translations are available: German, Russian, Modern Greek and now English. Leo's work is a narrative that deals with military events and the politics that follows from them. He was well acquainted with war and its practices and understood power politics. While not particularly highbrow, he had a fine grasp of practicalities. I judge that he drew on oral sources from serving Byzantine officers and reports passed through the imperial administration. The English translation is Talbot-Sullivan, *The History of Leo the Deacon: Byzantine Military Expansion in the Tenth Century*, Dumbarton Oaks, Washington DC, 2005.

Another historical text, John Scylitzes' chronicle, is significantly different from the work of Leo. Written in the time of Alexius Comnenus (1081–1118) by a high official, the work is a compilation of information from older historical works, including Leo the Deacon's. Skylitzes' chronicle was included in a larger compilation, George Cedrenus' *Chronographia*. Skylitzes' work was presented in full by the efforts of the editor Hans Thurn in 1973. Cedrenus exists in many manuscripts and Thurn's *edition principle* used nine manuscripts from the twelfth to the fourteenth century. I must make special mention of the *Codex Matritensis*, Madrid Bibl. nat.Vitr26.2, the famous 'Madrid Scylitzes'. This manuscript, probably from the time of the later Comnenian dynasty, has 574 illustrations, which appear to be well founded. Reproductions of these remarkable pictures grace most books on Byzantium; it is probably the most beautiful book that remains from the time of the Byzantine Empire. John Skylitzes was an acute observer, with a view of humanity worthy of Tacitus and an eye for detail similar to his younger contemporary, the Princess Anna. He understood real politics and was well informed regarding military affairs. His strengths and weakness well reflect the nature of Byzantine civilization. There is an English translation by John Wortley, *John Skylitzes: A Synopsis of Byzantine History 811–1057*, Cambridge UK 2010. This translation was done in conjunction with the French translation by Bernard Flusin with notes for both translations by Jean-Claude Cheynet. The critical edition of Hans Thurn (1973) is the basis for both translations.

The third text is Michael Psellus' *Chronographia*. While Psellus, who was a member of the city aristocracy, became a monk, this had more to do with political difficulties than personal piety. Psellus revived Plato and Platonic thought in Byzantium, replacing the older Aristotelian orientation. Some thought that Psellus emphasized pagan philosophers to the detriment of Christianity. However, Psellus was often welcome at court, sometimes in positions of influence and honour. The *Chronographia* covered the ruling emperors and empresses from 976–1078. But Psellus reflected Plutarch's *Lives* rather than Polybius. Excellent on character, with perceptive insight into the mysteries of human relations, the *Chronographia* is a literary work of art. But as history it has, as Sewter says in his introduction to his Penguin translation, an 'impression of vagueness' (p. 16). The definitive edition of the *Chronographia* is Émile Renauld, *Chronographie ou histoire d'un siècle de Byzance (976–1077)*, 2 vols, Paris, 1926/28.

Analysis of Literary Sources

Even with the literary source in hand, the text requires more than merely reading it. We, in our comfortable chair and heated or air conditioned rooms, can read the work just as we have read a favoured novel or newspaper. Very few Byzantines ever propped up a book in bed and read for enjoyment. A book of Skylitzes' *Synopsis* cost more to manufacture than the building of a residence in terms of skilled labour. The book was kept in a secure library, where a reader might sit at a desk with the book propped up in front of him and take notes or, more likely, take the book to an assembly room and read the text to an audience. This was the purpose of the book: to be read, either directly or indirectly, to a group of people. As an historical work, the book was seen as 'deep' background, to bring forth a sense of continuity with the past and to explore events to see how people in the past handled them. Of course, to be successful, the lector needed a touch of drama and detail to enliven his task. So the historical text was the framework upon which the lector made such points as appropriate.

This was the way that Greek books functioned. The historical tradition was clear since Herodotus and Thucydides: save the significant events of the past from fading into nothingness and explain what happened so people have an understanding of how to handle similar situations. (Herodotus 1.1.1; Thucydides, 1.22.4). The task of the historian was to describe what happened as clearly and accurately as he could. He was not in the job of persuasion, which was left to the reader. In our modern world these sentiments appear trite and empty. But that is because we can write and read and publish cheaply and widely. When the question is, what shall be recorded in a very expensive product and stored in a special room, the answer is not some document made to influence an opinion of the moment. The task of the Byzantine historian was to collect as accurate information as possible and present it in as objective form as he could. Still, errors come, mistakes happen: no historian is perfect.

Another issue presents itself concerning John Skylitzes. Despite his statement (Skylitzes 1–4) that he is a compiler whose primary interest is to collect and present information, 'finely ground up', for a quick and clear introduction to past events, certain modern commentators have attempted to find information and agendas in his work that simply are not there. To over-intellectualize ancient and medieval historians is often amusing but tells us more about those who do it than their objects. To rewrite histories is fun but not likely to be more accurate than the original. The specific problem revolves around Skylitzes' account of Basil II. As it happens, Skylitzes' is the only narrative account of Basil II's reign and it is not very good. Looking at Psellus' short account and Basil's novels, the Emperor was clearly not interested in spending money on anything without a return. Panegyrics, reign specific histories, monuments, these were not for Basil II. The reason Skylitzes' account of the reign is poor is because Basil was not interested in leaving a historical record any more then he was in leaving a viable long term successor. Skylitzes patched together military reports, local records, and accounts from older people concerning their relatives or friends. A number of his informants got their information from Skleros' supporters and Alexius I's generals' families. Skylitzes account is far from perfect but the information he did collect is good.

Military Handbooks

The Byzantine army was a very mixed bag, some units were well paid, well trained, professional; other units were scrapings from poor farms and bandit gangs. Some of their officers were well born well educated leaders of men; many were toughs who held their men together by a mixture of lust for plunder and fear of pain. Most of the soldiers and officers were small landowners living and working on 'soldiers' properties', hard men living hard lives. Except for the aristocratic officers from courtly families, few of these men were particularly literate. They could read a bill of sale or inventory with a sharp eye but lengthy literary works were not for them. Unlike the imperial Roman army, a fairly uniformly trained infantry force, the Byzantine army needed to hammer together motley groups of independent minded toughs on horses.

Fight they would and well. But who and how was the problem. The answer was a military manual.

Sometime between about 590 and 610, the army high command received a manual that explained the nuts and bolts of the Eastern Roman, now Byzantine, army's methods of operations and combat. Similar in form to the Justinian *Anonymous Byzantine Treatise on Strategy*, the new manual was often associated with the name of Emperor Maurice (582–602). The manual described methods of training, unit formations, passing orders, managing the baggage train, drills to perfect efficiency and methods of conducting combat. Included are information about the conduct of sieges and discussion of possible enemies' styles of fighting. As a training tool, commanding officers would have different sections read to subordinate officers collected together along with experienced soldiers giving examples and pointers. Particularly during the winter, the army officers, through discussion and debate, would develop a fairly uniformed approach to army management. This book continued in importance as long as the army of soldiers' holdings remained. The manual went through numerous editions, abridgements and adaptations, just like modern military manuals, but always functioned to hold the independent minded officers and soldiers to a common understanding of their roles.

Two of the adaptations of the manual are the *Praecepta militaria* and *de Velitatione bellica* by the Emperor Nicephorus. He wrote the first, *Principles of the Military Arts,* while he was a commander. The book is a comprehensive but very concise series of observations about how to manage an armed force in war. The work exists in one primary manuscript, State Historical Museum, Moscow, 436/298/285, fols 115–136. A scribe copied out this manuscript at Trebizond about 1350, certainly before 1361 when Trebizond fell to the Turks, as part of a collection of didactic literature. At some point, the book found its way to the monastery, *ton Iviron* on Mt Athos. The librarian Abessalom read the book and left marginal notes sometime around 1630. The Russian monk, Arsenii Sukhanov, bought the manuscript in 1651. The Patriarch of Moscow had sent him to Athos to buy books for the new Patriarch Library. Ultimately, the Patriarch Library became part of the State Historical Museum. Unfortunately, the book was unavailable at the time Eric McGeer was doing his work, but the Bibliothèque Nationale, Paris, had a microfilm of the text. Using computer technology, McGeer was able to investigate the manuscript. The editors, first J. A. Kulakovsky (1908), and also McGeer (1995), find the manuscript very corrupt, full of spelling and grammar mistakes.

McGeer found a practical solution for interpreting the *Praecepta militaria*. There was a series of writings by the imperial general, Nicephorus Ouranus (ca. 950–1011), collected in modern parlance as the *Τακτικ́*. The collection is quite large; it consists of paraphrases of the military manual into a simple Byzantine Attic, noting changes in military operations from the author's own time. Interestingly, only a small fraction of Ouranus' works have been published in the original, not to mention any translation. But McGeer constructed a text by joining together parts of three separate manuscripts to make a work complementary to the *Praecepta*. He considered that Ouranus, chapters 56 through 65, paraphrases the *Praecepta*. The three manuscripts are: Constantinopolitanus graecus 36 from the fourteenth century, in the Seraglio, Istanbul; Monacensis graecus 452 from the fourteenth century, in the Bayerische Staatsbibliothek, Munich; and Oxoniensis Baroccianus 131, in the Bodlein Library, Oxford. Const. graecus 36 actually extends only to chapter 43, and so does not enter directly into McGeer's edition but the manuscript clearly identifies the work as that of Ouranus. Monacensis graecus contains the complete section, chapters 56–65 on folios 109–28, in an easy hand but water damage has made writing on the page edges difficult to read or simply illegible. The Oxford Baroccianus appears to be more of a private effort rather than a manuscript for a library or even for sale. The handwriting is very small and difficult to read, as if the writer wanted to pack as many words on a page as possible. The text contains parts of many works; among them Ouranus' book on tactics chapters 4 to 9.32 and 65 to 178. The Oxford manuscript chapter 65 acts as control for the Monacensis manuscript, demonstrating that chapter 65 in Monacensis is indeed the corresponding chapter in the *Praecepta*. Eric McGeer has rescued Nicephorus Phocas' *Praecepta militaria* from time's wreckage.

The other book by the Lord Nicephorus, *de Velitatione bellica*, was more of an official publication. Written when Nicephorus was emperor, the book's language is very good Byzantine Attic Greek. There are many copies of the manuscript text but only three are important for editorial purposes, all of the others deriving from these three: Vaticanus graecus 1164; Barberinianus graecus ii 97 (276), both in Rome; and Scorialensis graecus 281 in the Escorial. All three texts are very similar, probably written in the same scriptorium in Constantinople about 1010. Only the copy in the Escorial is complete, the other two lack significant parts, but because of the close relations of the manuscripts, reconstruction of the text was clear. The first edition was completed by C. B. Hase when he made the first edition of Leo the Deacon in 1819. However, he used derivative manuscripts from the sixteenth century. I use the critical edition and translation by George T. Dennis SJ, in his book, *Three Byzantine Military Treatises*. The Greek title of the work is Περί Παραδρομῆς, which has the sense of 'regarding moving along side (of the enemy)' that is, 'harassing the enemy'. Dennis translates the title as *Skirmishing*. But skirmishing is part of the tactics of large forces to protect flanks or trouble a battle line. What the Lord Nicephorus describes is guerrilla war, that is, 'small war', harassing an enemy until either a major force arrives to deal with him or he gets frustrated and leaves. Otherwise, the translation is very good, and the work illuminates Nicephorus' military efforts.

The last major edition of the military manual that I use is by Leo VI the Wise, *Tactica*. The Emperor Leo VI (886–912) oversaw a reform of the Byzantine military establishment. He was very interested in military affairs and if, as has too often been said, he never set foot on a battle field, he certainly commanded men who did, and the Emperor saw to it that they had the supplies, soldiers, and support they needed. There are many manuscripts of the book. The primary one is the Mediceo-Laurentianus graecus 55, 4 in Florence. This is a large book, well written by one hand, from sometime around 950. Leo VI's son, Constantine VII, had his father's book included in a large collection of military handbooks written and put in a master volume for the imperial library. It is quite possible this book is that one or a close and contemporary copy of it. Complete copies of the book found their way into print in 1612 and then 1745. The current edition is, *The Taktika of Leo VI*, ed. trans. George T. Dennis, Dumbarton Oaks, Washington DC, 2010. Also, the commentary on the *Tactica* by John Haldon is full of good information and demonstrates how the *Tactica* is an outgrowth of the *Strategikon* manual.

Artefacts and Reconstructions

The study of military history has developed new methods of investigation since the 1970s. This is the proliferation of military reconstructions. Taking a couple of hundred people, giving them long staffs, and having them execute the manoeuvres described in the classical texts, tells us a lot. Some moves that historians pictured as easily done actually take a lot of training; other things, which many saw as difficult, just happened as part of the flow. Building a trireme and rowing it around is also instructive; the Olympia has some serious inaccuracies but has certainly taught the student of Thucydides important lessons. In Byzantine warfare, particularly at the time of Nicephorus Phocas, reconstructors have done a great deal of work. Besides the general medieval military reconstructions, throwing machines, horsemanship, weapon and armour construction, some investigators have looked at the specific armed forces of the tenth and eleventh century Byzantium. Much of this material, and so much else, is presented by the Osprey Publishing Company. Three publications in particular speak to Nicephorus' campaigns, Ian Heath, *Byzantine Armies 886–1118*; and Timothy Dawson, *Byzantine Infantryman c.900–1204*, and

Byzantine Cavalryman c.900–1204. While Heath worked on the analysis of pictures and sculptures to figure out what the Byzantine soldiers used for clothes, armour and weapons, Dawson was involved in the actual manufacture of armour and weapons. Further, using war re-enactments, Dawson tested Byzantine tactical schemes drawn from the Byzantine handbooks. These efforts illuminate the Byzantine texts.

Another area of Byzantine military reconstruction is war at sea. John H. Pryor and Elizabeth M. Jeffreys' marvellous book, *The Age of the ΔΡΟΜΩΝ*, deals with the construction of the Byzantine battleship, the Fire-Shooting Dromon. With a brilliant discussion of ship construction and operation, complete with a massive apparatus, Pryor and Jeffreys' work is a monument to Byzantine studies. Interestingly, the great Byzantine scholar, John Haldon, working with fabricators constructed a full-scale working model of a Greek fire thrower, using the design of a late Roman water pump and distilled petroleum.

Among efforts to recover Byzantine military thought, I cannot leave out the work of Edward Luttwak. In 1976, Luttwak published his *The Grand Strategy of the Roman Empire* that brought about considerable discussion of the Romans' methods of war. In 2009, Luttwak published a sequel, *The Grand Strategy of the Byzantine Empire*, which continues to demonstrate Luttwak's usual insightful thought.

I would be remiss not to mention one of the great reconstructions of Byzantine military activity: the rebuilding of sections of the great Theodosian Walls of Constantinople. Purists complain that the building project did not use original materials but the work was expensive enough as it was and the form, colour, and size are all correct. It gives a fine view of the fortifications of the Great City during the time of Nicephorus Phocas.

References

Arnold Toynbee, *Constantine Porphyrogenitus and his World,* , Oxford: Oxford University Press, 1973, pp. 575–605.

Basic collection of Byzantine historical works: CSHB, *Corpus Scriptorum Historiae Byzantinae*, ed. B. G. Niebuhr (Bonn 1828).

Alice-Mary Talbot and Denis Sullivan, *The History of Leo the Deacon*, pp. 50–51.

Ibid., 51–52

Hans Thurn, ed. *Ioannis Scylitzae Synopsis Historion*, edition princeps, Berlin, 1973.

John Skylitzes, *A Synopsis of Byzantine History 811–1057*, trans. by John Wortley, Cambridge UK, 2010.

Eric McGeer, *Sowing the Dragon's Teeth*, p. 4.

McGeer, *op. cit*, pp. 81–85.

Dennis, George, *Three Byzantine Military Treatises*, Washington DC: Dumbarton Oaks, 1985, pp. 140–141.

Leo VI, *The Taktika of Leo VI*, ed. Trans. George T. Dennis, Washington DC, 2010, pp. ix–xiii.

Pryor, John and Elizabeth Jeffreys, *Age of the ΔΡΟΜΩΝ*, Leiden: Brill Academic Press, 2011, pp. 607–631.

Empire and Horse Soldiers
The Origins and Development of the Byzantine Army

Introduction

T he empire of Augustus rested on an army of heavy infantry. The imperial army of the early and high empire was the last military force of the ancient Mediterranean city-state civilization. Athens and Carthage, Sparta and, of course, Rome were city states based on an urban mercantile and rural farming population. These people massed together in disciplined infantry armies and for centuries these soldiers fought each other. In the beginning of the third century AD, a new military technology appeared: the solidly seated, lance wielding, armoured horseman. Lance-bearing armoured horsemen appeared when horseback riding began, but they held to the horse with their knees and their opponents could easily knock them off the animal. However, at the beginning of the third century, armoured horsemen who sat solidly on their mounts appeared in the eastern Mediterranean world and used heavy lances against their enemies as sculptures show. Horsemen lived a very different lifestyle than the city folk. As this new technology entered the Roman Empire, societies began changing. Byzantium was the only part of the Mediterranean world that managed to adapt Classical culture to the new world of horsemen.

Roman Imperial Army

After the defeat of Marcus Antonius and the end of the thirty-year long brutal civil war, the Young Caesar, Gaius Octavius, commanded some sixty legions. This was a force of over three hundred thousand soldiers. These organizations were a mixed bag; some were very well trained and disciplined, others were a collection of rabble. The victorious Caesarians understood that this force was very dangerous and needed very careful management. They awarded many of the soldiers, no matter for which side they had fought, retirement and a plot of good farm land, dispossessing weaker and less threatening owners. Some, mostly Antonius' men, were settled in soldiers' colonies in the east; others, their own favoured men, acquired estates in Italy. The Caesarians took the best and most dangerous soldiers from both sides and reorganized them into twenty-eight legions, which were sent to the most threatened parts of the empire. Most of these legions ended up on the frontiers, along the Rhine, the Danube, and in the east facing the desert. Most of these legions had a very long existence: while they started out in dirt-walled camps, living in tents, slowly they built their camps in wood, then stone, until each legion base became a town. Retirees from the legion settled nearby with business and farms loosely connected with the legion so ultimately the legions became part of the landscape.

The imperial legions were a force of heavy infantry. Armed with a throwing spear, the *pilum* and the famous short sword, the *gladius*, the legionary was protected by strong torso armour, metal helmet, and large shield. The army deployed in manoeuvre units, the *cohortes*, made of six *centuriae*, each with eighty men. Ten *cohortes* made up the *legio*, for some 4,800 fighting men. Adding officers, reconnaissance, messengers and such, the legion was some five thousand and more men. So, at twenty-eight legions, the Young Caesar presided over some one hundred and forty thousand soldiers. Given the practice of raising auxiliary forces, less well armed but in a manner reflecting local traditions, this figure probably doubles to somewhere around three hundred thousand soldiers. Sending in the auxiliary troops to soften up the enemy, the legionaries followed them up and pounded the enemy into the dust. '...*ubi solitudinem faciunt pacem appellant*'.

For some two and a half centuries, the imperial Roman war machine dominated the Mediterranean world and its hinterlands without much change. The armour became heavier, the swords longer, and auxiliary forces using missiles such as arrows, spears, and throwing machines became more numerous. Then, starting with the death of Septimius Serverus in AD 211, the imperial army began to change. At first, the changes were internal administrative reforms. Serverus had substantially increased soldiers' pay and retirement benefits. Soldiers were allowed to marry and so have families on or close to military bases. This, of course, meant that the legions as institutions sunk deeper into their location. The military institutions needed more money and became less mobile. Then, Serverus' son, Serverus Antoninus (Caracalla), issued the Antonine Constitution of 212, which made all free people of the empire into Roman citizens. This began to end the distinction between legions and auxiliary units. Before, citizens formed the legions, and non-citizens were auxiliary. At the time, this was not a major event, the two forces were slowly merging into one another, but as a marker the extension of citizenship illustrated a number of developments on the imperial frontiers.

Because Augustus established the army on the frontiers of empire along the Rhine and Danube and in the east, a new form of social institution emerged in the Mediterranean world. The frontier society that emerged united the imperial military soldiers with a mix of local peoples and cultures, including businessmen and merchants from all sorts of areas. Their language was Latin and, with local variations, eventually spread through Britannia, along the Rhine and Main, through the lands that connect the Rhine valley with the Danube, and down along the Danube to the Black Sea. The frontier soldier culture centred in garrison towns and fortress settlements along the great rivers, spreading out on either side of the actual limit of empire for many miles. Main centres included the Rhine cities of Colonia Agrippina and Mogontiacum for the armies of the Germanies; along the Danube, there were Vindobona, Singidunum, and Sirmium, the centres of the Illyrian forces. The views of the officers and managers of this frontier culture regarding the nature of the empire differed greatly from the views of the rulers of the major urban centres around the Mediterranean. The military leaders began to see themselves as being the 'true' Romans and that the civilian urban centres' main function should be to support the armies.

In the east, from Armenia to Egypt, a different frontier society emerged. The Roman army there was connected directly to the main urban centres, the cities of Asia Minor, along with Antioch, Damascus, Palmyra, Jerusalem, and Alexandria. The soldiers of the eastern armies were involved with overseeing trade routes, caravans, and way-stations along the boundaries of empire. Besides desert and mountain raiders, their opponents were the cavalry forces of the Parthians. Once in a generation, some ambitious emperor would come, leading a force drawn from the west, and uniting with the eastern forces, would strike deep into the Parthian lands, only to withdraw loaded with loot. The challenges facing the eastern armies, except for putting down the revolts of the Jews, were considerably less than those facing the northern forces. Now, however, external forces began to drive new developments.

The Great Crisis Begins

On the Rhine and upper Danube front, the German tribes began to coalesce into larger confederations. During the reign of Marcus Aurelius, beginning about AD 166, a vast war erupted along the middle Danube. At that time, large forces of Germanic tribesmen pressed against the frontiers. Following them were their families and tribes. Behind these tribes, came more tribes; most of Free Germany was in movement. Different tribes formed larger groupings: the Alamanni are named first in AD 213, and then in the next decades we find the

Goths, the Saxons, and the Franks. While the Roman army and the Germans fought, both lived together in a close-knit world. Roman merchants, retired Roman soldiers of German ancestry, fugitives from Roman justice, captives and slaves lived in Free Germany and many Germans joined the Roman army, lived as forced settlers on Roman lands, and worked as slaves and also as free labour. Both sides were intimately connected with each other.

The main forces facing each other were heavy spear-throwing, sword-wielding infantry. Each side had some cavalry, generally manned by Germans, along with archers and support groups. Since the time of Augustus, all the imperial forces were stationed on the frontier. The only way an emperor could mobilize a large field army was to pull legions from one frontier and march the men wherever he wanted them to go. Alexander Serverus had pulled Rhine and upper Danube legions away for an unsuccessful war in the east. While the legions were in the east, Germans attacked across the Rhine, burning cities and ravaging the countryside. Alexander brought his army back to the Rhine and attempted to make peace with the Germans. The soldiers saw this as weakness, just like the emperor showed in the east; the soldiers rebelled, killing Alexander and proclaiming one of their commanders, Maximinus, emperor. The new emperor set out to invade Free Germany with the full support of the soldiers. The political crisis this started so badly so damaged the Augustan political system that it never recovered. However, the problems in the west, serious indeed, were not as disrupting as the problems that the Romans faced in the east.

The Horse Lords Come

For centuries, since the time of Pompey's victory in his war against Mithridates, Rome had a strong presence in the eastern Mediterranean. Beyond the imperial frontiers, there were the Parthians. These were an Iranian people, centred in what had been the lands of the Medes, a successor state to the eastern parts of the dominion of the Seleucids. Ruled by a King of Kings, the Parthian Empire was a coalition of peoples held together by an imperial family, the Arsacid dynasty. Holding most of Mesopotamia and its thriving cities, the empire stretched east toward India and north into the steppes of inner Asia. At times, the Parthians appeared to the Romans as easy pickings; Crassus had famously invaded Parthia while Caesar invaded Gaul and Pompey subdued Spain. At other times, when the Roman hold on the east was weakened, the Parthians raided the empire, collecting loot and slaves. This pattern of attack and counter attack continued for centuries. There was no question of permanent occupation of the main Parthian lands. Trajan attempted to add all of Mesopotamia to the empire but Hadrian quickly gave the lands up. Occupation was much too costly. The Parthian King of Kings was no less interested in raiding the Romans and seizing a frontier fort here and there but permanent occupation was out of the question. Then, if the Emperor and the King of Kings did not have a direct argument, there was always Armenia. A cadet branch of the Arsacid house ruled some of Armenia most of the time. These kings often recognized Roman suzerainty, begging for aid in quelling their turbulent subjects. That way, the Armenian Arsacids remained independent of their Parthian relatives. However, when the Romans were weak, and the Parthians strong, the King of Kings would enforce his suzerainty on the Armenian kings.

Coming from the east, new military technology and practice upset the balance of force along the Roman-Parthian frontiers. A new aggressive power toppled the Parthian dynasty in fierce campaigns. Adashir, King of Kings, grabbed power in 224. He immediately announced to the Romans that he would resume control over all those lands held by the Achaemenid Empire lost to the Great Alexander. He attacked the Roman city of Hatra in 229, ravaged the country side, but withdrew into the lands of the Medes. The Romans attempted to negotiate with Adashir but found their efforts going nowhere. Since Alexander Serverus' family's main holdings were in the east, his administration launched a massive attack against the new eastern power. Gathering troops from across the empire (AD 231–3), he advanced against the new Persian state in three directions. He sent his Asia Minor forces through Armenia to strike deep into the lands of the Medes; he sent a cross desert raiding party into southern Mesopotamia; and he led his main army of heavy infantry directly down the Euphrates, following the routes used by past emperors. Adashir met Alexander's army – Herodian describes what happened:

> the king (of Persia) attacked (the Roman army) unexpectedly with his entire force and trapped the Romans like a fish in a net; firing their arrows from all sides at the encircled soldiers, the Persians massacred the whole army. The outnumbered Romans were unable to stem the attack of the Persian horse; they used their shields to protect those parts of their bodies exposed to the Persian arrows. Content merely to protect themselves, they offered no resistance. As a result, all the Romans were driven into one spot, where they made a wall of their shields and fought like an army under siege. Hit and wounded from every side, they held out bravely as long as they could, but in the end all were killed. The Romans suffered a staggering disaster; it is not easy to recall another like it, one in which a great army was destroyed, an army inferior in strength and determination to none of the armies of old.

This passage of Herodian is important for our understanding of Roman military developments. Similar to the Athenian historians, the Greek Herodian wrote about his own time, using oral accounts that he sought from people connected with the events. This passage has three items of information, whether from the same person or three different people is unknown. First, the item about the Roman army being caught like fish in a net emphasizes the archery forces of the Persians. We can understand the enemy as light horse archers, riding around the Roman heavy infantry, cutting them all down. The next item goes on to say that the Romans could not respond to the arrow storms nor did they attempt a counter-attack. Rather, they hid behind their shields and we may see this as the 'turtle' formation. The result: the Roman army bunched together behind their shields where the Persians killed them all. In order to be able to do this, the Persian army needed a weapon that the Romans were unable to counter. In subsequent similar battles, this weapon was the heavy, lance-bearing horseman. We may assume that Adashir fielded an army of light horse archers, to pin and kill unprotected Roman soldiers and of heavy cavalry to break the massed formations that the Romans used for protection from arrows. The last item of Herodian's account states that this defeat was unlike any defeat known in living memory. The accepted judgment of those familiar with the imperial army was that the lost force was as good a force as possessed by the empire. We may understand from this observation that the Persian attack not only defeated the Roman army but surprised the Romans with a major tactical innovation.

The question this presents: what did Adashir throw at the Roman army that caused such a defeat? The answer is that the horse lords arrived. Here is a major turning point of the military development in the Mediterranean world. Some fifty years before, the same technological change overwhelmed the eastern continental power, the Great Middle Kingdom. Large armies of heavy infantry underpinned the Chinese Empire, just as they did the Mediterranean empires. In the decades following AD 180, horse lords, either external forces sweeping out of Inner Asia or Chinese frontier armies raised to face such invaders, smashed the Chinese heavy infantry, broke the empire apart, and led into a new world of fragmented states. These dominant horse lords had emerged in central Asia, where the great steppe lands are crossed by the inner Asian rivers, the Oxus, the Jaxartes, the Tarim, the upper Indus, the Panjshir and the Areias. Here, in what Arnold Toynbee called the Central Asian Roundabout, cultures swirled around each other, civilizations clashed and the nomads of the steppe collided with irrigation based cities.

The distant Iranian provinces of the Achaemenid Empire extended into the steppes of central Asia, intersecting with the nomad tribes whose lands reached toward the Gobi and China. Alexander the Great occupied the former provinces of the Achaemenids, defeating some tribes and making agreements with others. After Alexander's death there was a decade of chaos in these far provinces. They fell to the Seleucids who set up quasi independent satraps to manage these areas. Long before the Iranian great kings, cities had formed, using the rivers for irrigation. The Iranians encouraged city development; Alexander founded some cities and the Seleucid satraps founded more. By 250 BC the Seleucid Greeks, Iranian settlers, and local Iranian tribes formed a rather stable society, the Hellenistic Bactrian Kingdoms. But, by 140–130 BC, nomads from the high steppe overran the Bactrian lands. This event introduced a new cultural stratum to an already very complex sequence of ways of life, living side by side. The military traditions of the Iranians and Greeks merged with that of the nomads. To defend their towns against the nomads' light cavalry bowmen, the urban inhabitance developed the phalanx of heavy armed cavalry, armed with a lance solidly seated on their mount. Armoured horsemen were not a new idea, the Sarmatians had long had armoured cavalry, but here, the armour was better, the horses were heavier, and the unit fought as a disciplined body, delivering a sold and harsh shock to their enemies. By having light cavalry bowmen of their own, the urban dwellers could send them out to chase the nomadic horsemen and follow them with the heavy cavalry. The nomadic forces would have to retreat or, if they massed for an attack, the heavy horse would catch them. The ideal situation was to catch the nomads' encampment, harass it with the bowmen and then overrun with the heavy cavalry.

This tactical system quickly spread to Parthia, Armenia, and the European Steppe lands. It also spread east into China and south into India. The bowmen and armoured heavy cavalry were very effective but they were also very costly to the societies that adopted them. The armies of heavy infantry came from peasants, urban poor, and even convicts. The officers of such armies were literate land owners for whom command was simply a temporary occupation. The backbone of the army was the career under-officers who held the force together. This would not work for the horse soldiers. First, they had to live with their horses from childhood and, at the same time, learn to use their weapons. Then, the horse soldiers needed large areas of land upon which to graze, and more importantly, breed their horses. Moreover, they needed farms to grow grains to feed the horses and the men who handled the horses. At the centre of this enterprise, the Horse Master needed a great house, with stables, storage, and an armoury for his weapons. For protection, he would fortify his great house and so set up a micro state in which he was lord of his lands. Now a ruler who could convince these horse lords to support him, could sweep any competition away but the horse lords, if they became unhappy, could easily get together and find a new ruler.

Adashir founded the Sassanid dynasty. His power rested on the Savaran, the formation of heavy cavalry, mounted on Nisean chargers, protected by cuirass, helmet with face guard, and armoured horse. The Savaran fought with lance and sword. We can see Adashir's battle against the Parthian emperor at Hormozgan in AD 224 in large reliefs carved in the living rock at Firuzbad. Here, heavy cavalry fight in joust formation, lance to lance, both Parthian and Sassanian engaged in combat. Adashir himself unhorses Ardavan V, the Parthian ruler, while Adashir's son, Shapur unhorses Darbandan, the grand vizier. Adashir's continuing victories, followed by those of his son, Shapur, are a telling indication of a technical improvement, a force multiplier, which gave his cavalry a significant edge over their opponents. This was probably an improvement in the built-up saddle, or some form of stabilizing foot rest that allowed the horseman to stay more securely on his mount. Whatever it was, this innovation was a significant game changer, because cavalry came to dominate the battlefield rather than simply be an adjunct to heavy infantry. With this improvement, the horse lords had arrived.

The Great Crisis Continues

The upheaval started by the murder of Alexander Serverus finally began to settle in 238 with the sole rule of the boy emperor, Gordian III, under the direction of his praetorian prefect, Timesitheus. Shapur ascended the Persian throne in 240 and began to look to the west. After his forces took the town of Hatra, the Romans decided to attack the Persians with a large army, believing Alexander Serverus' defeat was just an unfortunate event. Later, the Romans claimed victory but, evidently, their pursuit of the Persian army led the Romans beyond their supply lines. Timesitheus died, Philip was appointed his successor, and the soldiers mutinied, proclaiming Philip emperor. Gordian III was dead. Shapur claimed he died in battle, Philip said he died of sickness, and many thought Philip had murdered him. The new emperor paid a great deal of money to Shapur and was allowed to retreat back to the Roman lines. Shapur proclaimed this a great victory. Philip died in 249. His successor, Decius, had trouble with many usurpers and then faced a massive invasion by the Gothic confederation on the lower Danube. Decius and his son were killed fighting the Goths in 251, the first emperor to die fighting the barbarians. Anarchy erupted in the empire as many usurpers attempted to seize the throne.

While the Romans were sorting out their political problems Shapur attacked Syria. The Savaran, Shapur's striking force, plundered rich farm lands and sacked Antioch, carrying away thousands of people and immense booty. The new emperor, Valerian, from a senatorial family, began to repair the damage done in the civil disturbances. He sent his son Gallienus to the western frontiers while he went east. Valerian carefully put together a powerful army to attack Shapur and revenge the damage the Savaran had done to the Romans (260). Shapur tells that Valerian brought an army collected from all over the Roman Empire; that he won a great battle over the Romans beyond Carrhae and Edessa; and that he took Valerian prisoner 'with our own hands' along with the Praetorian Prefect and a host of officials. The King of Kings then proceeded to recount all the many cities and lands he ravaged and plundered. The whole army and its administrative tail were lost. The following decade was a catastrophe for the Romans. The east passed from Roman control into the hands of the master of Palmyra, Odaenathus. The far west suffered permanent devastation of cities and withdrew from imperial control, setting up their own emperors to rule Gaul, Spain, and Britannia. The Danube frontier gave way and the tribes devastated the Aegean cities, particularly Athens and Ephesus. The military system of the empire was clearly bankrupt.

Gallienus Reforms the Imperial Army

Gallienus' time is very dark with respect to sources of information. The literary sources are lost and from what we can see from the remaining fragments, they were confused and terse at best. The chaos of the times overwhelmed people and no one really knew what was happening. Gallienus maintained his personal rule to 268, when he was murdered. From about 260, he managed to throw together sufficient forces to hold Italy, Africa, and a good part of the Balkans. In these battles, Gallienus devised a number of expediencies that became part of the Roman way of war. First, the infantry became lighter. The *contus*, a thrusting spear, replaced the *pilum*, the throwing spear. Instead of heavy armour, the soldiers now began to wear chainmail tunics and lighter helmets. Large oval shields replaced the old curved shields. The result was a more manoeuvrable infantry that could fight both as a solid unit and in loose order. This allowed the soldiers to effectively react to cavalry or missile attack. Also, the Romans invested in bolt-throwing machines, able to defend ground with far fewer soldiers.

While the infantry reforms were effective, the most important innovation of Gallienus was the development an independent cavalry formation. He set up cavalry regiments, *tagmata*, under their own commander. This is the first instance of this military institution that would eventually dominate Roman military structures. Gallienus organized a mobile force under his general,

Aureolus, who held the title *Hipparchon*. This force consisted of heavy and light cavalry, backed up by infantry units formed from detachments of the frontier legions (*vexillationes*). These cavalry regiments and their support units consisted, in good part, of hired troops rather than regular Roman soldiers. Gallienus and his successors saw the horse breeders as inherently unpredictable people. They took good farm land and turned it into pasture. The Roman estate was a balanced production institution that supplied jobs, and although many farm workers were slaves and serfs, they still had to be fed and housed, and the more they had children, the better for the estate owner. The estates also paid taxes; there was some immunity for senators, but there were still taxes to be paid. The Romans rather would purchase the horses and riding soldiers too, if possible, than dedicate the amount of land necessary to support corps of horse. This problem of horse breeding in the lands of extensive empires is a reoccurring problem: the Chinese were always faced with different versions of this difficulty as were other lands. Bring in the horse lords, and they take over; buy the horsemen from the outside, and pay the enemy. The Romans decided to buy.

Aureolus rebelled and Gallienus trapped him in Milan. But the commander of his cavalry cut Gallienus down in 268. The next emperor, Claudius II, continued Gallienus' reforms of the army. He took Milan, executed Aureolus and set out to re-establish the frontiers north of Italy. But he died of the plague in 270. Aurelian took over and using the new armed force, reunited the western provinces with the empire and, defeating Palmyra, he established direct rule in the east. Aurelian improved the imperial defences, constructing walls around major cities including Rome, pulled back from exposed positions, surrendering the most exposed section of the German frontier and evacuating Trajan's province of Dacia. While he continued to put the empire back in order, his soldiers killed him in 275. For the next ten years, the empire slowly regained cohesion but clearly, major reforms were coming if the empire was going to survive.

The New Empire of Diocletian and Constantine

Diocletian murdered his chief rival and became emperor in 284. He and his successors began a massive reform of the political and military institutions of the empire. The Emperor Constantine died in 337; in the fifty and more years since the accession of Diocletian, the Roman state experienced a massive transformation. Provincial administration changed. The old Augustan large provinces run by a governor with a small staff overseeing self governing towns assessing and collecting their own taxes were replaced by a vicar who oversaw a group of smaller provinces, each run by a governor whose large staff assessed and enforced tax collections. The old self-governing towns had disappeared, the victims of war and upheaval along with the demands for higher revenue. Because of the pressure on revenue, the administrations preferred to deal with larger estates than small holders because the larger economic structures were more profitable, unit for unit, and easier from which to collect. The basic structures of society shifted from the older urban-based collection of city states to a more rural society based on large farms. Cities still existed but they tended to be smaller and with more heterogeneous interests. These institutions are the foundations of the Later Roman Empire.

The structure of the armed forces also changed significantly. The large legions remained as administrative organizations, slowly sinking into the nominal provincial government. The soldiers on the frontiers became farmer-soldiers, *limitanei,* members of small units defending guard houses, watch towers, and local towns while their more soldierly, or better trained, or younger compatriots joined mobile units of elite cavalry and foot, in 'detachments', *vexillationes,* which formed field armies. These accompanied the emperor or high officials as personal guards and the nucleus of any large army that the emperor might need. Called the *comitatenses,* they were the main instruments and companions of those in power.

Modern commentators have criticized this division of forces in the Later Roman Empire. They see the separation of frontier forces from the field armies as weakening the frontiers and forcing communities in the interior to build expensive fortifications. The field army was more expensive to maintain than the old frontier legions and detracted from overall defence. However, the point they miss is the introduction of large and powerful horse armies. Here is a point that needs attention. The founder of modern analytic military history, Hans Delbrück, clearly said that the emergence of the barbarian tribes during the Later Roman Empire coincided with the development of a powerful cavalry. Further, Charles Omen observed that the end of the predominance of the Roman infantry forces was the rise of powerful cavalry. However, many modern commentators doubt the importance of cavalry as a decisive military arm. The reasons for this, as far as I can see, are involved with the ages-long debate about the collapse of the Western Empire.

Source material from the Later Roman Empire is voluminous. There is far more from this period than from the ages before or after. Most of these essays, letters, histories, laws and political treatises revolve around questions of the application of the faith of the Christian Church to the problems of the time. Since the Enlightenment, most commentators on ancient Rome have ignored most of these materials but, nevertheless, have invoked the strong moral content expressed by later Roman authors regarding the difficulties of their time. Of course, the writing by and about the Bishop St Ambrose, St Jerome, and the Bishop St Augustine not to mention by and about the emperors Constantine, Julian, and Theodosius are very important in the history of humanity, although the thrust of this importance is very controversial. While I certainly will not deny anything those ancient authorities had to say, my point here is that the basic difficulty facing the Later Roman Empire and society was the fact that they could not adequately absorb the new military technology that allowed horsemen to dominate the battlefield. While the churchmen had a lot to say, those who really made the decisions that produced major social results were the horse lords whose approach to the question of social management was summed up in the statement of a number of their leaders: they and their trusty knights would simply kill anyone who threatened the rule of the Prince of Peace.

A master of horses grew up from early childhood with his horses, either in a nomadic tribe that raised horses or on a horse-raising estate. Horses are temperamental and difficult creatures to handle. Sure enough, a gentle riding horse can pass from rider to rider but a warhorse is different. Feisty, head-strong, willing to take the bit in his mouth and charge ahead, this rather stupid creature needs a firm hand but also a degree of tenderness so that horse and rider move and think as one. Generally, the horse used by a superb cavalryman comes from a single blood line. This is because the actual working life of a horse is no more than a decade, at which time the cavalryman needs a new mount. Further, horses get sick, have hoof problems, and a whole host of such things, not to mention killed in battle. The cavalryman needs at any one time three to six mounts following him. Having the animals carefully chosen from one blood line allows a similarity in actions between animals. The breeding, raising, training of horses and of the men to ride them is a full time job.

Just as the horsemen are concerned over the pedigree of their mounts so they and their wives are concerned over their own pedigrees. The noble steed carries a noble rider. Or, as their critics were quick to point out, the difference between a cavalry horse and a cavalryman were minor. The Romans resisted the spread of the horse lord culture of large estates of horse breeders and riders. With the imperial stud farms, they produced sufficient horses. But the cavalry that system produced could not stand against those raised with their mounts. The Battle of Adrianople illustrates the problem.

The Battle of Adrianople, AD 378

From the reign of Constantine (d. AD 337) to the time of the Valentinian dynasty (AD 364), the empire successfully held off the northern Germans.

Emperor Valentinian I and his brother and co-emperor Valens launched successful attacks against the German tribes. After Valentinian died in 375, his son Gratian reigned in the West. His uncle Valens, ruler in the east, became senior emperor. The imperial frontiers appeared stable until 376, when a great disturbance broke out in the steppe lands north of the Black Sea. Here ruled vast horse-based tribal kingdoms of Goths extending from what are now the plains of Poland to the River Volga. Erupting into these Gothic lands came what appeared to be a vast horde of barbarian horsemen from the depths of the steppes. These were the Huns. Who they were, where they came from, and what they wanted, are answered in many modern accounts but there is little agreement. What is certain is that the Huns smashed the Gothic kingdoms, sent the survivors reeling, and seriously frightened them. The Goths from the steppes recoiled against their neighbours and soon whole Germanic peoples were at the imperial frontier, begging to be allowed into the empire.

The result, well told by the contemporary Roman historian Ammianus Marcellinus, was war. The Goths organized themselves into armies. The original group that came across the Danube into the empire seized weapons from the Romans; others came across the Danube armed and ready. Emperor Valens deployed a large army in Thrace with the intention of crushing the Goths. The Romans and Goths clashed near Adrianople on 2 August 378. Ammianus is our only literary source and his account is not very clear. What is clear is that while the Roman infantry units advanced against the Gothic foot, the Gothic cavalry of the Greuthungi and their Alan allies swept away the Roman cavalry and smashed into the Roman infantry. The Roman lines crumbled: the Goths wiped out a major Roman force and killed Emperor Valens. How the Goths managed to destroy the Roman army is unclear but a major factor has to be the force of the Greuthungi cavalry, described by Ammianus as '...*equitatus Gothorum cum Althatheo reverses et Saphrace, Halanorum manu permixta, ut fulmen prope montes celsos excussus, quoscumque accurse veloci invenuire comminus potuit, incitata caede turbavit.*' The effect of the Gothic cavalry charge, in Homeric simile, 'Like a lightning bolt from a mountain top,' is probably from an eyewitness account. The battle of Adrianople wreaked the Roman army of the east, opened the whole of Thrace to the Goths and their allies, and disrupted imperial administration.

The defeat rang throughout the empire. In an emergency, the imperial administration in the east chose a new emperor, not merely a product of political infighting but someone whom many believed to be the best possible candidate. This was Theodosius I (379–395). The new emperor was spectacularly successful in his efforts to rebuilt the imperial armies and strengthen the Roman state. His solution to the problem of an effective cavalry force was to hire non-Roman tribes and organize them as units in the imperial army. This, of course, followed Roman military tradition; the use of auxiliary units recruited from the 'barbarians' went back to the old Republic. Germans had been a part of the imperial army for centuries. Julius Caesar had hired German cavalry in his conquest of Gaul. Theodosius' *foederati*, as the hired Gothic units were called, provided a powerful striking force, which the Emperor used in recovering Thrace and reasserting the dominance of the imperial forces. Theodosius made good use of German military talent: one of his generals and advisors was a Vandal noble, Stilicho, and one of his generals leading a *foederati* unit was the noble Goth Alaric. Both gave Theodosius excellent service. To ensure imperial stability, after he overcame a western usurper, Theodosius placed his two sons on the throne, Arcadius in Constantinople, Honorius in Italy. When Theodosius died in 395, the empire was unified and stronger than it had been for a generation.

The Development of the Eastern Empire

Theodosius' successors' mismanagement destroyed that emperor's achievements and the Roman Empire. The two new emperors were very young when Theodosius died but he had placed them under the directions of his most trusted advisors. Unfortunately, these advisors betrayed his trust. In the west, the Emperor Honorius, aged ten, looked to the military commander, Stilicho, who was able but unscrupulous. In the east, Arcadius, aged seventeen, was at the centre of an imperial court, many members of which were manoeuvring for power. The east was significantly richer than the west and Stilicho decided to gain power over the eastern provinces nearest Italy, Greece and Moesia. The eastern court countered by sending the imperial general Alaric and his allied army of Goths against Stilicho. While Stilicho duelled with the eastern directed forces in Italy's north, he called on the Army of the Rhine for reinforcements. While these came as ordered, in December of 406, the Rhine froze and vast numbers of German tribes swept into Gaul and then Spain. The Germans sacked and burned the army headquarters and garrison towns. The Rhine frontier was lost. Within two generations, the society of the western province changed significantly. Wealth had always been land and now the land owners left their town houses and moved to the country. The gracious villas became comfortable manors. Now, besides raising staple crops, the land owners raised horses and bought into the horse lord way of life. The cities shrank, the old, who remembered the cosmopolitan imperial way of life died, and their children went off to find adventure on horseback. These children, raised with horses, were just as able riders as the Germanic noble tribesmen, with whom they intermarried. Those to whom war and violence did not appeal joined the Church and became priests and monks. Civil government disappeared, replaced by horse lord domination. From the ruins of the Western Empire emerged the kingdoms of the Franks, the Visigoths, the Angles, the Vandals, and the Ostrogoths.

The eastern provinces were different. Here the young and immature Arcadius stayed in Constantinople, under the thumb of his advisors. They indulged themselves with a never ending series of power struggles in which the victor held sway for a year or so and the losers suddenly died. The struggles polarized between those whose power rested on the Gothic units of the eastern army and those who supported 'Roman' nationalism. This disagreement exploded in the year 400, when the population of Constantinople rose against the Goths and other Germans in their midst and massacred thousands of them. Soon after, the Roman army turned on unsuspecting Gothic units and slaughtered them. The eastern army, purged of Germans, now had to rely on troops locally raised or non-German outsiders. The German forces and people that remained alive were shoved toward the west, where the Western administration could deal with them. In many ways the purge of the Germans weakened the Eastern Army but with the divisive German soldiers gone, the Eastern realm found a new degree of unity.

With the exit of strong German influence in the east, Arcadius' administration stabilized. Power passed to a group of Constantinople's distinguished citizens, people who combined the strengths of the old Hellenic culture with the power of the new Christian world in which they lived. A prominent member of the senate, Anthemius, became praetorian prefect of the east. His administration continued after Arcadius died (408) during the minority of Arcadius' son Theodosius II. The Church historian Socrates who wrote within living memory of these events, said about Anthemius, 'This man won the reputation of being the most intelligent of his time, and in fact he was. He did nothing without counsel, sharing with eminent men his deliberations on the proper course of action.' Anthemius and his circle envisioned a Roman state structured in civic institutions, the uniting of old Roman and Greek virtues with Christian values, diplomacy with war as only a last resort, and strong controls on the soldiers and their commanders.

Anthemius maintained the imperial forces but ensured that the army commanders recognized civil authority as paramount. Moreover, he changed the strategic structure of the empire: he turned Constantinople from an imperial residence and military base into the citadel and capital of the empire. Constantinople was defended by Constantine's walls, built like the Aurelian walls of Rome, as a typical city defence. Useful in a crisis, the walls could not hold out in a prolonged siege and anyway the city sprawled out into the countryside beyond the walls. Anthemius oversaw the design and construction of new walls, very large, encompassing wide areas so that they protected the whole city. Nowhere on earth were there such walls. Behind these walls the imperial establishment, the Great Church, the main business interests, and the military forces found safety and protection from the chaos that sometimes engulf the empire. Previously, the emperor and his administration moved around the empire rather regularly. Beginning with Theodosius II, the emperor might leave Constantinople, but the understanding remained: his home was Constantinople.

The army in the eastern section of the empire remained intact, unlike the armies in the west. The *limitanei* still guarded the frontiers, along the Danube, in Asia Minor, along the desert frontier in the east, and southern Egypt. A mix of light and medium infantry with a strong component of light cavalry, the *limitanei* guarded the frontier from raiders and infiltration. The total number of *limitanei* seems to have been a little under 200,000 men. The eastern section of the empire also had five field armies, two '*Praesental*', the other three in the main administrative units of the state: Thrace, Illyricum, and the East. Each provincial army consisted of from 18,000 to 15,000 men. The *Praesental* armies were about 15,000 each. Generally, cavalry formed about a third of the field armies and maybe a fourth or less of the provincial forces. This organization scheme considered the field armies (in the presents of the emperor) as final reinforcements for the provincial armies which, in turn, backed up the *limitanei*.

The army did recruit many Germans but as individuals and not groups. The commanders assigned them to different units to avoid building homogenous units. Now the truth is that the more homogenous a unit is, the better it will fight, so the East Roman administration purposely weakened its armies to avoid the problem of overly powerful and independent German armies taking over, as in the western sections of the empire. However, this was not seen as a significant weakness by the imperial administration. Rather, the masters of Constantinople developed a new strategy to handle serious threats. Edward Luttwak, the well known military commentator, makes the point that it is precisely this development that led to a uniquely 'Byzantine' style of international relations. The crux of this development was the intense effort to find another answer to the problem of aggressive neighbours besides fighting. Here, were applied all the arts of the masters of intrigue: bribery, either to individuals or groups, empty honours or lovely women, offering half a loaf because it is cheaper for the enemy to get that than to go for the whole. And, of course, the counter point of all of this: the sleight of hand, being able to take back with one hand what the other hand has given. Double dealing, targeted assassination, holding a possible rival in hand, all is fair game. This will give the operators of these methods a bad name but names are cheap and manipulating the enemy is good. While the western section of the empire fell apart, the eastern section increased in unity and cohesion using both intellectual skills to out think their enemies and strong, if not overwhelming, physical force to back up their positions.

The Development of the Byzantine State

The establishment of a stable Roman regime in the East was not easily achieved. The Court of Constantinople never saw itself as an independent entity but always maintained that it was part of the whole empire, responsible for and to the legitimate Western Court and the empire as a whole. As the power of the Western Court waned, Theodosius II sent aid as he was able. By 440, a Hunnic empire, under Attila, stretched along the Danube frontier, threatening both the Eastern and Western Empire. The Eastern Court, after suffering a series of defeats, offered to pay substantial tribute to Attila in exchange for peace.

While diplomacy had a hand in lessoning the military burden, the Eastern Court needed a large number of horsemen, both light and heavy, and drew these from Germanic tribesmen. The Germanic influences again increased at the Eastern Court. Theodosius II successfully balanced his administration between the Court faction, led by his eunuch chamberlain and the Germanic military faction led by the Alan general, Aspar. But, in the summer of 450, Theodosius died from a fall off his horse. Theodosius' sister, Pulcheria, allied herself with Aspar, marrying one of Aspar's lieutenants, Marcian, and proclaimed him emperor. It appeared at the time, that just like the west, a military Germanic warlord would take over. Marcian refused to pay the Huns once Attila began moving his forces against the Western Empire. The Master of Soldiers in the West, Aetius, organized a coalition of Roman and Germanic armies and defeated the Huns at Chalôns. Attila died soon afterwards and the empire broke up but Huns remained a threat to both sides of the empire.

In 457, Marcian died. The senate offered the imperial office to Aspar, recognizing that he held the commanding power in the state. Aspar, however, as both an Alan and Arian believer, understood that significant opposition would face his direct rule. Instead, he nominated another one of his lieutenants; this was Leo, fifty-six years old, who received the crown of the Roman Empire. But the empire Leo ruled had become very different from that of Theodosius II. The dynastic link that held together the two sections, East and West, had broken. Theodosius II and his sister were gone and the western line had ended with the murder of Valentinian III in 455. Now there was no Western Emperor, only a squabbling group of Germanic and Roman warlords, struggling for what power remained in the growing chaos. While the ongoing collapse of the Western Empire was a matter of concern in Constantinople, local problems were also pressing. The main concern was whether German warlords were going to run and wreck the empire.

Emperor Leo I oversaw the civil administration and slowly tried to weaken Aspar and the Germanic military factions. In the west, the Germanic appointed emperors, who Leo refused to recognized, tried to eliminate their Germanic warlords but were quickly killed for their efforts. Leo took note and moved slowly. In the southern part of Anatolia, north of the Tarsus Mountains was the land of the Isaurians, a wild country of brigands and unruly people. Never quite conquered or brought into the civil administration, the Isaurians had been contained by an internal frontier of the Roman Empire. Leo brought a gang of Isaurians to Constantinople under the command of an Isaurian leader, Tarasius. The emperor organized the gang, with some volunteers from other sources, into a new guard regiment, the *Excubitors*. Tarasius took the name Zeno, became commander of the imperial guards, master of soldiers in Thrace, and, in 467, married Leo's daughter, Ariadne. In this way, Leo built a counter force to the Germanic troops that Aspar was unable to thwart.

In the west, the warlord general Ricimer came to an agreement with Leo on a political settlement. The strategic threat that pushed the Western Empire into final ruin was the Vandal Kingdom in Africa. As Roman provinces, Africa supplied inexpensive food and high tax revenue to the imperial government. But the Vandals ended that. Unlike the Visigoths in southern Gaul and Spain, who recognized imperial suzerainty and kept peace of a sort, the Vandals maintained a militant independence and plundered Italy and the northern Mediterranean as they saw fit. Ricimer agreed to install Anthemius, Emperor Marcian's son-in-law, as western emperor and Leo began organizing a joint major military campaign to oust the Vandals. The Eastern Empire sent a number of coordinated armies to distract the Vandal forces. The main effort, commanded by Leo's wife's brother, Basiliscus, sailed in a large fleet and landed to the south of the Vandal capital, Carthage. The aged Vandal king, Gaiseric, ever wily, begged of Basiliscus a mere five days' truce so the Vandals could prepare for surrender. The inexperienced commander agreed, only to find the Vandal fleet bearing down on his anchorage with fire ships to the fore. The defeat was devastating. Any hope of a restored Roman Empire faded away in the aftershocks of Vandal victory. Ricimer soon ousted Anthemius, and the Roman Empire of Italy collapsed into the hands of a tribal chieftain, Odovacar, who ended the shadow imperial office in the west. Leo, using a series of military failures and charges of disloyalty, and with the support of the Isaurian Zeno, invited Aspar and his son to a banquet and had them killed. The Germans were now, for all intents, in absolute control of Gaul, Spain, Africa, and Italy. But Isaurian military interests in the administration, although unpopular, displaced the Germans in the east and the imperial government survived. Leo's reign ended in confusion, with battles in Thrace between competing bands of Ostrogoths when Leo I died in 474.

A period of confusion followed. Leo II was an infant, who soon died, and the husband of Ariadne (Leo I's daughter), Zeno, attempted to seize power, but he was thwarted by Leo I's wife's brother, Basiliscus. But, Basiliscus rested his power on the Ostrogothic forces in Thrace and the population of Constantinople disliked the Goths more than the Isaurians. Soon Zeno gained the throne. Even though Zeno remained unpopular, his reign was fortunate. The old Vandal King, Gaiseric, died and his successor did not have his burning desire for constant war. The eastern provinces of the Persian Empire were devastated by a steppe invasion. The Persians had no time for a Roman war. And, eventually, Zeno solved both the Italian and Ostrogoth problems by sending the Ostrogothic leader, Theoderic, to clean up Italy. Zeno died in 491. Ariadne Augusta nominated a high court official, Anastasius, as emperor. He was approved by the senate and the people of Constantinople. The reign of Anastasius was particularly successful. He removed the Isaurian faction from power. While small wars sputtered across the empire as usual, Anastasius maintained the integrity of the state without major challenge. The military upheavals of previous reigns settled down and the armed forces stabilized into a set pattern. Anastasius, as part of his general financial reforms, raised the soldier's pay significantly. Volunteers joined the army from the civilian base of the state: no longer were Germans or Isaurians needed. He also solved the problem of building hard fighting elite units.

The Byzantine Way of War

The order of battle under Anastasius remained similar to that portrayed in the *Notitia Dignitatum* (early in reign of Theodosius II). The *limitanei* still protected the borders. Often mounted infantry, these troops were more of a local militia and constabulary than an actual military force. The term *comitatenses* was not much used anymore but the main forces of the empire were collected in six major field army formations: Illyricum, Thrace, the East, and two mobile forces, Armies in the Imperial Presence I and II. The soldiers of these formations were known as *statiotai*. These were well trained and disciplined infantry from inside the empire, from Thrace, Illyricum, and Asia Minor.

The term *numerous* described the battalion sized units to which the *statiotai* belong. These are the successors of the older *vexillationes*, detachments of the imperial legions, now independent units. Commanders attached elite units to these field armies as necessary. There were two types of elite forces, both heavy cavalry. One was called the *foederati*, units of highly trained horsemen, coming from outside or inside the empire. No longer the older *foederati*, tribal units under their own leaders employed by the government, these organizations were successor units commanded by Roman officers, consisting of men from a variety of origins, working together as a military unit. The other elite units were the *bucellarii*, literally 'biscuit eaters'. These had existed for a long time but as private units of bodyguards for important Romans. They were hired men, trained to the needs of their private employer to protect life and property. Germanic leaders always had their own sworn companion body guards and the *bucellarii* served the same function for Roman commanders. However, the units expanded into a corps of heavy shock troops. There were two classes of *bucellarii*, the *hypaspistai*, shield bearers and *doryphoroi*, spear bearers. The shield bearers were the rank and file of the units and the spear bearers were officers. The army of Anastasius still included a sizeable number of people from beyond the imperial frontiers, now called allied troops, consisting mainly of light cavalry archers.

The dominant forces of the imperial armies were the heavy cavalry *kataphfractoi*, cuirassiers in mail, casques, greaves, and riding armoured horses. Besides sword and spear, these soldiers fought with powerful bow and arrow. Making up both the *foederati* and the *bucellarii*, these were queens of the Byzantine chess board. By the numbers, Anastasius' army appears to have had about 175,000 *limitanei*, 95,000 field troops, along with some 30,000 oarsmen for the transports and warships. The imperial administration in Constantinople held these forces well in hand. The military commanders were officers of a centralized state, not warlords able to decide on policy in their command area. Unlike the commanders in the Germanic successor states of the Western Empire, Byzantine generals were surrounded by civilian officials who counted every *numisma* spent and oversaw any dereliction of duty. The central government, unstable as it often was, rested upon a professional bureaucracy of accountants and lawyers that had existed since the time of Diocletian.

These officials had developed a basic outlook on the issue of war and peace. The commentator Edward Luttwak identified seven qualities of what he calls 'the Byzantine Operational Code'. This code crystallized at one time because its different parts are all interrelated. We first see it in the last half of the 5th century. The seven points are:

I. Avoid war if possible but be prepared to fight at any time.

II. Always keep any possible enemy under observation: know their methods and manners.

III. If at war, battle effectively, but emphasize small unit engagements against the enemy's supplies and camps.

IV. Emphasize manoeuvre over attrition.

V. In war, find allies who will attack current enemy.

VI. Subversion is the best method of victory.

VII. Fighting needs to be about finding the enemy's weaknesses and avoiding his strengths.

The reign of Anastasius ended in 518. By that time, the process that began when Theodosius I left Constantinople in the charge of his young son, Arcadius in 395, reached conclusion. The Roman Empire, founded by Augustus, reformed by Diocletian and Constantine, had started to morph into two separate societies, a Latin west and a Greek east. The west slowly transformed into a horse lord warrior culture while the east maintained the imperial organization, finding ways to keep the horse soldiers under bureaucratic controls. At Constantinople a new society emerged, based on Greek culture, Roman government and the Orthodox Church: the civilization we call Byzantium.

The Age of Justinian

Anastasius died without naming a successor. After the usual game of intrigue and betrayal, the commander of the palace guards, the *Excubitors*, ascended the throne as Justin I. Coming from a Latin-speaking small farming community in the Balkans, Justin was neither educated nor sophisticated. He had worked his way up the ladder of command in Constantinople; he brought his younger nephew to the Great City and saw to it that the young man had a fine education. This nephew took the name Justinian and supported his uncle as Justin slowly achieved prominence. Once Justin was emperor, Justinian was his right hand, helping Justin manage the empire. Justin died in 527, after a reign of some nine years, and Justinian ascended the throne without question. Like Augustus and Constantine, Justinian was a pivotal personality in Roman imperial history. While the empire was becoming Greek and local, Justinian emphasized Latin and the universal nature of Roman rule. In many ways Justinian is the last 'Roman' emperor: after him, there are only 'Byzantine' emperors.

For reasons that remain unclear, the reigns of Anastasius, Justin I, and the first half of Justinian I were unusually prosperous. The Eastern Empire flourished amidst booming markets, a return to growing cities, and agricultural plenty. Justinian determined to use this wealth in an effort to rebuilt and restore the empire. He reformed the administration, drawing up a new complex law code; reenergized the Church, attempting to find a unifying formula; rebuilt the centre of the Great City; and attempted to reunite the whole empire. Clearly, all of this effort failed, except the building program, because within a century of the end of Justinian's reign, the empire had become Greek, local, with a disunited church, huddling behind great walls. Why the emperor's efforts failed remains controversial.

The Germanic successor states of the Western Empire entered into their second and third generations. As these kingdoms aged, their administrations lost their original unity and intensity. Justinian saw that the Vandal Kingdom in Africa and the Ostrogothic Kingdom of Italy were ripe for conquest. The African lands fell rather easily in 533–4. Then Justinian's army invaded Italy in 535. The Italian war was far less successful than the African war because Justinian's forces collide with the Italian problem. This requires some discussion because the Italian Problem is important not only in Roman history but through medieval history and through modern times.

When the Roman Republic conquered Italy, before the Second Punic War, the Romans instituted a variety of regimes, some subject to their neighbours, others, privileged rulers in their own right: Roman citizens, to be sure, but self governing and internally self taxing. These communities were part of the upheavals that were called the Social War in the first century BC. During the civil wars that ended the old Republic, these communities supported one side or the other, expending lives and property. Eventually, these communities united under the Young Caesar supported his assumption of imperial power as Augustus. Under the early empire, Italy was a diverse land of privileged, self-governing communities, exempt from the burdens of imperial administration and taxation. That's the way the Italians liked it. In the imperial crisis of the third century AD, many in the imperial administration believed that Italy should pay a 'fair share' of imperial costs. But the problem was that while the Romans united Italy, they never united the Italians. The different Italian communities had no intention of surrendering their self governing independence and refused to cooperate with the imperial administration. After Diocletian and his successors subjected Italy to direct imperial rule, the Italians incessantly hindered the administration, constantly lodging legal appeals, demands for personnel changes, and open revolts to establish friendlier emperors. That is why the Italians welcomed the Germanic warlords and had no problem dispensing with the western emperor.

The Ostrogothic Kingdom was a rather ramshackle affair but that suited the Italians. When Justinian restored imperial rule, many Italians wanted no part of the restored burdens. Of course, because some communities opposed imperial rule, others because of that fact, supported the empire. The Italian war dragged on and on.

Justinian's Armies

The wars of Justinian are well recorded in the works of two contemporary historians: one, Procopius, as good as any classical Greek military narrative and the other, Agathias, certainly adequate. But equally interesting, there was a military handbook, written for officers that described the training of the soldiers. This text is included in the *Codex Mediceo-Laurentanus graecus 55*, a book commissioned by Constantine VII Porphyrogenitus and held in the imperial library for centuries. This volume contains the most significant late Roman and Byzantine strategic texts. Because the first few leaves of this specific text are missing, fairly clearly the text was defective when it was copied into Constantine VII's book. The text was old when Constantine chose it. The book appears to date from the age of Justinian. Called, the *Anonymous Byzantine Treatise on Strategy*, the work gives a concise and succinct account of managing the forces of the state for offence and defence. Together, the narrative histories and the training manual described an army that became the standard Byzantine armed force.

The queen of the Byzantine chess board remained the heavy cavalry. Like the queen in chess, the use of heavy cavalry did not always appear as the decisive move on the field of battle. Rather, because the piece is so powerful and expensive in the terms of equipment and training yet still vulnerable to unseen attack, its use is restricted to either a massive finishing sequence of moves or used in desperation to stave off defeat. Most of the time for a good player, the queen is simply an observer of the events on the board, her mere presence a substantial contribution to the fight. Supporting the heavy cavalry is the light archer cavalry. Far less expensive, yet a substantial investment, the light cavalry screened and assisted the heavy cavalry. If faced by an infantry unit that assumed a tight formation, the archer cavalry shot at it until the formation beaks up, then the heavy cavalry charged. Cavalry engagements were a swirling mass of light horse as the heavies manoeuvred for best position to charge their opposite number.

The infantry is not to be forgotten: here the mass and staying power of the force resided. The main infantry formation was defensive. For offence there was the cavalry. As a defensive formation, the infantry had dispensed with the chequered board formations of maniples so typical of the legions of the high empire. With their short sword, *pilum*, and lose formations, the maniples were offensive in action. Now, with a long sword and stout spear, the infantry formation was to hold their ground, protecting their base and providing refuge, if need be, to the cavalry. The manoeuvring of a large number of armed men without confusion in the middle of falling arrows, charging horses, dead, and dying men, was difficult. The army officers' answer, as always was drill. The basic unit of the formation is the file. Each man has a place in the file, which he must know without question. A file is also a collection of messmates so the men know each other well. The first man in the file is the most well armoured, the man just behind him is also well protected. The rear man of the file is well protected. In between the men have less armour, and may even have bows or throwing spears. The files are organized in ranks. Each man must know in what his place in the file belongs. Then, of course, this whole moves, keeping rank and file. The only way to really do this is to march in step, each man stepping at the same time with the same foot. To march in step, drums beat a rhythm and a little song never hurts. And this is what the infantry does every day. Besides cavalry and infantry, the treatise includes an excellent section on teaching archery, laying out a camp and a fort, and a host of general information the new officer needs to consider.

In the later part of Justinian's reign, other developments of the imperial army include the downgrading of the *limitanei* into a local militia. No longer paid by the imperial government, the border soldiers became full-time farmers. But, the impressive series of fortifications that Justinian built was thought to make their task easier. Also, Justinian reintroduced a field army in Armenia to reinforce the Army of the East.

Events after Justinian I

Bad management and unpopular decisions bedevilled the later years of Justinian's reign. When he died in 565, Justinian was in his low eighties. Theodora, who often moderated Justinian's less than optimal actions, had died in 548; Justinian grew into an old self-willed autocratic man who accepted no opposition. Nor did he ever appoint a successor. For a brief moment there was a vacuum in the empire when the old man finally succumbed to nature's debt but a nephew, Justin II, quickly ascended the throne. He was the son of Justinian's sister and husband to Theodora's formidable niece, Sophia. Justin II proved a competent if not brilliant administrator. The government had sufficient revenue; the religious problems did not break out into violence; the eastern frontier managed with the usual vicissitudes. The Balkans remained difficult but under control, with the Avars constantly challenging imperial authority and the Slav tribes settling in different places. In the west, however, the Italian problems kept coming. Local Italian interests in the Po valley decided that managing Lombard rulers was more profitable than managing the Greeks and the hard won unity of Italy fell apart. Africa remained loyal and calm as did southern Spain. Justin II suffered a mental breakdown in the mid 570s and Sophia chose a successful general, Tiberius Constantine, to manage affairs. After Justin died in 578, Tiberius Constantine succeeded to the throne.

The new emperor was competent. Revenues continued to be adequate. The never-ending wars in the east and the Balkans continued as did the fighting in Italy. Tiberius Constantine did develop an administrative innovation that proved in the long run to be very important. In Italy, instead of the usual apparatus of civil officials running military officers, the Emperor appointed an *exarch*, an official who combined both civil and military authority in one. To foreshadow: this unitary command structure later became a main factor in the administration of the Byzantine Empire. Tiberius became sick and died in 582. His successor was the successful military commander Maurice.

The reign of Maurice presents historians with a significant problem of interpretation. When this emperor ascended the throne, the Eastern Roman Empire appeared as strong as it had ever been: after he fell, the whole Eastern Roman Empire collapsed; did Maurice's somehow weaken the imperial structure so that it collapsed? Certainly, at the time, this did not appear so. During Maurice's rule, the Danube frontier, while under strong pressure, remained strong and fortified; the Persian frontier, also under pressure, remained strongly held. Indeed, Maurice reigned for twenty years, successfully fighting wars and managing the state. He reformed the army into a pattern that would continue to exist for centuries. These are explained in *Maurice's Strategikon*, a military manual used throughout the rest of Byzantine history. This book, probably written by the Emperor, described the imperial army as Maurice wanted it. A remarkably full and informative narrative, the handbook demonstrates a remarkable understanding of the military problems facing the empire.

Maurice's Army

Before we look at the vicissitudes of empire, let us consider the army as Maurice described it and as it remained for centuries. The elimination of the semi private character of many units, particularly the *bucellarii* and *foederati*, was a major objective of his reforms. Maurice reorganized military units to fit a single standard model. For cavalry, the basic unit was the *bandon* or *tagma*, of about 400 lances. Two or three *tagmata* together made a *moira*, also called a *chiliarchy*. Two or three *moiras* made a *meros*. Each *moira* should have no more than 3,000 lances and no *meros* should have more than 6,000 or 7,000 lances. The *meros* should be divided into a right, centre and left or van, middle, rear. Here, I must note a point about numbers: a 'lance' (my terminology from medieval Western European usage), that is a mounted soldier, is actually a small unit of five to seven men and at least six or seven horses. The war horse is not ridden for transportation and certainly not to carry materials. The soldier himself needed a hackney, the groom, weapons keeper (or esquire), cook, and washer woman each needed a horse and actually the whole group needed two or three more horses, and maybe a couple of slaves. So when the numbers say the bandon has 375 men, we are actually talking about a little less than 2,000 people. So when the emperor says that we should have no more than some 7,000 lances, we are talking about better than 30,000 people on the move. Now, these are not necessarily all together in one spot but are rather spread out along the line of manoeuvre, participating in all sorts of interesting businesses. The infantry are also organized into *tagmata* and so forth, but in general are spear carriers and each file shared a tent and mess. Even so, each file would have a number of helpers, relatives or slaves.

The imperial army collected the *tagmata* together into the field armies. Since Justinian had disestablished the older *limitanei* these field armies represented the whole military force. Under Tiberius Constantine, *tagmata* of *foederati* combined into a field army, called the *Foederati*, representing the older Army in the Imperial Presence I. The older Army in the Imperial Presence II was reconstituted as the *Optimates*. Many *tagmata* of Germanic soldiers, now called *Gothograeci* composed this unit. A third major unit formed under Maurice, the *Bucellarii*, smaller and more select, used as a personal guard and elite reinforcement. A probable number of soldiers in each unit are: for the *Bucellarii*, some 600 total; for the *Optimates*, some 2,000 total, in other words, a *moira*; and the *Foederati*, between 6,000 and 7,000 men, a *meros*. In total, the elite corps of the Emperor Maurice's forces was some 10,000 mounted soldiers, backed up by *tagmata* of the older field armies, the Army of Thrace, of Armenia, and of the East.

For twenty years Maurice managed the empire and the frontiers successfully. He had the reputation of being tight with the *numisma*. Often, his efforts to improve efficiency and maintain tactical superiority were said to be simply money-saving tricks. In 602, civil unrest in Egypt delayed the wheat fleet to Constantinople. This caused a rise in the price of bread and led to riots in the city. Meanwhile, the imperial army and the army of Thrace were on campaign in the Balkans north of the Danube. Maurice upheld the field commanders' order for the army to spend the winter in the field north of the Danube. While there were obvious tactical advantages to this plan, the soldiers intensely disliked the idea and they mutinied. Originally, the demand was to simply remove the field commander, but the city also rose and the situation quickly exploded out of control. A soldier, Phocas, became emperor amidst the intramural fighting of competing factions.

The End of Antiquity

When Phocas started his reign in 602, he faced opposition from many different groups in the aristocracy and army. He solidified his position through prosecutions and executions. Phocas' political and management abilities were poor: he instituted a persecution of Christian heretics and decreed that all Jews convert to Christianity. Refugees fled to the Persian court, to Africa and Italy. In 603, the Persian Shah, in support of a supposed son of Maurice, attacked in the east. As the political situation went from bad to worse, Heraclius, the Exarch of Africa, proclaimed himself and his son as consuls in opposition to Phocas, in 608. In 610, his son, Heraclius, led an expeditionary force to Constantinople and was well received by all factions. By the year's end, Heraclius the younger became emperor and Phocas had found a painful end.

While the new regime took over in Constantinople, the eastern provinces of the empire grew more chaotic. The Persian forces pushed deep into the empire, fragmenting the centres of political control. By 611, the Persians occupied strategic points in Syria; by 612, they penetrated Asia Minor; by 612, they took Antioch, Emese, and Damascus; in spring of 614, the Persians stormed Jerusalem and later in the year took Egypt. A number of difficulties had allowed Roman control to slip away in the east besides Phocas' misrule. Under Theodosius II as under Justinian I, the empire was Roman and Latin. Despite the fact that most of the government and church officials spoke Greek, the language of administration remained the old imperial tongue. This kept a distance between the imperial officials and the population they ruled. Copts, Syrians, Jews, Armenians, Greeks and so forth bent the knee to the Latin-speaking overlords. But, after Justinian died, under Justin II, Tiberius Constantine, Phocas, and now especially Heraclius, the empire became Greek in language and the mystique of the Romans faded in the face of the knowledge that it was the Greeks who ruled. Cultural and religious differences came to the fore and chaos followed. The Persians taxed and plundered as they willed but they did not so much conquer the lands they occupied as administered the chaos around themselves. Many enclaves remained Roman in name, even if their attitude toward the regime in Constantinople was doubtful.

Heraclius faced a divided city, administration, and empire when he gained the throne. First, he had to pull the parts back together; for that, he needed an army. The Army of the East was in Cappadocia, defending itself none too well; Heraclius dismissed the army's commanders in 612. Nevertheless, the Emperor's campaign to relieve Antioch failed in 613. The Danube frontier had collapsed when Phocas marched on Constantinople: Avars followed by Slavic tribes spread into the Balkans, threatening even the imperial city. The Avars allied with the Persians and Heraclius tried to negotiate with both in 615 but the effort failed. After putting down a rebellion in Italy during 616–618, Heraclius began collecting the means of pushing the Persians back to Persia. His efforts came to a head in the winter of 621–2, when the Emperor told the senate, aristocracy, and church leaders, that he was going back to Carthage and would stay there unless they gave him all that they could to fight against the Persians. The Church surrendered its treasures, the senate and aristocracy surrendered land. Using the gold to recruit new soldiers, giving the land as payment, Heraclius built a new powerful force of horse soldiers. The Emperor strengthened the old field army of Armenia, which remained in Armenia; the Army of the East stayed in Cappadocia; the Army of Thrace settled in Phrygia. Heraclius broke up the old Army in the Imperial Presence, the *foederati*, which he attached to the Army of the East. He then established a new elite field army, the *Opsican*, settled in Bithynia. He folded the corps *Optimates* into the *Opsican* corps, setting them along the Bosporus on the Asian side. Heraclius gave the soldiers land instead of pay, believing that the men would fight for what was theirs more than for an abstract idea.

The ensuing campaigns are the widest sweeping in imperial history. Our knowledge of them is, unfortunately, very imperfect. In the final analysis, all we really have is a bald list of events: mobilizing the imperial armies in spring of 622, Heraclius struck at the Persian forces in Asia Minor, defeating a strong contingent; the next year, Heraclius tried to talk the Avars into leaving the vicinity of Constantinople but they attempted to kill him in the process; in spring, 624, Heraclius marched into Armenia, sacking Persian bases, striking into the lands of the Medes and burning a main Zoroastrian temple. Then the Emperor encountered and defeated the main Persian commander Shahbaraz near Lake Van in winter of that year; Heraclius and his army wintered in Armenia; the next spring, the Emperor withdrew through the Cilician Gates with Shahbaraz following. Meanwhile both the Avars and the Persians besieged Constantinople from land and sea; in 627, Heraclius made overtures to Shahbaraz, who had fallen into disfavour with the Persian Shah. Finally, in summer 627, the Emperor contacted and made an alliance with a powerful group of Turkish tribes in central Asia, joining them to his army in order to attack and destroy the Persian forces. In the fall of 627, Heraclius led his army from Tiflis with his Turkish allies to the River Tigris in a winter campaign;

on 12 December 627, Heraclius, his army, and allies decisively defeated the Persian army at the Battle of Nineveh. The Persian government collapsed and in spring 628, Heraclius signed a peace treaty with the Persian administration, allowing them to evacuate the areas they were occupying. The war ended on terms that were favourable to the Eastern Empire.

As the Persian forces withdrew in 629, Heraclius and the imperial administration began returning to the eastern provinces. In 630, the Emperor celebrated his victory in Jerusalem. The restored authorities called many of those who supported the Persians to account. Mobs massacred dissidents and this included many Jews in Galilee and Jerusalem. Local populations in Syria, Palestine and near areas were not all pleased with the return of the imperial government. While the empire settled back into power, other events, very important but unperceived by the imperial leaders unfolded in the Arabian lands. When Heraclius was occupied in his Persian war, the Prophet Muhammad was spreading the Word of Islam. The Prophet died in 632 and by 634, a united Muslim force began sweeping into the Syrian provinces. The great Arab conquests had begun.

The Arab armies attacking the empire were different from anything seen before. The Late Romans had allied or fought with Arab forces near the imperial or Persian borders for centuries. But the forces coming from deep in the Arabian lands were very different. One innovation greatly changed the desert military environment: the north Arabian wood-framed camel saddle, secured to the top of the animal's hump. This allowed the camel raising tribes to transport a large number of men and supplies through the previously impassable desert. Fighting from camel back was not a good idea, but camel-mounted infantry and cavalry, leading their horses from camel back, meant that large forces could now go where the infantry and cavalry of the empire did not expect. Moreover, the Arab forces were intrinsically lighter than the imperial forces. The Arabian horses, few in number, could ride circles around the *tagmata* of the emperor. Arab archery was very good. Arab infantry, in loose order, could steal in, strike, and retreat faster than the heavy infantry could respond. Arab swords cut floating silk while imperial swords shattered iron.

The decisive Arab victory over the empire was the month long campaign along the Yarmuk River, where now Israel, Lebanon, and Syria met. The later Byzantine, Armenian, and Arab sources are confused and conflict about what happened but the basic facts remain that the Arab forces outmanoeuvred the imperial army, trapping the infantry and destroying them. The elite cavalry escaped and the imperial forces retreated into Asia Minor. The empire lost whole provinces without military answer through the 640s to the 670s. The imperial forces did not just give up, they fought constantly, but in the end the Muslims prevailed.

The Army of the Byzantine Empire

When the military chaos of the seventh century finally settled, a new army and society had formed. The Eastern Roman Empire, spreading from the Danube to the Nile and from the Euphrates to the Adriatic was gone. Now the Byzantine Empire centred on Constantinople, held Asia Minor, islands in the Mediterranean, and bits of Greece, Macedonia, Thrace and Italy. The core of the state was the military settlements in Asia Minor. These were the old army corps of the Eastern Empire, now settled on 'soldiers' land' each property responsible for equipping and maintaining a soldier. The Byzantines applied the term *theme* to the administrative structure overseeing these properties. By about 660, there were five themes, each under a general. In Armenia, the *Ameniakon Theme* replaced the old Armenia field army; the *Thrakesion Theme*, settled in Phrygia, was the successor to the field army of Thrace; in central Asia Minor, the *Anatolikon Theme* was the remains of the Army of the East; near Constantinople, on the Asian side, the *Opsikion Theme* was the successor to the elite Army in the Emperor's Presence. There also emerged the *Cibyrrhaeot Theme* on the south shore of Asia Minor, consisting of naval personnel for the fleet. The *themes* were very successful as an organization. They continued as a main organization of the Byzantine Empire until the 1080s and the Battle of Manzikert. Consisting of both cavalry and infantry, they successfully defended the empire against their Muslim and steppe enemies for three hundred years. The emperors, however, found that their support was often in question when opponents arose within the empire. By the 740s or so, the emperors had begun to organize new professional units around Constantinople that replaced the old Armies in the Emperor's Presence.

The soldiers' properties that made up the *themata* supported both horse raising and the training of horse soldiers. Clearly certain elite families had large estates that also raised horses but it was the small holdings that produced the largest number of well trained cavalry. The Byzantine government, particularly when in the hands of the elite military families, exercised great care in maintaining the small soldiers' properties. Most of the cavalry was heavy because light cavalry were mercenaries from the steppe. Even the elite units came, ultimately, from the soldiers' property because the field armies recruited their personal from the territorial units. Unlike Western Europe, the horse farmers were not semi-independent warlords, living on manors in their personal fortresses, always at swords points with their neighbours and governments. Rather, the economic social base of the Byzantine army was a regulated series of properties that supported small units of soldier's families. This is how the Antique World of the Eastern Roman Empire had passed away and yet the Byzantine Medieval World did not experience the chaos of the European west.

Conclusion

The theme of this appendix is how the technological innovation of the armoured, lance-bearing horseman changed the Mediterranean world. Coupled with his elder brother, the light bow-bearing horseman, the heavy cavalryman broke the heavy infantry armies from which classical civilization emerged and ended the dominance of the infantry armies and the urban society of which they were a major part. Economic and social structures provide a framework in which people operate but the ever-fluctuating nature of human personality always provide unexpected responses to seemingly intractable problems. The thesis is that the Eastern Roman civilization, while caught in the same ongoing maelstrom of the ending of Classical civilization, found a different solution to the challenges of the time than either the chaos of the western Europe or the advent of Islam in the Near East and North Africa. By managing their horsemen in a highly controlled way, the Eastern Romans allowed the emergence of Byzantine civilization, preserving much of their existing traditions while at the same time adjusting to the new technology of warfare. This cultural conservatism allowed the development of a fragment of the Classical World to continue for centuries into the Medieval World, providing a bridge over which much of the collected wisdom of the ancient Greeks and Romans passed to the Modern World.

References

Roman Imperial Army: Boris Renkov, 'Military Forces of the Late Republic and Principate', in Sabin et al., *Cambridge History of Greek and Roman Warfare*, vol II, pp. 35–6.

Latin quotation: Tacitus, *Agricola*, 30.5 (They make a desert and call it peace)

Changes in army during late Serveran dynasty: discussion of *Constitution Antoniniana*, in Brian Campbell, 'The Serveran dynasty' in Bowman, C. A. H., vol. XII, Cambridge UK: CUP, 2005, pp. 17–8; also see Brian Campbell, *The Emperor and the Roman Army, 31 BC–AD 235*, Oxford: OUP, 1984, especially pp. 365–414.

The great crisis begins: see Malcolm Todd, The Early Germans, Oxford: Blackwell, 1995, p. 55.

The horse lords come: For a contemporary view of these events, see Herodian: Cambridge Mass. LCL, 1969, VI 8–9, VII 1–2.

For background and detail, see A. N. Sherwin-White, *Roman Foreign Policy in the East*, Norman OK: University of Oklahoma Press, 1983, especially pp. 186–226; also, important compendium of information, Rose Mary Sheldon, *Rome's Wars in Parthia, Blood in the Sand*, Edgeware UK, 2010, especially pp. 154–85.

Roman-Persian wars: some commentators suggest that the Romans overemphasized Persian desire to expand in order to hide their own aggressive moves. Herodian, who lived through these events, seems to be well informed and saw the Persians as hostile. For a discussion see Michael Dodgeon et al., *The Roman Eastern Frontier and the Persian Wars AD 226–363*, London: Routledge, 1991, p. 352, note 12.

Quotation, Herodian, VI, 5, 9–10.

Developments in Inner Asia: see William McGovern, *The Early Empires of Central Asia*, Chapel Hill: University of Northern Carolina, 1939, pp. 311–33; Owen Lattimore, *Inner Asian Frontiers of China*, Boston: Beacon Press, 1962, pp. 429–68; Dennis Sinor (ed.) *The Cambridge History of Early Inner Asia*, Cambridge UK: CUP, 1990, pp. 151–76; John Hall, *Through the Jade Gate to Rome*, www. Booksurge.com: John Hall, 2009, a comprehensive description of Central Asia during the high Roman Empire; Rafe de Crespigny, *Imperial Warlord, Biography of Cao Cao 155–220 AD*, Leiden: E.J. Brill, 2010 (marvellous book on Chinese military history).

Inner Asian roundabout: Arnold Toynbee, *A Study of History*, vol XII, London: OUP, 1959, p. 119.

Sassanid warfare: Kaveh Farrokh, *Sassanian Elite Cavalry, AD 224–642*, Oxford: Osprey, 2005; *Shadows in the Desert, Ancient Persia at War*, Oxford: Osprey, 2007, pp. 170–81.

The Great Crisis Continues: The internal history of the empire, from the death of Alexander Serverus (235) to the accession of Valerian (253), is well displayed in David Potter, *The Roman Empire at Bay*, London: Routledge, 2004, pp. 217–256 and Pat Southern, *The Roman Empire from Serverus to Constantine*, London: Routledge, 2001, pp. 64–77.

Source problems: see the most accessible literary sources of the third century crisis, Thomas Branchich et al., *The History of Zonaras, from Alexander Serverus to the Death of Theodosius the Great*, London: Routledge, 2005, pp. 40–58 and commentary pp. 73–120.

Sassanid history: Michael Dodgeon et al., *The Roman Eastern Frontier and the Persian Wars AD 226–363*, London: Routledge, 1991, pp. 34–48, especially 'Inscription of Shapur at the Kaaba of Zoroastre', *Res Gestae Divi Saporis*, in Dodgeon, *op. cit.* p. 57.

Gallienus Reforms the Imperial Army: regarding Gallienus, Lukas De Blois, *The Policy of the Emperor Gallienus*, Leiden: E.J. Brill, 1976, especially pp. 23–83 for military policy; John Bray, *Gallienus*, Kent: Wakefield Press, 1997, especially pp. 65–6, 75–6, 144, 180–2 for new type of army; Brian Campbell, 'The Army' in CAH XII, pp. 111–6.

Problems of the horse trade: for a discussion of the horse trade in early medieval China, see David Graff, *Medieval Chinese Warfare 300–900*, London: Routledge, 2002, especially, pp. 125–130; for early modern India, Jos Gommans, *The Rise of the Indo-Afghan Empire, c. 1710–1780*, Delhi: 1999, especially pp. 68–103.

The new empire of Diocletian and Constantine: among important current accounts of the age of Diocletian and Constantine are: Timothy Barnes, *Constantine and Eusebius*, Cambridge Mass: HUP, 1981, especially, pp. 3–27, 245–260; Bill Leadbetter, *Galerius and the Will of Diocletian*, London: Routledge, 2009, especially, pp. 26–47; Noel Lenski, *The Cambridge Companion to the Age of Constantine*, Cambridge UK: CUP, 2006, especially, pp. 35–110, 183–254; Charles Odahl, *Constantine and the Christian Empire*, London: Routledge, 2004, especially, pp. 15–41, 221–244; Paul Stephenson, *Constantine Roman Emperor Christian Victor*, New York: Overlook Press, 2010, especially, pp. 87–112, 190–214; Stephen Williams, *Diocletian and the Roman Recovery*, New York: Methuen, especially, pp. 39–150.

Military problems of the New Empire: Edward N. Luttwak, *The Grand Strategy of the Roman Empire*, Baltimore: John Hopkins Press, 1996, pp. 130–45; Arthur Ferrill, *Roman Imperial Grand Strategy*, New York: University Press of America, 1991, pp. 43–51; Arthur Ferrill, *The Fall of the Roman Empire*, London: Thames and Hudson, 1986, pp. 43–9; Hans Delbrück, *The Barbarian Invasions*, Lincoln: University of Nebraska, 1980, pp. 269–84; Charles Omen, *The Art of War in the Middle Ages*, London: Greenhill Books, 1991, vol I, pp. 11–16.

The Battle of Adrianople AD 378: quotation, '...the Gothic cavalry led by Alatheus and Saphrax, combined with a force of mounted Alans, returned to the battlefield. They struck forth, like a lightning bolt from a high mountain, and disrupted all the Roman forces in their path and killed them' (Ammianus XXXI, 12. 17).

Reconstructions of the battle: Alessandro Barbero, *The Day of the Barbarians*, New York: Walker and Co., 2007; Michael Kulikowski, *Rome's Gothic War*, Cambridge UK: CUP, 2007; Lenski, Noel, *Failure of Empire*, Berkeley: University of California, 2002; and Simon MacDowall, *Adrianople AD 378*, Oxford: Osprey, 2001; Ian Hughes, *Imperial Brothers, Valentinian, Valens and the Disaster at Adrianople*, Pen and Sword, 2013; Adrian Coombs-Hoar, *Eagles in the Dust, the Roman Defeat at Adrianople, AD 378*, Pen and Sword, 2015.

Theodosius' accomplishments: see Stephen Williams and Gerard Friell, *Theodosius the Empire at Bay*, New Haven Conn: Yale University Press, 1994.

The development of the Eastern Empire: for problems in the Western Empire, see Samuel Dill, *Roman Society in the Last Century of the Western Empire*, New York: Meridian, 1958, especially pp. 285–382; Guy Halsall, *Barbarian Migration and the Roman West 376–586*, Cambridge: CUP, 2007, especially pp. 320–70; Penny MacGeorge, *Late Roman Warlords*, Oxford: OUP, 2002, especially pp. 69–164; John Michael O'Flynn, *Generalissimos of the Western Roman Empire*, Edmonton Canada: University of Alberta, especially pp. 129–49.

For problems in the Eastern Empire, see: J. B. Bury, *History of the Later Roman Empire* (2nd edition), New York: Dover, vol I, pp. 106–38, especially pp. 134–36; Alan Cameron, et al., *Barbarians and Politics at the Court of Arcadius*, Berkeley: University of California, 1993, pp. 301–336; Stephen Williams et al., *The Rome that did not Fall*, London: Routledge, 1999, p. 25.

Quotation from the Church historian: Socrates 7. 1. 1, 3.

The building of Constantinople's great wall: Byron Tsangadas, *The Fortifications and Defense of Constantinople*, Boulder Co: East European Monographs, 1980, pp. 7–15.

For the eastern Roman army, See Warren Treadgold, *Byzantium and its Army*, Stanford University Press, 1995, for a discussion of the figures, pp. 44–59; summary in Stephen Williams et al., *The Rome that did not Fall*, London: Routledge, p. 106; Edward Luttwak, *The Grand Strategy of the Byzantine Empire*, Cambridge Mass: HUP, 2009, pp. 49–94.

Development of a eastern Roman identity: see the especially intriguing work by Fergus Miller, *A Greek Roman Empire*, Berkeley: University of California, 2007, particularly pp. 84–129; also, Warren Treadgold, *A History of the Byzantine State and Society*, Stanford: Stanford University Press, 1997, pp. 97–8, 100–1, 149–51, 152–155; R. C. Blockley, *East Roman Foreign Policy*, Leeds UK: Francis Cairns Ltd, 1992, pp. 71–9; Luttwak, *Grand Strategy*, pp. 415–8.

The Byzantine way of war: Anonymous, Byzantine Treatise on Strategy, text in George Dennis, *Three Byzantine Military Treatises*, Washington DC: Dumbarton Oaks, 1985, pp. 11–135, see especially, pp. 29–37, 47–61, 129–35, information about text, pp. 2–5; Luttwak, *Grand Strategy*, pp. 258–65 doubts that this text is indeed from the age of Justinian but I think he is misled by the use of terms in the text.

Text and translation, George Dennis (translator) *Maurice's Strategikon*, Philadelphia PA: University of Pennsylvania, 1984, especially pp. xii–xiii.

Justinian's empire: For a current overview of Justinian's reign, see Michael Maas (ed.), *Cambridge Companion to the Age of Justinian*, Cambridge UK: CUP, 2005, especially Michael Maas, 'Roman Questions, Byzantine Answers: Contours of the Age of Justinian', pp. 3–27.

For Justinian's wars see, Anthony Kaldellis, *The Wars of Justinian*, Indianapolis, 2014, an excellent new English version of Procopius' great history.

Events after Justinian: the best narrative remains J. Bury, A History of the *Later Roman Empire from Arcadius to Irene (395 A.D. to 800 A.D.)* , vol II, London, 1889, pp. 67–94; see also, Norman Baynes, 'The successors of Justinian', in CMH, vol. ii, *The Rise of the Saracens and the Foundation of the Western Empire*, Cambridge, 1926, pp. 263–301; Michael Whitby, 'The Successors of Justinian', in CAH, *Late Antiquity: Empire and Successors*, A. D. 425–600, Cambridge, 2000, pp. 86–111.

Upheaval and Collapse of Eastern Roman Empire, emergence of Byzantine Realm: Bury, *Later Roman Empire* (1st edition), vol ii, pp. 197–206, 227-248; Greek literary sources translated with commentary, James Howard-Johnston, *The Armenian History Attributed to Sebeos*, Liverpool: Liverpool University Press, 1999, vol II, pp. 65–94; Geoffrey Greatrex and Samuel Lieu, *The Roman Eastern Frontier and the Persian Wars, part II, AD 363–630*, London: Routledge, 2002, pp. 182–228; for current narrative Walter Kaegi, *Heraclius Emperor of Byzantium*, Cambridge UK: CUP, 2003; Iranian sources, Parvaneh Pourshariati, *Decline and Fall of the Sassanian Empire*, London: I.B.Tauris, 2008, pp. 130–53; best analysis of sources, James Howard-Johnston, *Witness to a World Crisis, Historians and Histories of the Middle East in the Seventh Century*, Oxford, 2010; also see now Peter Crawford, *The War of the Three Gods Romans, Persians, and the Rise of Islam*, Pen & Sword, 2013.

Muslim conquest of Syria and the Near East, Donner, Fred McGraw, *The Early Islamic Conquests*, Princeton NJ: Princeton University Press, 1981, pp. 81–156; John Glubb Pasha, *The Great Arab Conquests*, Englewood Cliffs: Prentice-Hall, 1964, pp. 155–88; Hugh Kennedy, *The Great Arab Conquests*, Philadelphia PA: Da Capo, 2007, pp. 66–97; Walter Kaegi, *Byzantium and the Early Islamic Conquests*, Cambridge UK: CUP, 1992, pp. 88–146; Barnaby Rogerson, *The Heirs of Muhammad*, New York: Overlook Press, 2006, pp. 159–69.

For a good overview of early Muslim capabilities, see David Nicolle, *Armies of the Muslim Conquest*, Oxford: Osprey, 1993, especially pp. 8–14, and David Nicolle, *Yarmuk 636 AD*, London, Osprey, 1994, particularly, for camel saddle, p. 11.

There is a large amount of literature on the battle of the Yarmuk, for a good discussion of the problems and reconstructions of the battle see, Kaegi, *Heraclius*, pp. 239–44; Nicolle, *Yarmuk*, complete.

The emergence of the Byzantine realm: well discussed in J. F. Haldon, *Byzantium in the Seventh Century*, Cambridge UK: CUP, 1990, p. 253; also see Arnold Toynbee, *Constantine Porphyrogenitus and his World*, London: OUP, 1973, pp. 224–251.

Land and Soldiers

After the catastrophes of the seventh century, the soldiers of the defeated armies settled on lands they found empty or pushed the weaker owners away. The theme commands emerged as the institutional support for these holdings. While the times of crisis continued, this system worked well enough. The soldiers defended their farms from marauding raiders sweeping toward the Aegean and provided the field armies with reinforcements as imperial offensives advanced against the enemy. However, once the wars settled down to a frontier society, raiding and counter raiding, the economy improved. The value of the soldiers' holding rose significantly. The expansion of the monetary economy during the late Amorian and early Macedonian dynasties made investment in farmland profitable. This was especially true of farms that would produce cash crops. Farms near the seacoast could produce grain and staples while farms on the interior could produce fruits, nuts, and oil. As investors picked up land to develop such establishments, they bought up soldiers' properties. Many soldiers were stuck between investors looking to buy investment property and large estate owners who would protect their positions in the military establishment by subsuming the soldiers' communities into their own estates and maintain the soldiers as dependant tenants. In the early tenth century, army officers and imperial officials became concerned about the rise of large estates along with a significant increase of rural poor. The problem called for a legislative solution.

Novel of the Lord Emperor Romanus I the Elder Concerning the Right of Pre-emption

The first legal effort to restrict the sales of soldier's holdings was issued in the reign of Romanus I Lecapenus in the early 920s. In this, Romanus invokes a right of first refusal of the seller's relatives and neighbours, which he said was traditional but had been ignored. Romanus I specifically added a provision that pointed to the *dynatoi* as culprits in these transactions. The Emperor granted the pre-emption right to, first, the land owner's family, widely considered, and second, members of the fiscal unit that constitute the village to which the plot of land belonged. The *dynatoi* are described as those who are able to intimidate sellers or bribe them with some advantage. There was no specific test to identify the *dynatoi*, common knowledge sufficed. Moreover, *dynatoi* were not to receive any such property through adoption nor gift of any kind. If authorities found that an improper transaction had happened, the property returned as a soldier's holding without compensation to the *dynatoi*, who must also pay the purchase price as a fine to the treasury. A ten-year statute of limitation applied.

Novel of the Lord Emperor Romanus I the Elder Concerning Land Transactions

Emperor Romanus issued a far stricter novel in September 934. This was, in good part, a reaction to the effects of the terrible winter of 927–8. For one hundred and twenty days frost continued, killing animals and orchards, causing great disruption to the growing season. Famine stalked the land; many died. Small farms failed, food disappeared, and lenders recalled loans. Lenders, powerful neighbours, and those who had food at hand acquired large numbers of small holdings. The results were a growth in the holdings of the powerful and masses of poverty-stricken peasants who could supply no longer the harness and trappings of a Byzantine soldier. Romanus had mobilized his forces in his successful campaign against Melitene in the spring of 934. Many officers and soldiers no doubt informed the Emperor of the rural distress, adding to what he saw himself. When he issued the novel, Romanus appears genuinely shocked by what he found. Quoting Psalms 12: 5, 'For the oppression of the poor, for the sighing of the needy, now will I arise, saith the Lord,' the Emperor goes on, 'If God, our Creator and Saviour, Who made us emperor, rises in retribution, how will the poor man who awaits only the eyes of the emperor for intercession, be neglected and altogether forgotten by us?'

The Emperor decreed that the small holdings belonging to village communities were inalienable. He particularly pointed out,

> ...*the illustrious magistroi or patrikioi, nor any of the persons honoured with offices, governorships, or civil or military dignities, nor anyone at all enumerated in the senate nor officials or ex-officials of the themes, nor metropolitans most devoted to God, archbishops, bishops, higoumenoi, ecclesiastical official, or supervisors and heads of pious or imperial houses (philanthropic organizations), whether as a private individual or in the name of an imperial or ecclesiastical property, dare either on their own or*

through an intermediary to intrude into a village or hamlet for the sake of a sale, gift, or inheritance – either whole or partial – or on any other pretext whatsoever.

Any such transaction was voided: the land was to return to the original seller without compensation to the buyer. However, if the price was fair and the sale not forced, the property was to revert to the seller but he was to repay the buyer in full within three years. The buyer could remove and take with him any improvement, if its construction was not forced from the efforts of the poor. Moreover, the Emperor decreed that this ruling covered all such transactions back to the time before the famine, fall of 927.

Novel of the Lord Emperor Constantine VII Porphyrogenitus Concerning the Encroachment of the Powerful upon the Communities of the Poor

Romanus I Lecapenus was removed from office in a *coup* by his sons in 944. They, in turn, fell from power at the hands of the junior emperor Constantine VII Porphyrogenitus in 945. Romanus had grown old as emperor and Constantine's new administration revitalized policy. Both emperors, however, agreed about the need to protect small holders' property. The village communities organized tax collection and provided recruits for the thematic forces. The decay of the villages caused by loss of properties to large estates lowered revenue and weakened the thematic army. While Romanus reacted because of the famine of 927, Constantine enforced a standing policy. Constantine issued his decree in March 947. All transactions in which small holdings were bought by powerful persons and houses, imperial and pious, using improper influence were forbidden. Any such transaction happening since Constantine assumed power was void. The purchaser was to receive no compensation for returning the property including any improvements he may have constructed on the property. The question of property bought for a fair price, at which time the property was to revert to the original owner or to the village as a community, the repayment schedule of three years remained unless the seller was indigent, i.e. had personal property of less than fifty *numismata* (a definition going back to the fourth century). Constantine concludes his decree noting difficulties that might arise, giving advantage but not without limits to the interest of the 'poor'. Constantine included military properties in his efforts to salvage the village communities but he also issued a decree specifically protecting soldiers' holdings.

Novel of the Lord Emperor Constantine VII Porphyrogenitus Concerning the Encroachment of the Powerful upon the Communities of the Poor

The Emperor issued his decree regarding *stratiotike ktemata* (military lands or soldiers' property – an estate capable of supporting a soldier and his family) sometime in 945–7. This is the first legal recognition of a specific class of small holdings tied to the military. Clearly such small holdings had existed in local and traditional customs for centuries but were not distinguished from the rest of the small holdings. Constantine saw the soldiers' properties as critical for the survival of the army and of the empire. 'We therefore establish by law the same rule which until now unwritten custom has determined': the cavalrymen holding *strateia* are not permitted to sell the property that support their *strateiai*, the specified amount of a *strateia* being set at the value of four pounds of gold for immovable property. Regarding the sailors of the *kibyrrhaiotai* theme, their *strateia* was said to be valued at two pounds of gold.

Constantine defined a military property as that needed to support a horse soldier or sailor and required the army and navy to list these properties on military roles. The result was a registry of properties worth some four or two pounds of gold that were inalienable and had to supply a fighting man. This decree moved soldiers' property out of the realm of small holdings and into the military administration. The decree proceeded to outline different situations that might apply to different holdings of the *strateia* all revolving around the point that,

> *We deem it fitting to turn to the persons of the* stratiotai *themselves and discuss what has recently befallen them. There was a time which saw a general upheaval of affairs and an irresistible onslaught of misery, when every last one of the high and mighty in haste to carve out unlimited lands for himself enrolled the wretched owners in a list of slaves, with nary a thought that his actions were reprehensible, but instead believing himself ill-treated if someone else seemed to surpass him in greed.*

Moreover, the problem was not only with the *dynatoi* but, because the habits of the mighty prove contagious to the populace, spread to army officers and others in lower levels of administration. Constantine's decree proved practical. While questions arose regarding restitutions of claims, these problems had administrative solutions. Two edicts, one by Constantine and one by his son and successor, Romanus II, easily dealt with such difficulties.

Nicephorus II Phocas Adjusts Regulations Regarding Soldiers' Property

A number of issues presented themselves to Emperor Nicephorus who produced decisive and effective solutions. First, there were questions of how to expand the *stratiotai* to newly acquired lands. The Emperor understood that the new Armenian lands were both a springboard to further advances and also a barrier behind which the empire might find protection. But, the instability and 'wandering' qualities of the Armenians as seen by the Byzantines convinced Nicephorus to regulate the soldiers' properties differently in the small Armenian themes that he founded. He decreed that the Armenian *stratiotai* be reassigned if their holder was gone for three years. Moreover, if the Armenian soldier went over to the other side and then returned, he immediately lost his *stratiotai*. However, in either case, if he was a good soldier, he would receive another *stratiotai*, presumably in new occupied territory.

Second, difficulties with the division of rights regarding land ownership emerged. Constantine VII's legislation emphasized the rights of the poor as opposed to the *dynatoi*. Like all such efforts at reform, while many received important benefits from the new rules, some took advantage of the system. The forty years' limit allowed some old wrongs rectification but opened opportunity for some imaginative operators to discover or invent evidence of lost soldiers' properties. Spotting a choice property, a 'poor' individual would file suit against a landowning *dynatoi*. Evidence was found or manufactured and the individual gained the land. However, this did not necessarily produce a soldier; rather at times, violent and wicked people used the land to cause harm to neighbours. In some cases, the suitors chose the plot that held the estate's manor house. Nicephorus, who belong to a great eastern house, understood the problem. He did not want to diminish the rights of the *stratiotai* holders but to allow the program to disrupt estates and villages would give no advantage. The Eemperor decreed that while the basic program would continue, the sales or transfer of *dynatoi* lands were restricted to *dynatoi* as *stratiotai* were restricted to soldier holders. This clarified in a practical manner the way through the morass of litigation. As an added benefit, Nicephorus decreed that if a suit prevailed in which the ground under a manor house was condemned, the *dynatoi* could redeem the land for three times its assessed valuation.

Third, land values rise as the army becomes more effective. To keep values in line, Nicephorus ruled that land of a soldier's property must be of at least four pounds of gold value, as before, but a soldier who holds a *stratiotai* must count lands that he may hold up to twelve pounds value. This increases the amount of land registered as soldiers' holdings.

Fourth, the Emperor was not happy seeing lands fall into hands of the monasteries. Nicephorus saw nothing but good coming from the monastic life, hospices, and homes for the aged; he doubted that properties and wealth did much to improve those institutions. He recommended that anyone who wished to help support such institutions do so: by assisting existing institutions not by founding new one

Novel of the Pious Emperor Basil the Younger Concerning Powerful Persons Who Acquired Land from the Poor, Subjecting Them to Punishment from the Time of the First Legislation of the Emperor Romanus the Elder

Some sixty years after Romanus I issued the first land decree, the Emperor Basil issued a major decree, January 996. This decree summarized and codified the issue of land holdings and remained enforced for a century when it was reissued hundred years later. Basil, following Romanus I, focused on small holdings military and non-military. He emphasized Romanus' reason regarding protecting the poor from the encroachments of the powerful but he also added the problems to the imperial establishment of the expansion and ambition of the *dynatoi*. Clearly the great houses threatened the very structure of the empire.

Basil based his decisions on his own personal observation,

> *...on our travels through the themes of our empire or while setting out for campaigns, we beheld with our own eyes the encroachments and injustices taking place every day.*

He saw that the powerful had sufficient wealth and influences to withstand any legal challenges from the poor. In order to provide sufficient protection to the small holders, Basil abolished the forty-year statute of limitation and then set the burden of proof on the powerful. The only acceptable proofs were authentic documents made before the famine. Moreover, the poor could reclaim the land and improvements without any compensation for the evicted powerful. Besides grabbing lands from small holders, the *dynatoi* had taken lands from the imperial treasury. Basil assumed that the only way *dynatoi* could acquire lands from the imperial treasury was with the cooperation of corrupt officials. He ruled that the treasury right of resumption of imperial lands extended back to Caesar Augustus.

The legislative efforts to protect small holdings clearly ran counter to the interest of the owners of the great estates. Some of these estates were owned by people tied to the government in Constantinople. Their lands were within reach of the Great City, near the coast of the Aegean and Black Sea. Other estates, almost independent principalities, were in the interior and further reaches of Asia Minor. Just about fifty years after Basil II died, under the pressure of Seljuk forces and continuing civil war, the themes disintegrated and the cities in the east fell to the invaders, as the last native Roman army of professional soldiers disappeared. Byzantium remained but her army now became a mercenary force, hired as needed. The lands along the coasts of the Aegean and Black seas remained as part of the empire but the heartland of Asia Minor was lost.

References

The primary source for information about the Byzantine government's effort to protect soldier's property is found in the *Synopsis basilicorum major*, a reference guide to the Byzantine law code, the *Basilica*. The *Synopsis* had appendices containing the texts of many novels including those regarding small holdings and soldiers' properties. There are numerous copies of the *Synopsis*, dating from 950 to 1250. However, the texts differ in some minor and few major areas. Establishing a definitive text is very difficult. But the basic concepts remain clear. The texts in their different forms are presented with extended discussion in Eric McGeer, *The Land Legislation of the Macedonian Emperors*, Toronto, 2000.

Romanus I Lecapenus' legislation regarding preemption: McGreer, *Land*, pp. 37–48.

Romanus I Lecapenus' legislation concerning transactions: McGeer, *op. cit.*, pp. 49–60.

Great famine: Skylitzes, 225.

Constantine VII's legislation to protect villages: *Ibid.*, 61–76.

Nicephorus II adjusting the regulations regarding soldiers' property: *Ibid.*, 86–108.

Basil II strengthening small holders' rights and increased penalties for those who abused them: *Ibid.*, 111–131.

The Byzantine collapse in the east: see Warren Treadgold, *Byzantium and its Army 284–1081*, Stanford, 1995, pp. 215–19; Speros Vryonis Jr, *The Decline of Medieval Hellenism in Asia Minor*, Berkeley, 1971, pp. 107–112.

Appendix IV

The Great Palace

The Byzantine Caesars ruled their state from a residence and ceremonial centre in Constantinople. Constantine constructed the first palace in the city, between the Hippodrome and east coast of old Byzantium. After Emperor Arcadius ascended the eastern throne (AD 395) Constantinople remained the residence of an emperor for almost six hundred years to the beginning of our narrative. Slowly, different emperors added buildings, remoulded old structures and added decorations. By 962, the complex of buildings was immense, stuffed with antique statues, mosaics and trophies. This is the setting for the drama of life in Byzantium. Here servants and empresses, eunuchs and soldiers, emperors and bureaucrats, ecclesiasts and hermits danced in the stately minuet of politics in Constantinople.

The Hippodrome defined the west side of the palace as Hagia Sophia did the north. The west and south faced gardens and playing fields that backed up to the Sea of Marmara. Constantine connected his palace to the Hippodrome with a structure called the *kathisma*, which consisted of an imperial box allowing the occupants to see the races and the audience to see them. The structure sat against the main halls of the palace. The old Constantinian palace was surrounded by buildings and gardens having various functions. Near Hagia Sophia, built in its present form by Justinian (d. 565), on the main street, the Mese, was the Milion, the monument that marked the centre of the city. The street turned and continued along a corridor between the imperial baths of Zeuxippos on the southern side and the Augustaion Court to the north. The main palace gate, the Chalke (the Bronze House) was at the end of this corridor. Just beyond the gate, on the north stood the Magnaura, the great audience hall with the mechanical lions and elevating throne. In the centre and toward the south were the schools, also called *Triklinos* of the *Scholae* and of *Excubitores*. The *Scholae* and *Excubitores* were organizations of the field army and these were the banquet halls for the higher military officers, so these structures held the administrative offices of the imperial army. To the south of these army offices, there extended a series of more 'banquet' halls, the *Triklinos* of the Augustus, the Hall of the Nineteen Couches, and the halls of the Daphne Palace. Intermixed among these rooms were apartments, gardens, terraces, and walks. Just beyond these buildings there was another complex centred on the *Chrysotriklinos* (Golden Hall) audience hall and the *Bucoleon* imperial residence.

The Golden Audience Hall and the Bull and Lion Palace became the centre of the emperor's interaction with the personnel of the imperial administration. The imperial family and their relatives' business ran out of this complex but the business of state ran out of the old palace. Some suggest that the old palace was simply derelict, an almost unused group of buildings between the imperial residence and the Bronze House in front of Hagia Sophia. Proximity to power is always useful. Somebody was there. The best speculation is that the governmental administration ran out of offices in the old palace. Just as the old Roman administration ran out of a series of small booths in the Basilicas so the large rooms of the old palace provided space for the higher personnel, record rooms and hearing rooms of the Byzantine state. When major events required the halls be cleared, the palace servants packed up the booths and made the halls ready for the emperor. It is even probable that the emperor moved his personal household to the west, to the Golden Hall, because the press of business increased as the economy improved through the eighth, ninth, and tenth centuries. Evidently the press of business grew so great that Emperor Nicephorus II had a fortified wall driven through the palace complex, isolating the Golden Hall and the Bull and Lion Palace. John Skylitzes complains that of all the nasty things Nicephorus did, removing beautiful structures surrounding the Golden Hall and Bull and Lion Palace, was the worse.

Imperial Chambers

In the lifetime of Basil II, the Emperor and his family lived and worked in the Golden Hall complex. The *Bucoleon* Palace, some of the walls of which are still extant, was a large rectangular two-storey masonry building overlooking the Sea of Marmara on one side and interconnected with the Golden Hall on the other side. Surrounding the building were gardens and terraces stretching off in the east to the imperial polo grounds. The rooms were small by modern standards with thick stone walls covered by hangings. The corridors led to a stairway descending to an antechamber behind massive silver doors that led to the Golden Hall.

The *Chrysotriklinos*, Golden Hall, was an octagonal domed structure of three storeys and was the model for Charlemagne's hall at Aachen. Heavy arches formed the first storey, that led up to a second storey of light soaring arches opening to a balcony which, in turn, led to a clear storey of arched windows under the dome. The hall was some fifty feet in diameter and the dome peak was some fifty feet above the floor. Each of the eight arched openings led to a chamber with a specific function. On the east side, the opening led into a large apse, with an image of Christ in the half dome above the imperial throne. During the day to day business in the Golden Hall, the emperor sat on a gold-coloured chair on the left side of the great throne. The arched opening opposite the throne held a massive silver doorway, covered by curtains, which led to an exterior porch, the *Tripeton* where there was a large time piece. The opening to the left of the throne held the Chapel of St Theodore, which contained a vestry for imperial robes. The next chamber, called the Pantheon, was a waiting room for imperial officials. Beyond that, there was the stewards' quarter. Before this entrance, there sat the bench for the *papias*, keeper of the palace keys. On the south side, there were entrances to the private quarters. The central door, of massive silver, led to the anteroom of the stairway to the imperial quarters. On one side, there was the vestry for high Church officials and inside that chamber a separate entrance to the private quarters that led directly to the empress's rooms. On the other side of the great door there was the *aristeterion*, a small dining room where the imperial family and their children joined the emperor for dessert at the end of imperial banquets.

Procession Through the Palace

The clearest way to see the structure of the building complex was to follow the emperor as he proceeded through the Great Palace on an official procession. Five days a year the emperor led a grand procession from the Golden Hall through the palace to Hagia Sophia: Easter, Pentecost, Transfiguration, Nativity, and Epiphany. On the day before the Holy Day, the servants of the Grand Chamberlain made a formal entry into the Golden Hall and informed the emperor of the next day's importance. The emperor then issued orders for the procession. The servants deliver the orders to the servants of the imperial residence, the leaders of the two main demes (heads of civil administration of city), the commanders of the army, the commander of the walls, and commander of the watch. Then the servants gave official notification to the *eparch* (mayor) of the city to ensure that the streets leading to the palace were decorated with laurel, rosemary, and sweet-smelling flowers.

Very early next morning, the head servant and all the attendants of the *Chrysotriklinos* went into the imperial residence and waited there. When the Great *Papias* (eunuch head of palace security and keeper of the keys) opened the doors of the *Chrysotriklinos*, they entered and sat down at the curtain before the apse called the Pantheon, on the left side of the room. Then, the *vestitores*, officers of the wardrobe, entered the *Chrysotriklinos* and proceeded to the chapel of St Theodore, in an apse on the left side of the hall. Here, some took up the Rod of Moses (a relic that appeared as an archetypical crosier), while others took out the chests which held the imperial robes and crowns. The *Spatharioi* (swordsmen guards) took the imperial arms and armour. Special servants took the imperial regalia and placed them in the octagonal chamber of the old Daphne Palace (this was a smaller chamber that allowed the interconnection of a number of important rooms.) The special servants went to the *Onopodium* (a formal garden shaped like a race track) where the *Spatharioi* joined them.

While these preparations continued, the emperor emerged from the private quarters, dressed in a *skaramangion* (a formal silk robe with gold facings on sleeves, hems, and slits). The emperor prayed at the apse under the picture of Christ then turned and met the servants who had been waiting in the Pantheon area. The servants clothed him in his golden bordered *sagum* (a type of cloak, reaching down to above the knees). The emperor then proceeded through the main door and went to the treasury and down a gallery lined with pictures of saints to a waiting room where well wishers received him. The entourage proceeded to the *Onopodium* where servants presented ceremonial candles at the old and venerated chapel of Our Most Blessed Lady. The company prostrated thrice and holding their lit candles repeated the prostrations at the adjoining chapel of the Holy Trinity. The procession then entered the Baptistery. Three great beautiful crosses stood there and at a signal of the head servant, the emperor's personal attendants lit the candles in the chamber. After prayers the procession continued, to the Banquet Hall of the Augustus where the courtiers waiting there acclaimed the emperor. The emperor, accompanied only by his personal servants, went through the octagonal hall of the Daphne Palace to the Chapel of St Stephen, which now held the imperial robes. The emperor and the whole court standing in the Church of St Stephen adored the great cross of Constantine with three prostrations amidst candle light. Next the procession went to the upper floor, to the living chambers of the Daphne above the octagonal hall. Here, servants of the patriarch presented the orders for the ecclesiastical arrangements of the ceremony.

Once all these preparations were made, the emperor descended to the octagonal chamber of the Daphne. The head servant announced that the emperor was ready for the formal robes. The *vestitores* then came and arrayed the emperor in the imperial robes. Once finished, they withdrew. The emperor's personal attendants surrounded him and placed the crown on his head. Fully arrayed, the emperor proceeded again to the Banquet Hall of the Augustus. There, to receive the emperor, stood the high officials of the secretariat, next to the gilded table that held the gold and jewelled basins for official inks. Standing at the Golden Hand, just outside of the great door, the high imperial servant bowed and presented the high civil officials, district governors, army generals, and frontier commanders. These men, the rulers of the realm under the emperor, saluted their master. At a sign from the emperor, the high servant chanted, 'He commands.' Turning at the Golden Hand, the emperor proceeded to the *Onopodium* where the admirals and captains of the fleet along with the *Spatharioi*, holding the emperor's armour, received the imperial company with acclimations.

Turning about, the emperor led the courtiers and high officials down the corridor to the Great Consistory Hall, which now held the Great Cross of Constantine and Moses' Rod, brought in the morning from the imperial chapel. Here, the legal secretaries, notaries and legal experts greeted the emperor with applause. From the Consistory, the procession went to the Hall of the Candidati, where the patriarch's administrative clergy received the imperial company. The emperor kissed a presented cross. The emperor then went to the octagonal dome at the entrance of the schools where sat the centre of the imperial military command. Under the dome was a beautiful silver cross before which the emperor and his company made triple prostrations. The procession continued to the adjoining Hall of Nineteen Couches. As the emperor entered the hall, a double line of sceptre bearers received him. In the large hall, the chief judges, imperial lawyers, and administrators had gathered and saluted the emperor. He stood on the great rostrum at the end of the hall, decorated by the guilds of cloth manufacturers and silversmiths. Purple hangings and spectacular draperies were accented with silver and gold. On either side of the rostrum stood high ranking foreign envoys, including Saracens, Franks and Bulgars. Below them were the guild masters and the official regulators of business in the city. After the congregation offered prayers and wished the emperor long life, the emperor walked to the great door and the congregation in the hall formed into a procession to follow him.

The emperor and his entourage led the whole congregation through the corridor to the Hall of the Schools, the centre of the military command. From this hall, the emperor went to the entrance of the chapel of the Holy Apostles and prostrated himself, his entourage following, three times. After the servants lit candles at the door to the chapel, the entourage tuned and faced the inner door of the great bronze gate of the palace, the Chalke. With organs playing, the emperor received the demarchs, leaders, of the Blue and Green Demes. These organizations, represented the aristocracy and common folk, oversaw the registration of individuals, births, deaths, property transfers and supplied units of men for the defence of the walls and the city watch.

The Chalke was a large structure. Two sets of doors faced each other across a high domed hall. The innermost doors opened to a great bronze door, which opened to the domed room. There were two sets of great entrance doors, which opened on to the last leg of the main street of the City, the Mese. Within the domed chamber awaiting the emperor and his entourage stood the College of Physicians on the left and the College of the Gymnasiums on the right. Together, the groups intone a greeting, wishing the emperor long life. At the great bronze door, the College of Musicians greeted the emperor. The emperor proceeded to the space between the Great Bronze Gate and the outer gates facing the street; this area was called the Bar of the Bronze Gate. Here the leader of the Blue Deme introduced representatives of the White Deme, representing members of the court, who stood behind him. Moving out of the gates into the Augustaion Court, the leader of the Green Deme introduced representatives of the Red Deme, representing the armed forces, to the emperor. The emperor, his entourage, and the following procession, crossed the Augustaion Court to enter Hagia Sophia. Here, we will leave the emperor and his officials. The complex choreography demonstrating the nature of Byzantine church and state continue to play out in the celebration of the Holy Sacraments but we will return to the palace.

The Emperor and the Palace

Processions like this took place five times a year. If the senior emperor was busy with other affairs then junior emperors would preside. For Romanus I, it would have been Constantine VII, our source of information. For Nicephorus II and John I, the junior emperors were the young brothers, Basil II and Constantine VIII. Under Basil and Constantine, Constantine VIII resided most of the time. We can easily assume that while the *De Ceremoniis* speaks only of the emperor, the empress and the imperial princes and princesses accompanied the emperor. The purpose of the procession was to meet and greet. Just as the emperor and his close associates saw the high officials and their associates so the officials met the emperor and his friends. The two groups could exchange ideas and receive clarifications without going through 'official channels'. They renewed old friendships, and established new acquaintances. The logic of the meet and greet procession relates to the fact that the officials worked in the spaces through which the emperor walked. He could look at their work product and his associates could comment on them. This is where the real business of running the empire took place. This work had gone on for centuries and continued until 1185. When the City rose against Andronicus, a mob invaded the Great Palace and plundered it. We can be certain that one of the objectives of the plunderers was to destroy the paperwork that held the government together. When the rebels destroyed the coordinating centre of the imperial administration, the Byzantine state received a serious wound. The Angelus emperors were never able to reconstruct the administrative system and so the wound proved fatal, leading to a downward spiral of centrifugal forces that ended in the catastrophe of 1204.

References

General accounts: Constantine VII *de cerimoniis*, initiated at the start of self rule, 945. A later redaction was made in the reign of Nicephorus II 963–9. Two contemporary texts, Lipsiensis I, 17 in Leipzig, almost complete, and Chalcensis 133 (125) + Vatopedensis 1003 first part in Istanbul and second part in Mt Athos (p. 162).

A. G. Paspates, translator, William Metcalfe, *The Great Palace of Constantinople*, London, 1893.

Gilbert Dagron, *Emperor and Priest*, Cambridge UK, 2003 (ET *Empereur et Pretre*, 1996).

Featherstone, J. M., '*De Cerimoniis* and the Great Palace', in Stephenson, *The Byzantine World*, New York, 2010.

Procession through the Palace: Constantine VII *de cerimoniis* is the basic source; see J. B. Bury, 'The ceremonial book of Constantine Porphyrogennetos', *English Historical Review* 22: 209–27, 417–39 (1907); A. G. Paspates, *The Great Palace of Constantinople*, London, 1893, pp. 290–297; Gilbert Dagron, *Emperor and Priest*, Cambridge UK, 2003, pp. 84–92.

The emperor and the Palace: looting of palace; Nicetas Choniates in Harry Magoulias, *O' City of Byzantium, Annals of Niketas Choniates*, Detroit, 1984, p. 191.

Bibliography

Introduction to References

Byzantine Background – General Treatments of Byzantine History

The basic collection of Byzantine literary sources, including all of the chronicles and most of the various descriptive materials remains the CSHB, which is the *Corpus Scriptorum Historiae Byzantinae*, ed. B. G. Niebuhr (Bonn 1828–).

While there were many accounts of Byzantine history written before the mid nineteenth century, usually a close translation of the *Chronographia* of George Cedrenus, the first academic history was George Finley's *History of Greece after the Romans* in many volumes. The volume on the Byzantine Empire from 716 to 1057 was first published in 1852, with a definitive edition coming out in 1856. This is a sound and well written account based on the chronicles collected in the CSHB.

Following the ideas of Lord Acton, Cambridge University began the project of developing definitive multi-volume histories in 1902. Volume IV of the *Cambridge Medieval History, the Eastern Roman Empire (717–1453)*, edited by J. R. Tanner, C. W. Previté-Orton, and Z. N. Brook came out in 1923. This is a well constructed political history by many hands. It remains informative. In 1966, a revised edition of CMH came out. This is titled, *The Byzantine Empire*, in two parts. Part I, *Byzantium and its Neighbours*, a volume of some 1,100 pages and part II, *Government Church & Civilization*, some 500 pages, ed. by J. M. Hussy, assisted by D. M. Nicol and G. Cowan. This book is a superior collection of information on many facets of Byzantine politics and life. In 2008, a third *Cambridge History of the Byzantine Empire, c. 500–1492*, came out. Edited by Jonathan Sheppard, this is a collection of articles concerning Byzantium that are in the *New Cambridge Medieval History*. This is essentially an updating of the 1923 volume, covering new research and exploring concerns of the early twenty-first century.

A number of significant and comprehensive accounts of the Byzantine Empire came out in the mid twentieth century. Russian academic institutions pursued Byzantine studies. The Russian scholar A. A. Vasiliev wrote a three-part Byzantine history published in Russia in 1917, 1923 and 25. By 1928, Vasiliev had produced a two-volume history in English published by the University of Wisconsin, updating and revising the Russian text. Eventually, Vasiliev produced French and Spanish editions, each time updating the text. In 1952, Vasiliev pulled all the information together in a new English edition (Madison, 1952). Professor A. A. Vasiliev died in 1958. The book is comprehensive and detailed, written in textbook style.

Another Russian Byzantine scholar, George Ostrogorsky, wrote a comprehensive history in German for the series *Handbuch der Alertumswissenschaft*, published in 1940. At the time, Ostrogorsky was a professor at the University of Belgrade. In 1952, he produced a second German edition; this was translated into English in 1957, as *History of the Byzantine State*. In 1963 Ostrogorsky produced a third German edition, which was translated into English as the second English edition. The *History of the Byzantine State* covers social and economic developments in a political context. This book is one of the best histories of Byzantium.

Warren Treadgold, who had written a number of important works about Byzantium in the late twentieth century, produced *A History of the Byzantine State and Society*: Stanford, 1997. In many ways, this book is a successor and expansion to Ostrogorsky. Social, economic, military and political events are carefully woven together. As of the early twenty-first century, this is the best account of Byzantium.

The current college text book, by Timothy Gregory, *A History of Byzantium* (Wiley-Blackwell: 2nd edition, 2010) is a fine and thorough introduction to the subject. Well balanced, up to date in regard to current scholarship, Gregory's book is a good place to start a study of Byzantium.

Origin of Byzantine Society-Constantine and the Later Roman Empire

Emperor Constantine was controversial in his own time and he has remained so ever since. Any study of his life must begin with Eusebius' *On the Life of the Blessed Emperor Constantine*, best approached in Averil Cameron and Stuart Hall, *Eusebius Life of Constantine*: Oxford, 1999. Since 1981, when Timothy Barnes' *Eusebius and Constantine* came out, there has been a renewed effort to understand the Emperor using some new material and a more nuanced approach. This is a mixed bag of books but some very insightful works are included. Of great interest are: H. A. Drake, *Constantine and the Bishops*: Baltimore, 2000; Charles Odahl, *Constantine and the Christian Empire*: New York, 2004, 2nd edition, 2010; Paul Stephenson, *Constantine Roman Emperor*

Christian Victor: New York, 2010; Timothy Barnes' rethinking about the emperor, *Constantine: Dynasty, Religion and Power in the Later Roman Empire*: Wiley-Blackwell, 2011; and David Potter, *Constantine the Emperor*: Oxford, 2013. Each author approaches Constantine from a different direction and so complements one another rather than contradicts each other.

Also important for the age of Constantine: Jonathan Bardill, *Constantine, Divine Emperor of the Christian Golden Age*: Cambridge, 2012, who explains the emperor through his monumental works and how they expand meanings in the literary sources. Noel Lenski, editor, *The Age of Constantine*: Cambridge, 2006, presents an up-to-date account of the social economic issues of the time.

The Later Roman Empire is well represented in the older literature by J. B. Bury, *History of the Later Roman Empire from Arcadius to Irene (395 to 800)*: New York, 1889; *History of the Later Roman Empire from the Death of Theodosius I to the Death of Justinian*: New York, 1923, and Ferdinand Lot, *The End of the Ancient World*: English translation, New York, 1931. These are well written works, based on the literary and primary sources, and so always have something to say. All works on the Later Roman Empire were superseded in 1964 when A. M. H. Jones's *The Later Roman Empire, 284–602: a Social, Economic, and Administrative Survey*: New York, 1964, came out. This work is still important today because of the comprehensive nature of Jones's treatment of the sources.

In 1971, Peter Brown changed the historical landscape with his book, *The World of Late Antiquity AD 150–750* (London). The Cambridge Ancient History series had said that the ancient world ended with Constantine. The Cambridge Medieval History series had said the Medieval Ages began with Constantine. So the pedagogical structure had been since the Renaissance. Here, however, was the nucleus of a new subject: Late Antiquity, a bridge from the Greeks and the Romans to the Carolingians and the Umayyad Empire. This is the time, of course, of the transition from Eastern Roman to Byzantium. Whole new perspective and changing narratives explained events in ways not understood before. The archetype account of this new subject is the new *Cambridge Ancient History, XIV, Late Antiquity Empire and Successors*: Cambridge, 2000. Other texts covering the transition from Roman to Byzantine include Walter Kaegi, *Heraclius, Emperor of Byzantium*: Cambridge, 2003; James Howard-Johnston, *East Rome, Sasanian Persia and the End of Antiquity*: Burlington VT, 2006; Idem, *Witness to a World Crisis*: Oxford, 2010; Gerrit Reinink and Bernard Stolte, *The Reign of Heraclius (610–641) Crisis and Confrontation*: Leuven, 2002. Each of these volumes is a treasure when compared with the treatment given in previous accounts.

For Byzantine understandings of their origins, the best sources are their own histories. For their view of the world before them, the main work is the *Chrononography of George Synkellos a Byzantine Chronicle of Universal History from the Creation*, translated and annotated by William Adler and Paul Tuffin: Oxford, 2002. Written in the first decade of the ninth century, the Synkellos drew on many sources to explain how history culminated in the Roman Empire. The Synkellos died before he could finish his project and it fell to Theophanes Confessor to complete the project. His *Chronicles of Byzantine and Near Eastern History AD 284–813*, translated and edited by Cyril Mango, Roger Scott with the assistance of Geoffrey Greatrex: Oxford, 1997, gives a detailed description of the events from Diocletian to Michael I.

The Reformation of the Byzantine Empire and the Imperial Dynasty

The emergence of Byzantium from the Eastern Roman Empire has intrigued many people. John Haldon has produced the most interesting studies on the subject. His *Byzantium in the Seventh Century*: Cambridge, 1990, rev. edition 1997, is a profound statement of the matter. Even better, Leslie Brubaker and John Haldon, *Byzantium in the Iconoclastic Era, c. 680-850*: Cambridge, 2011, covers the issues and problems in great detail with perception and insight.

Histories of the Byzantine 'middle' empire abound. Two very good ones are Romilly Jenkins, *Byzantium the Imperial Centuries AD 610–1071*: New York, 1966 and Mark Whittow, *The Making of Byzantium, 600–1025*: Berkeley, 1996.

Literary Sources

Collection: *Corpus Scriptorum Historiae Byzantinae*, ed. B. G. Niebuhr (Bonn 1828).

Byzantine Authors

Constantine VII *de cerimoniis*:
Two contemporary texts, Lipsiensis I, 17 in Leipzig, almost complete, and Chalcensis 133 (125) + Vatopedensis 1003 first part in Istanbul and second part in Mt Athos
Edition: J. Reiske, 2 vols. 1829, 1830.
The Book of Ceremonies, English translation accompanying Greek text, 2 volumes, by Ann Moffatt and Maxene Tall, Canberra 2012 (Byzantina Australiensia 18).

Basileus Leo VI translated and edited George Dennis, *The Taktika of Leo VI*: Washington DC, 2010.
  Also see John Haldon, *A Critical Commentary on the Taktika of Leo VI*: Washington DC, 2014.
Leo the Deacon:
  Hase, C.B., *Leonis diaconi Caloënis Historiae libri decem*: Bonn, 1828.
  Talbot, Alice-Mary and Denis F. Sullivan, *The History of Leo the Deacon*: Washington DC, 2005.
  Liudprand of Cremona, *Complete Works*, Paolo Squatriti (translator), Washington DC: Catholic University Press, 2007.
  'Heron of Byzantium', translated, Dennis Sullivan: *Siegecraft, Two Tenth-Century Instruction Manuals*: Washington DC, 2000.
Imp Mauricius Augustus, translated, George Dennis, *Maurice's Strategikon*: Philadelphia PA, 1984.
Nicephorus II Phocas, *Praecepta militaria*: in Eric McGeer, *Sowing the Dragon's Teeth*: Washington DC, 1995.
Nicephorus II Phocas, 'Skirmishing' in George Dennis, *Three Byzantine Military Treatises*: Washington DC, 2008.
Michael Psellus:
  Note, only one twelfth century manuscript of the *Chronographia* survives.
  Michael Psellus, *Chronographia*, ed. Konstantinos N. Sathas, *Bibliotheca greaca medii aevi*, vol 4: Paris, 1874.
  Michael Psellus, *Chronographia*, ed. J.B. Bury: London, Methuen, 1899.
  Michael Psellus, *The History of Psellus*, edited with critical notes and indices by Constantine Sathas. 1st AMS ed.: New York, AMS Press, 1979. Reprint of the 1899 ed. of Chronographia, published by Methuen, London.
  Michael Psellus. *Chronographia*, editor and French Trans E. Renauld, 2 vols: Paris, 1926–18.
John Skylitzes:
  Thurn, Hans, editor, *Ioannis Skylitzae, Synopsis Historiarum*: CFHB, 1973.
  Wortley, John, *John Skylitzes, a Synopsis of Byzantine History, 811–1057*: Cambridge UK, 2010.
Cross, Samuel and Olgerd Sherbowitz-Wetzor *The Russian Primary Chronicle*: Cambridge Mass, n.d.
Sears, David, *Byzantine Coins and their Value*: London, 1974.

Secondary Sources

Barbero, Alessandro, *The Day of the Barbarian* (ET *9 Agosto 378: IL Giorno dei Barbari*), New York: Walker & Co., 2007.

Barnes, Timothy, D. *Constantine and Eusebius*, Cambridge Mass: HUP, 1981.

Blockley, R. C. *East Roman Foreign Policy*, Leeds UK: Francis Cairns Ltd, 1992.

Bowman, Alan K., Peter Garnsey, Averil Cameron, *The Crisis of Empire AD 193–337*, CAH XII, Cambridge UK: CUP, 2005.

Branchich, Thomas, et al., *The History of Zonaras from Alexander Serverus to the Death of Theodosius the Great*, London: Routledge, 2009.

Brubaker, Leslie and John Haldon, *Byzantium in the Iconoclastic Era c680–850*, Cambridge UK: Cambridge University Press, 2011.

Bray, John, *Gallienus*, Kent Town (Australia): Wakefield Press, 1997.

Bury, J. B. *History of the Later Roman Empire*, 1st edition, London: Macmillan and Co. 1889.

Bury, J. B. *History of the Later Roman Empire*, 2nd edition, New York: Dover, 1958 (original edition, 1923).

Butler, Alfred, *The Arab Conquest of Egypt and the Last Thirty Years of the Roman Domination*, Oxford: OUP, 1998 (first published 1903).

Campbell, J. B., 'The Army' in Bowman, CAH XII.

Campbell, J. B., *The Emperor and the Roman Army*, Oxford: OUP, 1984.

Carr, John C., *Fighting Emperors of Byzantium*, Pen and Sword, 2015

Coombs-Hoar, Adrian, *Eagles in the Dust, the Roman Defeat at Adrianople, AD 378*, Pen and Sword, 2015

Crespigny, Rafe de, *Imperial Warlord, a Biography of Cao Cao 155–220 AD*, Leiden: Brill, 2010.

Curta, Florin, *Southeastern Europe in the Middle Ages 500–1250*, Cambridge UK, 2006.

D'Amato, Raffaele, *The Varangian Guard 988-1453*, Osprey, 2010.

Dagron, Gilbert, *Emperor and Priest, the Imperial Office in Byzantium*, Cambridge UK, 2003.

Dawson, Timothy, *Byzantine Cavalryman c900–1204*, Oxford: Osprey, 2009.

Dawson, Timothy, *Byzantine Infantryman c900–1204*, Oxford: Osprey, 2007.

De Blois, Lukas, *The Policy of the Emperor Gallienus*, Leiden: E. J. Brill, 1976.

Decker, Michael, *The Byzantine Art of War*, Yardley, 2013.

Delbrück, Hans, *The Barbarian Invasions, History of the Art of War*, vol II, (English translation of *GESCHICHTE DER KRIEGSKUNST IN RAHMEN DER POLITISCHEN GESTCHITCHTE*, vol. ii, by Walter J. Renfroe, Jr), Lincoln, Neb: University of Nebraska, 1980.

Dennis, George, *Three Byzantine Military Treatises*, Washington DC: Dumbarton Oaks, 1985.

Dennis, George, *Maurice's Strategikon*, Philadelphia PA: University of Pennsylvania, 1984.

Diehl, Charles, *Byzantine Empresses*, New York: Knopf, 1927.

Dill, Samuel, *Roman Society in the Last Century of the Western Empire*, New York: Meridian Library, 1958 (reprint, original, 1899).

Dodgeon, Michael, Samuel N.C. Lieu, *The Roman Eastern Frontier and the Persian Wars AD 226–363*, London: Routledge, 1991.

Donner, Fred McGraw, *The Early Islamic Conquests*, Princeton NJ: Princeton University Press, 1981.

Farrokh, Kaveh, *Sassanian Elite Cavalry AD 224–642*, Oxford: Osprey, 2005.

Farrokh, Kaveh, *Shadows in the Desert, Ancient Persia at War*, Oxford: Osprey, 2007.

Featherstone, J. M., '*De Cerimoniis* and the Great Palace', in Stephenson, *The Byzantine World*, New York, 2010.

Ferrill, Arthur, *The Fall of the Roman Empire, the Military Explanation*, London: Thames and Hudson, 1986.

Ferrill, Arthur, *Roman Imperial Grand Strategy*, New York: University Press of America, 1999.

Fine, John Jr, *The Early Medieval Balkans*, Ann Arbor, 1983.

John Freely and Ahmet Çakmak, *Byzantine Monuments of Istanbul*, Cambridge, 2004.

Garland, Lynda, *Byzantine Empresses*, New York: Routledge, 1999.

Gregory, Timothy, *A History of Byzantium*, Malden MA: Blackwell, 2005.

Glubb Pasha, John Bagot, *The Great Arab Conquests*, Englewood Cliffs NJ: Prentice-Hall, 1964.

Gommans, Jos J. L., *The Rise of the Indo-Afghan Empire, c 1710–1780*, Delhi: OUP, 1999.

Graff, David A. *Medieval Chinese Warfare, 300–900*, London: Routledge, 2002.

Greatrex, Geoffrey, and Samuel Lieu, *The Roman Eastern Frontier and the Persian Wars, part II, AD 363–630*, London: Routledge, 2002.

Grégore, H. and J. R. H. Romilly, 'The Amorians and Macedonians 842–1025', *The Cambridge Medieval History, IV: The Byzantine Empire, part I Byzantium and its Neighbours*, Cambridge UK, 1966.

Haldon, J. F., *The Byzantine Wars*, Stroud, Gloucestershire: Tempus, 2000.

Haldon, J. F., *Byzantium in the Seventh Century*, Cambridge UK: CUP, 1990.

Haldon, John, *The Palgrave Atlas of Byzantine History*, New York: Palgrave, 2010.

Hall, John E., *Through the Jade Gate to Rome*, www.booksurge.com: John Hall, publisher, 2009.

Halsall, Guy, *Barbarian Migration and the Roman West 376–568*, Cambridge UK: CUP, 2007.

Holmes, Catherine, *Basil II and the Governance of Empire*, Oxford, 2005.

Herodian vols I II, trans. Whittaker, Cambridge Mass: Loeb, 1970.

Herrin, Judith, *Women in Purple*, London, 2001.

Hodgson, Marshall, *The Venture of Islam*, vol II, Chicago, 1974.

Howard-Johnston, James, commentary, *The Armenian History Attributed to Sebeos*, Liverpool: Liverpool University Press, 1999.

Howard-Johnston, James, *Witness to a World Crisis*, Oxford, 2010.

Hughes, Ian, *Imperial Brothers, Valentinian, Valens and the Disaster at Adrianople*, Pen and Sword, 2013

Hutton, William, *Constantinople the Story of the Old Capital of the Empire*, London, 1909.

Jenkins, Romilly, *Byzantium the Imperial Centuries, AD 610–1071*, New York: Vintage Press, 1966.

Kaegi, Walter, *Byzantium and the Early Arab Conquests*, Cambridge UK: CUP, 1992.

Kaegi, Walter, *Heraclius, Emperor of Byzantium*, Cambridge UK: CUP, 2003.

Kaldellis, Anthony, *The Christian Parthenon*, Cambridge, 2009.

Kazhdan, Alexander, (ed.) *Oxford Dictionary of Byzantium*, Oxford: Oxford University Press, 1991, vols. I–III.

Kazhdan, Alexander and Giles Constable, *People and Power in Byzantium*, Washington DC: Dumbarton Oaks, 1982.

Kennedy, Hugh, *The Great Arab Conquests*, Philadelphia PA: Da Capo, 2007.

Kreutz, Barbara, *Before the Normans, Southern Italy in the Ninth & Tenth centuries*, Philadelphia: University of Pennsylvania Press, 1996.

Kulikowski, Michael, *Rome's Gothic War*, Cambridge UK: CUP, 2007.

Laiou, Angeliki (ed.) *Economic History of Byzantium*, Washington DC: Dumbarton Oaks, vols. I–III.

Lane-Poole, Stanley, *A History of Egypt in the Middle Ages*, London: Methuen, 1925.

Lattimore, Owen, *Inner Asian Frontiers of China*, Boston: Beacon Press, 1962 (orig. 1951).

Leadbetter, Bill, *Galerius and the Will of Diocletian*, London: Routledge, 2009.

Lenski, Noel, *The Cambridge Companion to the Age of Constantine*, Cambridge UK: CUP, 2006.

Lenski, Noel, *Failure of Empire*, Berkeley: University of California Press, 2002.

Luttwak, Edward, *The Grand Strategy of the Byzantine Empire*, Cambridge Mass: HUP, 2009.

Luttwak, Edward, *The Grand Strategy of the Roman Empire from the First Century AD to the Third*, Baltimore: John Hopkins Press, 1976.

Mango, Cyril, *Byzantine Architecture*, New York: Electa, 1985.

MacCormack, Sabine, *Art and Ceremony in Late Antiquity*, Berkeley, 1981.

MacDowall, Simon, *Adrianople AD 378*, Oxford: Osprey, 2001.

McCormick, Michael, *Eternal Victory*, Cambridge UK: Cambridge University Press, 1986.

McGovern, William Montgomery, *The Early Empires of Central Asia*, Chapel Hill: University of Northern Carolina Press, 1939.

Maas, Michael, 'Roman Questions, Byzantine Answers: Contours of the Age of Justinian', in Maas, *Cambridge Companion to the Age of Justinian*.

McGreer, Eric, *The Land Legislation of the Macedonian Emperors*, Toronto Canada: Pontifical Institute of Medieval Studies, 2000.

McGeer, Eric, *Sowing the Dragon's Teeth: Byzantine Warfare in the Tenth Century*, Washington DC: Dumbarton Oaks Studies XXXIII, 2008.

Miller, Fergus, *A Greek Roman Empire*, Berkeley: University of California Press, 2007.

Nicolle, David, *Armies of the Muslim Conquest*, Oxford: Osprey, 1993.

Nicolle, David, *Yarmuk 636 AD*, London: Osprey, 1994.

Dimitri Obolensky, *The Byzantine Commonwealth, Eastern Europe, 500–1453*, New York, 1971.

Odahl, Charles Matson, *Constantine and the Christian Empire*, London: Routledge, 2004.

Omen, Charles, *A History of the Art of War in the Middle Ages*, London: Greenhill Books, 1991.

Partington, J. R., *A History of Greek Fire and Gunpowder*, Baltimore, 1999, reprint, original edition, 1960.

Paspates, A. G., *The Great Palace of Constantinople*, London, 1893.

Potter, David R, *The Roman Empire at Bay AD 180–395*, London: Routledge, 2004.

Pourshariati, Parvaneh, *The Decline and Fall of the Sasanian Empire*, London: I.B.Tauris, 2008.

Pryor, John and Elizabeth Jeffreys, *Age of the ΔPOMΩN*, Leiden: Brill Academic Press, 2011.

Ramsay, W. M. *The Historical Geography of Asia Minor*, London, 1890, reprint, Cambridge UK, 2010 (also e book, Elibron Classics).

Renkov, Boris, 'Military Forces' in Sabin, et al.

Runciman, Steven, *The Emperor Romanus Lecapenus & his Reign*, Cambridge, 1929.

Steven Runciman, *The Medieval Manichee*, London, 1960.

Tarn, W. W, *The Greeks in Bactria and India*, London: CUP, 1951; there is a third edition, with an update by Frank Holt, Chicago: Ares Press, 1984.

Todd, Malcolm, *The Early Germans*, Oxford: Blackwell, 1995.

Tougher, Shaun, *The Reign of Leo VI (886–912)* , New York, 1997.

Toynbee, Arnold, *Constantine Porphyrogenitus and his World*, London: OUP, 1973.

Toynbee, Arnold, *A Study of History*, vol XII, London: OUP, 1959.

Treadgold, Warren, *Byzantium and its Army 284–1081*, Stanford: Stanford University Press, 1995.

Treadgold, Warren, *A History of the Byzantine State and Society*, Stanford: Stanford University Press, 1997.

Tsangadas, Bryon C. P, *The Fortifications and Defense of Constantinople*, Boulder Co: East European Monographs, 1980.

Sabin, Philip, Hans Van Wees, and Michael Whitby, *The Cambridge History of Greek and Roman Warfare*, vol II, Cambridge UK: CUP, 2007.

Sheldon, Mary Rose, *Rome's Wars in Parthia, Blood in the Sand*, London: Valentine Mitchell, 2010.

Shepard, Jonathan (ed.), *The Cambridge History of the Byzantine Empire*, Cambridge UK: Cambridge University Press, 2008.

Sherwin –White, A. N., *Roman Foreign Policy in the East*, Norman OK: University of Oklahoma Press, 1983.

Sinor, David (ed.) *The Cambridge History of Early Inner Asia*, Cambridge UK: CUP, 1990.

Sophocles, Evangelinus, *Greek Lexicon of Roman and Byzantine Periods*, New York: Charles Scribner, 1900.

Southern, Pat, *The Roman Empire from Serverus to Constantine*, London: Routledge, 2001.

Stephenson, Paul, *Byzantium's Balkan Frontier*: Cambridge UK, 2000.

Stephenson, Paul, *The Legend of Basil the Bulgar-Slayer*, Cambridge UK, 2003.

Stephenson, Paul, *Constantine Roman Emperor Christian Victor*, New York: Overlook Press, 2010.

Treadgold, Warren, *Byzantium and its Army 284–1081*, Stanford: Stanford University Press, 1995.

Treadgold, Warren, *A History of the Byzantine State and Society*, Stanford: Stanford University Press, 1997.

Turnbull, Stephen, *The Walls of Constantinople*, Oxford: Osprey, 2004.

Toynbee, Arnold, *Constantine Porphyrogenitus and his World*, Oxford: Oxford University Press, 1973.

Ware, Timothy, *The Orthodox Church*, New York, 1993.

Index
Important People and Events

Index II
Byzantine Army, Organization and Operations